Wakefield Press

The Vanished Land

Richard Zachariah began his career as a journalist at the Melbourne *Age* in 1964. Throughout his life he spent equal time on the land as a farmer and horse breeder, and working in London and Sydney as a newspaper and television journalist and broadcaster. His schoolboy love affair with Victoria's Western District grew into a bewilderment at the withdrawal of those dominating pastoral dynasties who so impressed him with their elan and the qualities that allowed them to rule this special place. Richard Zachariah died aged 80 in April 2025.

By the same author

The Home Show
(with Maggie Tabberer)
ABC Books, 1991

Zachariah
Macmillan, 1999

Disappearing dynasties *of* Victoria's Western District

RICHARD ZACHARIAH

Wakefield Press
16 Rose Street
Mile End
South Australia 5031
www.wakefieldpress.com.au

First published 2017
Reprinted 2023, 2025

Copyright © Richard Zachariah, 2017

All rights reserved. This book is copyright. Apart from
any fair dealing for the purposes of private study, research,
criticism or review, as permitted under the Copyright Act,
no part may be reproduced without written permission.
Enquiries should be addressed to the publisher.

Cover designed by Liz Nicholson, designBITE
Typeset by Michael Deves, Wakefield Press

National Library of Australia Cataloguing-in-Publication entry

Creator: Zachariah, Richard, author.
Title: The vanished land: disappearing dynasties of Victoria's Western
          District / Richard Zachariah.
ISBN: 978 1 74305 501 4 (paperback).
Notes: Includes bibliographical references and index.
Subjects: Zachariah, Richard.
          Western District (Vic.) – History.
          Western District (Vic.) – 20th century – Social life and customs.
          Victoria, Western – History.

Contents

	Introduction	1
1	Hexham Park	5
2	The Unmapped Heart	17
3	Learmonth, Lion of the Western District	25
4	The Scots	39
5	The Wool Boom	48
6	In the Limelight	60
7	Landmarks	64
8	The Middle Ground	73
9	Up in Smoke	84
10	Coming in from the Cold	91
11	A Lost Land	97
12	Blue Blood, Bluestone	109
13	A Pillar Falls	120
14	Succession	127
15	The Great Land Grab	138
16	Lost for Words	146
17	Northern Lights in the Western Sky	153
18	Plain Speaking	166
19	A Voice of Reason	172
20	A Manifold Misunderstanding	179
21	The Last Squatter	186
22	The Pistol under the Pillow	197

23	Last Man Standing	207
24	A Mann and his Daughter	213
25	Two Weeks' Work in One	219
26	The Practical Stockman	224
27	'The Equal of Anyone'	230
28	Diary of a Farmer	237
29	A Gentleman Politician	243
30	Life on Loan	249
31	The Incomers	255
32	The New Medici	262
33	Melbourne Land Boomers and the New Order	274
34	Generational Shift	290
	Epilogue	297
	Acknowledgements	305
	Additional reading	307
	Index	309

For Sarah

Introduction

Let no one say the past is dead. The past is all about us.
                               Oodgeroo Noonuccal (Kath Walker)

The Western District is not my home, but I lived there between the years of eight and fifteen – years that close the distance between a boy and a young man. It was the strip along which I had my first experiences of everything, of finding what I have continued to love. When I visit now, it's like coming back to my memory. I remember the silent space of where I grew up, the pantomime of feeling, that blameless in-between time of my first sweet brush with intimacy – and my first experience of pain. It is best I don't live here.

I was in Hamilton during its 'belle époque', when wool was gold. As a uniformed schoolboy, I watched in wonder as women in smart suits by Balenciaga stepped from Rolls-Royces to shop in the market town's Gray Street. But now, more than fifty years on, there is a faltering spirit across those broad acres. The Western District, once a pastoral powerhouse, the haven of a social elite and bedrock of its political supremacy for a century and a half, has today become just another rural region at the mercy of city-based speculators and international marketeers. The great pastoral dynasties have departed, defeated by economic rationalism and lack of will, disengaged from a land that, if you let it, pushes imagination beyond what one can actually see.

Out there, I think the past is my new horizon. I am a reservoir filled by old rain. This is my place to drift across memory. Driving on an empty road at night amid the spent volcanoes, I see the lights of a faraway homestead wink like grounded stars. I imagine the unseen inhabitants clustered under high ceilings in their eyrie, watching firelight flicker as they contemplate the changed circumstances of their lives. Do they remember when it was the old manorial way, when to own land in the Western District was to rule?

As a school boarder among graziers' sons at Hamilton College in the 1950s, I received a smorgasbord of farm-stay invitations. It was a taste of honey from many pots. To call that time a wool boom gives no hint of the ambience, of the release unexpected money brought after the austerity of war. Hamilton became the wool capital of the world, where luminous Gatsbys rounded up their flocks in Daimlers, jolting across the open paddocks. But since then there has been an unwelcome reckoning. The sap has gone, towns have died, communities shrivelled.

There are no heroes in this story; it's about human loss and the demeaning of country as home. That is the wound that makes me want to write about the Western District as its people adjust to life in a different place, away from those blessed moors that are now an abandoned land.

I first saw the Western District on a nondescript May afternoon in 1953. My family – Mum, Dad and four kids – were irritably cramped in an Austin A40, bouncing over the plains towards an uncertain future five hours from Melbourne, our home.

My father, Harry, had accepted the role of headmaster at Hamilton and Western District Boys' College. Later, I discovered the dark rider: if he didn't make it work, the Presbyterian Church, which owned it, would shut it down. A boarding school for farmers' sons, it was struggling for numbers. Low commodity prices meant low enrolments.

INTRODUCTION

Hamilton and Western District Boys' College

My mother, Joan, was Brighton-bred and saw no reason to move from the fragrant suburb on the shores of Port Phillip Bay. She was apprehensive about beginning a new life at the age of 37. And she was forced to drive on this endless road with four kids tumbling over her because my father had avoided the responsibility of getting a driver's licence. Her resentment of his failure was palpable as the car came to rest in deep red gravel beside the Hamilton Highway.

We spilt onto stalky white grass. While my sisters scattered toward a plantation of sighing sugar gums, I retreated across a gravel drain. Waist-high kangaroo grass scraped my legs, alerting me to what might be hidden. I didn't go far.

Then I saw them – a mural of crucified magnificence, a 40-foot span of black-brown velvet wings and feathers hanging from six freshly killed wedge-tailed eagles. Their heads bent in death startled my eight-year-old imagining. I looked into their hooded eyes, some open, clear enough to see a thousand miles. The dark splendour of these wild creatures with the hooked beaks, deadly talons and diamond-shaped tails was threatening even in death. I was sure some local farmer had killed the birds out of fear.

I hurried back to my father, who explained there was a bounty on their heads. The farmer had hung them on the fence as proof for payment – and as a warning to other eagles who might dive from the sky to steal newborn lambs. Uncomfortably perched on my father's knee, I was happy with his explanation. The executed criminals had brought it on themselves.

Later, I learnt the science. Wedge-tailed eagles steal carrion – dead lambs, not live ones – and eat small native animals as well as feral cats, rabbits and even foxes. I lived through the withdrawal of the cruel bounty, and then saw them protected by government order. Today, they fly unfettered across the open skies of the Western District, using their sublime aerial skills to ride the thermals of solitariness. I suspect that they're angry at having been persecuted for an imagined crime.

Their majestic survival is a victory for enlightenment. These days, it is the humans whose feathers are ruffled. The people I knew have become the endangered species.

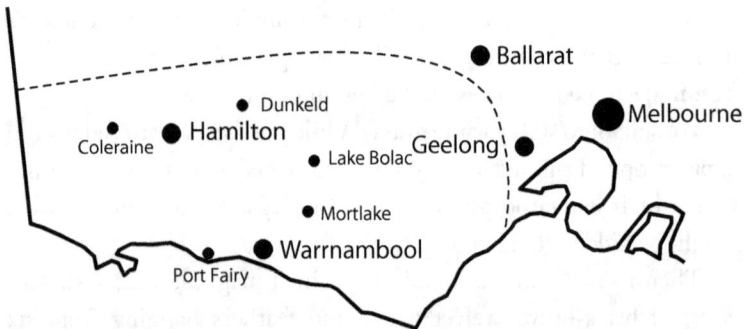

The Western District of south-west Victoria

1
Hexham Park

We write to discover what we think.

Flaubert

A keen July wind touches us. I'm standing at the entrance to Hexham Park, which my old friend David Armstrong sold at a time of rural recession a decade ago. The paddocks are invisible under a plague of pine trees. A hundred and fifty years of the Armstrongs' Western District hegemony has faded like a rainbow in the sky.

The Camelot of my boyhood dreams is gone. No one at this moment feels safe from talk of grief.

When he greets us, David is amiable and brave. Artist Robert Whitson is there with me to paint what is left of the beloved place.

David's key to the gate doesn't work. The locks have been changed by the new owners, one of the timber companies whose tax-driven tree ventures have disfigured the Western District. Hexham Park, once a haven of undulating paddocks and river flats, is now a vivid scar of pine trees over sprayed weeds.

David is apologetic as we climb the locked gate and walk the mile-long red gravel drive to his forsaken birthplace.

The only familiar thing is the drive itself. The magical fields of memory have been submerged beneath the discordant pines. Nothing lives in monoculture; even the rabbits have hightailed it.

I think back to our golden summers of rabbiting with the dogs, gingerly sinking our hands down dark burrows, eating bread and sausages cooked over a fire and fending off the magpies that swooped on us under the mulberry tree.

I remember a day stalking tiger snakes, walking warily toward the Hopkins River through long, dry grass. David had shot one here the day before – hit it through the head with one bullet. He was a good shot, but I reckoned it was a fluke.

I had the .410 shotgun, its spreading pellets a much better bet with snakes, but there was no sign of them. They'd probably retreated from the dogs, sliding under logs or into the cracks that opened up in the ground under the sun.

We'd given ourselves crew cuts like our hero, the Olympic swimmer Jon Henricks, hacking at our hair with a pair of Mrs Armstrong's sewing scissors while she looked on and laughed. 'Nothing that the barber in Mortlake can't fix,' she said. Mrs Armstrong was like that – she treated us as men. There wasn't much we couldn't do.

We weren't yet teenagers but she let us drive the ute, chasing rabbits and shooting foxes, spotlighting possums. We rode horses and helped with whatever was going on. At lunch, we could have a beer-and-lemonade shandy if we felt like it. 'It's better to learn at home than make a fool of yourself in public,' she said.

Now, down by the river, we unloaded the guns, put them against the river gum and stripped off. Walking out along a half-submerged tree trunk, we slipped and slid into the deep hole under the red-gum branch. I dived down a shaft of sun, the sliver of light like a torch in the murky river. I could only see three feet in front of me. There were fallen trees, submerged branches lurking like a hangman's noose, and no-one for miles.

It was our place – no-one ever came here but us and the dogs we brought with us each day. At the age of eleven, we'd sit beside the river with our guns like two old men.

There's no chance now. Our hunting country has been buried under a khaki plague. No more the freedom of space, to walk the paddocks, to tend the lambs and feed the cattle on carpets of frost, to fill the woolshed on a Sunday evening with willing dogs and unwilling sheep, then lie by the fire at night in sweet exhaustion. They were my days on this heavenly plain.

We talk listlessly as we walk. I skirt around the subject that preoccupies me. It was David who closed his family's final chapter here. In the 1850s, his Scots ancestors escaped the bloody border wars of Dumfriesshire to buy or lease thousands of acres of plains country and build a colonial mansion fit for a king. They revelled in the deep volcanic dirt, so much richer than their own soils, which the Scottish journalist Neal Ascherson has described as 'skin over bone'. Here was security of tenure with no armed invaders.

Yet today, when we reach the stately home they built in 1872, all that remains is rubble in a mound of debris.

I find it hard to convince Robert that one of the district's finest homes formerly commanded this dismaying site. There were 22 rooms around an atmospheric quadrangle, a distinctive two-storey courtyard with verandas and palms that could have staged a Tennessee Williams play of the old American South. The tiled piazza would have been perfect for the familiar themes of timeworn families living out loneliness in vast houses hauntingly like this one. The faded grandeur of the South may have been more vivid than the acts played out here, but the pattern of rural alienation is a familiar one.

Incredibly, a marble arch hangs on, attached to a crumbling wall. I once saw that wall lit by oil lamps, their shadows holding the shape of David's Gran, who sat alone at a table with a knee blanket for warmth. Gran lived there with a housekeeper, an English-born woman called Evie, and she had rugs on her lap even on the hottest days. She'd sit in a huge, dark room and read by lamplight, or peer through the draped windows. I don't remember her saying a word to us.

Her smoky outline remains imprinted on that bare wall today, though the boy who peered through the vast window is sixty years

Hexham Park in its heyday
[Courtesy State Library of Victoria, H81.155/50]

Hexham Park ruins

The gates at Hexham Park, and below, pines, pines, pines

David Armstrong among the ruins

on, wrapped in the immovable memory of that silhouette and the shadowland of locked rooms behind it.

When the whole family lived there just a couple of years before, there'd been a person whose job it was to light the candles and lamps each night and set the fires in winter. But now the two women only had use for a few of the twenty-odd rooms, and the house took on the mystery of emptiness.

At night, David and I went over to shoot possums. We'd patrol the grounds, carrying guns and powerful torches, stopping to look through the few windows lit by the mellow, melancholy glow of lamps. Gran would still be sitting in the same place, perhaps with a few more rugs and a dinner tray on her lap.

We'd back away and turn our torches into the tall tops of the pine trees, seeking the shining eyes of our prey, the big brushtail possums. We never shot the ring-tails, because they didn't do the damage. But the brushtail was a fruit bandit and liked nothing better than to create a home in the roof of the old house. Brushtails would piss through the ceilings, leave food lying around, encourage rats, bang around the place and sometimes die in the roof, creating a dreadful stink.

David and I were once crawling on our bellies in the roof when we cornered a live possum. I passed my gun up to David between his legs, but just as he reached down, it went off with a huge bang. It missed both of us, but went within inches of his young manhood.

I remember Evie, the housekeeper, had a relationship with an organiser attached to the despised Australian Workers Union. It was an explosive mix of politics and etiquette – a unionist, the shearers' rep, courting a lady employee in the big house. No one intruded, but there were disapproving whispers about inappropriate behaviour 1950s-style. David and I would see a dust plume in the drive and know it was him, aware of his unpopularity but unaware of the reason for his nocturnal visits, a memory that still brings a delicious shiver of daring and élan.

There is nothing left of the old house today. We pick our way gingerly over the few remaining bluestones, most of which have been taken away to be used for a rebuild elsewhere. David tells me the place was blighted, sinking into its failing foundations. 'As kids, we couldn't go to that western side of the house, there was such a dangerous lean.' In 1953, at the apex of the wool boom, his father gave up. He was told it would cost £22,000 more to repair the old house than to build a new one, which was soon under construction in an adjoining paddock. It had the luxury of electricity, which was supplied by a generator in a shed at the back.

Now that house too is deserted. The timber men have no wish to live in the moribund enclave they have created.

We move in a desultory group away from the 'new' house where we had such joy. David tells me the eucalypts on the house boundary have died of thirst, their moisture stolen by the invading pines.

The old house was liveable for less than a hundred years, just a blink given Europe's plethora of thousand-year-old buildings. Even our former school, Hamilton College, built in the same year, is still in use today. Yet Hexham Park's bluestones had surely been cut and laid in the certain knowledge that the Armstrong men, now they had found what they had searched the world for, would forever farm from their base on Hexham's hill. Why else would they bother raising such a splendid, romantic monument? Or was the cashed-up generation that built the grand houses simply driven by a desire for social eminence?

Either way, Hexham Park's demise is emblematic of the Western District's malaise. To me, it's a sign of a generation's predilection to surrender – in equine terms, to sprint rather than to stay. In the florid air of desolation hang questions of heirlooms and legacy. Problems of succession and the vagaries of rural markets have trumped the forefathers' wishes that the land beneath our feet remain in Armstrong hands.

When we leave, I am pleased to be out on the Hamilton Highway. I look at the locked front gate, which was once an entrance that was never closed, with an open cattle grid beside a gabled mailbox bearing the moniker 'Hexham Park' sheltered by a lambertiana tree. In the 1940s, David's grandfather would swing his car into the entrance, recklessly disregarding oncoming traffic. Warned that he would one day be killed in a head-on, the old boy replied, 'Everyone knows I live here!' Now even the sign has gone.

Later, over a cup of tea in a nearby Mortlake café, we break the cone of silence, more with relief than grief. David tells me that in the end, Hexham Park had become no-man's land for him. A decade after quitting the place, he doesn't wrestle with ideas of familial duty. He doesn't meditate on the forsaken land or the lost continuity of family ownership. He has survival firmly in his sights. The rest is for others, like me, to contemplate.

For David, the offer to buy his property was divine intervention, a release from the grind of selling commodities at less than their cost of production. The chance of escaping this conundrum was an overwhelming reason to flee.

David's conversation is veined with these sentiments, which were sharpened by a health setback in his last years fighting the land. His sons from an earlier marriage had rejected an offer to take over their birthright. And sown deep in his attitude toward the hereditary title is his fractured relationship with his father Ian.

I remember his father as a quiet man who was tragically killed in a car accident, shanghaiing young David into managing Hexham Park. But for David, this sudden ascension was tinged by a brutal reminder of the past.

He remembers playing with matches as a four-year-old and accidentally destroying a hayshed. Ten minutes later, his father hunted him down and whipped him for his indiscretion, forging a fear of his father that lasted through all their days together on Hexham Park.

David's decision to leave was probably born on that day. I can understand his relief half a century later, when at last he could be punished no more.

He is now comfortable in Warrnambool with his wife and teenage daughter, negotiating his investments and gazing at the ocean from his seat above the sand hills. Once, in a different place, all he could see was his problem, and Hexham Park was a dream for others to have.

I feel uneasy as I leave Mortlake. I know it's nostalgia for my youth, Hexham Park a fictional glow, a luminous centrepiece of a more reliable past. But knowing this only heightens the disquiet. Hexham Park has been allowed to flicker out like fire in the snow, the disintegration and loss beyond anything I could imagine. Exasperation overwhelms forgiveness.

Flaubert was right: I am beginning to understand how I feel by writing about it.

David's story of forsaking inherited land for a safe haven by the southern ocean is repeated in Victoria's other coastal towns, where émigrés from the savannah compete for houses in the dress circle, play bridge endlessly and congregate for cocktails and dinner at the Barwon Heads golf club or in Port Fairy's riverside restaurants.

They fiercely deny experiencing regret, but I don't believe them. What of abandoning the blood, the grace of title, the grassy moors and the seasons, the ultimate need to do the work? I fear faulty memory and varnished truth will obscure the Western District malaise. The story of surrender will not be popular, particularly with those members of the lost tribe who are close to me.

Reviewing his writing life, Graham Greene reckoned that writers give up their friends. I suspect it will happen to me as I seek to make sense of David's painful explanation. If I am honest, I am stunned by his disowning of grief knowing his wife Pauline had fought the good fight to save the land she now sheds tears over.

From Mortlake, I drive west toward my home, a small farm and vineyard in the Adelaide Hills. It too is threatened by the forces of economic rationalism. I am no stranger to the vicissitudes of depending on the land.

The Western District's winter emerald accentuates my bleak mood. I cannot comprehend the departure of those who inherited this God-given land. I am aggrieved at their disregard for their forefathers, who were wise enough to know that the abundant volcanic soil in their hands would nourish their families forever.

My journey home takes me across the vast marginal desert of South Australia's Mallee, a place of perpetual challenge for those who farm there. As I travel across its moonscape, my memories of the Western District warp into a Utopian mirage. But that is how it was for me, growing up in the years of the golden fleece, when owning that land was a guarantee of success. So how have the squatters' descendants, mainly the fifth generation, failed in the past twenty years?

Losing a farm is subtler than having a business fail in town, where merchandise is seized, liquidators are sent in and people go broke overnight. Having owned land for 150 years provides a shelter of good manners from the gathering storm. But grace can only extend so far. For many sons and daughters of today, it was only a matter of time before they were forced to market their heritage to managed investment schemes, city millionaires, corporates or foreign raiders with Chinese or Arab names.

Though the commercial pressures were real, I believe it was the families who failed the land. Their leaving was a miscarriage of nerve. I cannot accept their cavalier attitude to bequeathed property, my intolerance quickened by the fact that I am not one of them, burdened by inheritance or expectation. I am merely a headmaster's son, almost trade.

At the same time, I know that Australian agricultural survival has always favoured the brave, its uncertainties palpably unforgiving. The treeless plains of the Western District have a particular habit of staring back, finding you or finding you out. One grazier told me the land's intimidating power could propel him back inside the house when he faced a lonely morning in the paddocks with no help or expectation of reward. Nobody looks at land romantically if it's sending them broke.

Australia's rural exodus has been a shared and bitter experience, but the defeat has been greatest in the Western District, where the prominent and formerly successful have given up. The roll call of former squatting families is a long one. The Austins, Armstrongs, Afflecks, Blacks, Clarkes, Cooks, Currs, Chirnsides, Croziers, Fairbairns, Grimwades, Hoods, Huttons, Kininmonths, Learmonths, Manifolds, McDougalls, Mackinnons, Moffatts, Millers, Palmers, Peppins, Rowes, Rutledges, Shaws, Russells, Ritchies, Wilsons and Yuilles all ruled major landholdings. Practically all have left; those who remain are in reduced circumstances or in the hands of daughters. Their ancestors built dynasties they hoped would last forever, but now the families are gone.

This is no matter of dirt-poor farmers walking off some dustbowl. It is a ruling class abandoning the volcanic soil of Australia Felix, the continent's most fertile land, leaving country they had held since the 1850s or even earlier. And, while the Western District has danced on the stage at Australia's richest moments, it has barely been seen in the miserable endgame. My project in this book is to bring that forsaken land to light.

2

The Unmapped Heart

I have begun my journey through landscape and memory without a map, because the Western District doesn't have one. When I called the Victorian tourist office to ask for a map, a woman there passed me on to the Lands Department. But the Lands Department too was stymied. An official eventually told me there were individual shire maps but nothing to show where the Western District began and ended.

Escaping the cartographer, the open savannah invites mythology. There is infinite charm in infinity – to chart it would be like mapping your own soul. For me, the Western District lives and breathes without the restriction of maps. But, like most living things, it has veins. Three highways run east–west across the district – the Hamilton, Glenelg and Princes – while the Henty Highway bisects it from north to south, running from Portland to Horsham.

Today I'm travelling west from Geelong, where the Hamilton Highway lifts me onto the sun-kissed grassland. This is a stretch of the imagination that always excites a fierce longing in me. Here, just moments beyond Geelong and its freeways, where built environments crowd and muddle, the eye can relax in space. The land stretches into the sky, and lush spring pastures paint the greens from avocado to emerald.

A little north of here, near Shelford, is a spot where you can see the curvature of the earth, so mesmerising is the level surface. It's a view that doesn't need embroidering, a magnetic introduction to the Western District. These are the 'dreaming grasslands', in the words of journalist Tony Wright, a Heywood boy.

The wool town of Inverleigh is at the cutting edge of the Western District, although you'd never guess. On the way into the township, I pass a sign welcoming visitors to the 'Golden Plains Shire' and inviting all comers to 'Discover The Western Plains'. The Western District isn't mentioned. The proper noun has been pensioned off by the Shire's marketers.

Like all the towns on this edge of the Western District, Inverleigh is now being drawn into the orbit of the large conurbations to the east. The store on the main street has had a makeover and now offers freshly ground coffee, and the old bluestone pub sells craft beer, obviously aiming to develop a more sophisticated – and affluent – clientele.

Further south, a four-lane freeway has transformed the old pastoral town of Winchelsea into a commuter hub. Suburban brick-veneer bungalows now crowd around Thomas Austin's original property at Barwon Park, with its two-storey bluestone mansion built in 1871 to accommodate visiting royalty in style.

Still further west is a railway town enjoying a vogue, with a four-lane divided highway coming its way. Perched above the Barwon's alluvial plains, Birregurra is smart with three trains to Melbourne and back each day. It's here that the Western District meets the Melbourne-Geelong commuter belt as people seek relief from the city and chase a weekend swim on the Bellarine Peninsula or at the beaches along the ever-lengthening Great Ocean Road. In my youth, the road ended at Apollo Bay, but commercial interests have now extended it most of the way to Warrnambool.

Birregurra has eight realtors rather than the historical two. It's at a sensitive stage of development. It has the luxury of an influx of wealth, including AFL maestro Gillon McLachlan, a grandson of 'The Last Squatter', Trevor Clarke (Chapter 21), but other new arrivals are people of modest means. Now that the town is sewered, there's pressure to subdivide rambling gardens and build affordable houses. The battle to balance old and new in Birregurra is on in earnest.

When I think of the towns to the north-west, the contrast is stark. As a teenager, I knew Streatham, Skipton and Lake Bolac as the heart of a grazing and cropping nirvana, but today those towns are bereft and sinking, while proximity to a big city has handed Birregurra freshly painted cottages, organic cafes, a destination restaurant and a burgeoning future in lifestyle real estate.

Then I see the miracle of crops. Vast areas of sheep country have gone under the plough, defying traditional claims that the wet, heavy soil would drown any monetary return. Farmers have confounded the rules by raising the beds 15 centimetres and creating depressions between them to drain water. Once drained, the rich volcanic soil pushes up white and red wheat in unprecedented quantities, interspersed with ripening canola in swathes of ludicrous hi-vis yellow.

Steel mammoths with rubber legs rumble through widened gates where utes once bumped along. Workers give way to machines ruled by laptops and satellites, driven by GPS-RTK autosteer, replacing manpower and emptying the towns.

Back down on the Princes Highway, the rolling country gets lusher as my path meanders towards the dairying district around Camperdown. A tractor pulls a silage trailer, filling the view ahead. Slowly we overhaul the farmer and pass his cows, which are waiting in muddy anticipation of breakfast.

The alluring topographical diversity of the Western District's south-eastern corner is the antithesis of the volcanic plains up north. The view leaving Camperdown is an extended green carpet, smudged by orderly dark stands of sheltering pines, now in the distance turned the colour of ripe olives.

Birregurra's imposing Anglican Christ Church

The main street of Birregurra, and above, the church

Pastoral country near Camperdown

Mortlake Memorial Drive

To the south is Timboon, another dairy town, where the farmers grizzle that they spend nine months of the year in gumboots, with a huge trace elements bill at the end. These days, it has attracted lifestyle investors dazzled by the allure of the physically magnificent Great Ocean Road. Never straying far from the coast, this southern trail is the Western District's glitter strip. It attracts émigrés from the grasslands, along with a pile of Melbourne retirement money chasing the Australian coastal dream in beach townhouses and deep dirt farms with a good restaurant up close.

There are few rivers in the southwest, or indeed in the whole of the Western District. Its volcanic past and the 30-metre depth of the lava flows mean that most of the water drains underground. My route to Warrnambool will eventually take me across the Hopkins River, but there are few other waterways or even creeks. Here, rains end in swamps or saline crater lakes like Lake Keilambete.

The locals at the Terang pub say Lake Keilambete should be a spa, and they're right. In Europe it would be a landmark, with a five-star hotel for the rich who want to recuperate there. The Corangamite shire, however, refuses even to build a road to the lake. The only way to enter is to jump a wire fence, then squelch over mud flats and slime to the edge of the lake, where you can float like a cork on gravity-defying water twice as salty as the sea.

Down here in the south, they work close to the earth. They produce milk and grow spuds on smaller acreages, accessing some of the best soil. Agronomist Bruce Allen nominates the paddock in front of the historic Glenormiston homestead near Terang as being as fertile as any in the world. While their more socially celebrated neighbours controlled bigger runs with lighter soils and less rainfall, the southerners can point to squatter Niel Black as one of their own. This canny Scot from Argyll knew something when he chose to settle at Glenormiston and not up north.

More than 160 years later, the region experienced a brief dairying

The famous Glenormiston Agricultural College closed in 2014 from lack of patronage; the propery is now locked

boom after the export industry discovered an Asian appetite for milk and butter products More than $220 million was poured into the pockets of dairy farmers around Warrnambool in 2014, when the local milk and butter co-op became a takeover target. One farmer who had reluctantly supported the co-op out of loyalty by buying shares each year walked away with a $20 million dividend when it was sold to Saputo, a $10 billion dairy processor based in Canada.

On the plush south-west coast around Warrnambool, Tower Hill and Port Fairy, the Irish take over from the Scots, the two groups divided by the Hamilton Highway. For years, the Anglo/Irish gulf morphed into an electoral advantage that had Liberals on their knees in gratitude. A sectarian split between Protestants and Catholics divided the ALP and kept the Liberals in power. Local Liberal members were aware of the Irish issues in the south, stepping lightly around legalised abortion and state aid when in Warrnambool lest they stem the flow of Catholic preferences.

The Irish influence is unmissable when you go to the Warrnambool races at the May carnival on the edge of winter. It's like stepping onto the Curragh just south of Dublin. Men with ruddy faces are clad in Donegal tweed, their women dressed for a day out in worsted wool and sensible boots. They mix with their neighbours, forming a sea of cloth caps as they place bets with a long line of bookmakers between rounds of whiskey at open bars.

And the racing is steadfastly that of Ireland, with hurdlers and steeplechasers resisting activists' agitation. So far, the 'Bool has held true to its tradition. Viewing the Grand Annual Steeplechase from high on the hill above the stands is one of the great sights of Australian racing, though it's endangered as society moves closer to agreeing that jumping horses is animal cruelty.

Coastal Warrnambool is subject to southerlies that begin in the Southern Ocean and suffer no interference before bashing into the landscape, distorting hardy cypresses until they look like old men bent on sticks. At the nearby resort town of Port Fairy, set on the Moyne River, perpetually green hills roll down to rows of stone cottages that seem to grow out of the ground. Across the river and up the hill is millionaires' row, where retired graziers gaze at the brave fishing boats entering the Southern Ocean. In private, do they stare into the restless sea, bearing the weight of their decisions?

3
Learmonth, Lion of the Western District

Visiting outback Australia, the English writer Bruce Chatwin discovered the Aboriginal custom of measuring a journey in songs rather than kilometres. Out of this visit came *The Songlines* (1987), which lit up an ancient culture by interpreting the dreamtime as a parallel reality that exists alongside our quotidian existence, preceding us and lasting long after our deaths. Chatwin believed that our time-challenged lives would be enhanced if we discarded the angst of measuring kilometres so that a destination became a way of seeing and redefining ourselves.

The *Songlines* mythology came to me travelling in a car with Peter Learmonth, a fifth-generation Western District dictionary of ownership, bibliography of people and compendium of history. In the spirit of Chatwin, he measured our trips by properties passed and people remembered. Kilometres were irrelevant, never mentioned.

Peter, 84, had kindly agreed to guide me through his Western District, tracing a very personal map. His family's association with the region began in the 1840s when his ancestors built a homestead at Batesford, on the Moorabool River west of Geelong.

Peter's own first memory was of being set alight 'like a candle' by an exploding donkey engine in the kitchen of Koolamurt, his father's property, on Boxing Day 1939. 'I was eight and playing with

Peter Learmonth

the engine, which was connected to my Meccano set and driven by methylated spirits. I lit it and it went up, setting me on fire. I rushed outside with my top half ablaze. We had a lady who looked after us, and she came with a coir mat, wrapped me in it and put out the fire that was consuming me,' Peter says. 'A big part of me only had bone left.'

There followed an unlikely conjunction of circumstances that saved his life. The local party-line phone, unmanned on the Boxing Day holiday, was answered when the postmistress responded to its unusually persistent ringing. Next, the Coleraine doctor picked up, minutes before leaving for a Portland vacation. Peter was placed in a cold bath with a case of tea leaves. For three-and-a-half months he clung to life, unmoving, stricken in those days before skin grafts. A saga of survival began, engulfing him in more than 40 operations to re-join skin to bone and rebuild his upper body. At 12, he spent months in an adult recuperation ward for ex-servicemen at Melbourne's Heidelberg

Mount Elephant

A stone wall near Mount Elephant, typical of the region

THE VANISHED LAND

Chatsworth House, and below, the woolshed at Chatsworth

Boortkoi Homestead

Repatriation Hospital, trading in cigarettes and other small presents that the charities supplied to the troubled men.

In the next bed was Ted Kenna, a young man from Hamilton who had been awarded the Victoria Cross for his bravery during a firefight in New Guinea. When he won the award, he also won £400. Peter told me, 'I asked him what he was going to do with it, and he said, "Pay for my mum to come down and see me."'

We were now driving into the land where Peter had spent his working life – fifty years as a stock and station agent, confidante of the mighty and the meek. Ballarat, where we started, wasn't part of the Western District, Peter said. He set the boundaries of the District as running from Skipton in the north to Geelong in the east, the ocean in the south and Casterton in the west.

Heading for Skipton, we passed lifestyle properties, a maze of human endeavour and management styles that didn't necessarily enhance the landscape's aesthetics. We swung onto the road through Smythesdale, a commuter town that boasted a large pony club. The town was ringed by pine forests, unsightly gorse growing wildly in the light clay soil. Out of town, we tacked down to the road to Lismore, and Peter was easing into the saddle by the time we reached Cape Clear.

'This country hasn't the quality or depth of soil that the Western District has. If you buy sheep here for export, you have to be terribly careful. The stock look prime fat but weigh light. They have to be 55 kilos live to come out at 48 kilos. Then you are in trouble. You have to go further south or north to get the heavier fattening country.'

In his view, the best country needed to be multi-purpose. 'It must be able to grow fine wool, fat lambs, beef cattle and crop. The best country starts at Skipton and runs through to Glenthompson. You go north to Ararat and Tattyoon and south from Skipton to Mortlake to Hawkesdale and back up to Caramut.'

Now Peter was driving across country, aiming to meet the Geelong–Skipton road, and we were starting to see the richer soils of the Western District cut in. Peter drew it to my attention. 'The land has got a better depth of soil, not light country like we have driven through. That comes quickly when you get rain and goes off when you get heat, while the true Western District hangs on.'

We reached the Devil's Kitchen, a sharp intersection where roads bend sharply and drop steeply. It was a dangerous spot. Though Peter didn't know of any drivers being killed, he said there had been casualties among the stock.

'Many a loaded truck has come to grief, including loads of sheep going from Lake Bolac to Newmarket in Melbourne. The drivers would be going too hard. They'd be tired and the old single-axle trucks – over they'd go. We had to shoot the injured animals or get dogs to round up the loose ones. I got to know some blokes around here with dogs, and they lent us paddocks to put the sheep in overnight.'

On the Lismore Road above the Devil's Kitchen, the view opened up. We were now in Peter's beloved country, and he was singing its song. 'The Alexanders own this country on the right and are now mostly cropping. This year they are going to crack it with a bumper crop. On the left is a very big property, Glenfine, that has a classic bluestone homestead.'

He told me Glenfine originally belonged to the Rowes, who sold about 5000 acres to Max Howell, 'a lovely man who married a Beggs. He sold it to the meat people, the Gilbertsons, and it has been on-sold to an American teachers' superannuation fund, who have invested around $1 billion on places all over Australia.'

On our right was Naringal, another Rowe property. It had been in the family since 1841, and was eventually passed down to Bill Rowe. Peter describes him as 'a lovely man with a very good war record … a very smart fellow but not a farmer.' Bill Rowe sold the farm in 2011 to Graeme Croft, a Melbourne aged-care operator and developer. Its asking price was $7.5 million.

Peter recalls the burst of activity that followed. 'Croft completely fenced the place, put in a feedlot for cattle, a piggery, bought more land, did the house up and refurbished the Edna Walling garden. It was a model farm property. Five years later, Croft said there wasn't enough water here, so he sold the 5500 acres to a local for $17 million.'

The buyer was a young man named Alastair Wills, who belonged to an old family from Streatham and had married a woman whose parents were very wealthy. Peter says, 'He and his family already had cropping, some prime lambs, would have around 10,000 acres around here. When he bought Naringal, he asked the owner if he could get started cropping immediately. Croft said, "OK, but I haven't given you possession." Wills moved his tractors in on a Friday, and by Sunday night he had 500 acres of crop in. He pulled every new fence out, and now it's an enormous cropping property. Got rid of the feedlot and the pigs.'

It's quite a Western District story. An old family sells to a businessman, who does the property up, makes a dollar and sells it back to another Western District family who have had an injection of cash from off farm. The shifts in the use of the land are new, though.

Now approaching Lismore, we were right in cropping territory, passing wheat, canola, beans and barley. 'This was all classic sheep country,' Peter said. The falling volume of sheep sales was a sign of how things were changing, he said. 'We held two sheep sales in Lismore every year, selling 20,000 head. Today you'd be lucky to get 5000.'

He added, 'Lismore itself is holding its own economically rather than thriving. The well-established families and big properties contribute to its economic health.'

Outside Lismore, on the road to Skipton, we passed Titanga, a heritage-listed property with a Gothic gate lodge and a single-storey bluestone homestead and woolshed. Both were designed in the 1870s by a firm of Geelong architects, Davidson and Henderson, who were responsible for the inimitable style of many homesteads in the Western District.

One of Titanga's claims to fame was that John Currie, who bought it in the 1880s, experimented with planting various species of native trees there, and his grandson P.H. Lang expanded the plantation in the early twentieth century, so the property now had a unique collection of mature trees from all around the region. Among them, Peter reminded me, was the sugar gum, which had been recognised as the species most suited to the Western District.

We could now see the unmistakable outline of Mount Elephant, the largest of the region's scoria cones. The famous Mount Elephant Station once extended all the way to where we were now. It included the land around the mountain but not the mountain itself, which was owned by a local who extracted road material from it. Peter told me, 'He was eventually stopped when it began to impact on the natural beauty of the place.' Even from this distance, I could see the scars that the quarries had left.

Peter ran through the property's changing ownership. 'It passed through the Chirnsides and Curries before James Fairbairn bought it in the 1920s.' Fairbairn went on to become a government minister, but was killed in a plane crash outside Canberra in 1940.

Peter told me Mount Elephant was next sold in the 1940s to the Melbourne stockbroker John Baillieu, who was buying up a suite of significant properties across Victoria. The last sale was in 2010, when Baillieu's son Antony sold the property to a Swedish count, Carl Gustav Wachmeister, for more than $20 million.

Peter recalled, 'I did some work on Mount Elephant, usually dealing with managers who were hard to get on with.'

The home station had gradually been reduced from almost 16,000 hectares to a bit over 3300, partly as a result of soldier settlement. 'Over to the right is soldier settler country – used to be part of Mount Elephant,' Peter said.

I asked him about the effects of soldier settlement around here. 'The impact was spasmodic,' Peter replied. 'Some towns really benefited from the increase in population – Mortlake, particularly.' He ran through some of the local businesses that thrived as a result. Eric Golsworthy had a team of carpenters building new houses and sheds on the soldier settler estates. He also had a prosperous hardware store that sold everything from shovels to timber. Golsworthy employed twenty men and did so well that the company had to move into larger premises.

The Delaneys were another family that benefited. 'They had trucks, carted scoria to all these soldier settlers, built the roads. Delaney was in a big way, and he bought a property through that business.'

We were now approaching Darlington, a village whose high spot had always been the historic Elephant Bridge Hotel, a bluestone

The Elephant Bridge hotel – drinks currently in abeyance

oasis built in 1842. For years, squatter Roger Cumming of Jellalabad used to prop up the Elephant Bridge, writing songs and occasionally strumming his guitar for a dwindling number of melancholic locals. Now he was gone and there had been a makeover at the Elephant Bridge. It boasted skinny flat whites, wraps and focaccia. White stucco walls and polished concrete floors gave it the imprimatur of being on trend. Breaking all class rules, it was drawing patrons from across the region. On one of my visits, the hotel was hosting a large dairying family from down south at Noorat, a booking that once would have crossed the social divide between Irish Catholic southern dairy farmers and northern Protestant pastoralists. These days the pub is suffering from the population drain and is temporarily shut.

From Darlington, standing in military order, thousands of sugar gums outlined the borders of the station properties. Established before inhibitors like superphosphate and introduced grasses, the trees were a living testament to Lang and the other settlers who threw seed among the welcoming native grasses.

Walk into a windbreak of sugar gums beside the Hamilton Highway and you hear their music. Breezes rattle the leaves, and branches rub to make a haunting sound. The English composer Edward Elgar once posed the tantalising question: 'The trees are singing my music – or have I sung theirs?'

The tuneful gums have a practical purpose. When they fall, they heat up living rooms and kitchens in wood-burning stoves, leaving minimal ash and making a mockery of the introduced cypress pines, which are hard to manage and are now attracting their own regime of diseases. On one trip through the district, I saw an outbreak of rust-coloured fungal pathogens among some pines south of Mortlake.

We passed the Jamiesons' property at Stony Point. Peter remembered, 'Old Mr Jamieson was one of the greatest gentlemen I ever knew, a hard worker with no airs or graces. One day of 100 degrees in the shade I came past and he was outside his front gate in shorts and a singlet, digging stones out so he could mow a firebreak. His son Robert married Rosie Mann, and they had three children.' But over tea and wraps at the Elephant Bridge, we had already learnt that Rosie Jamieson was in the process of selling her property and beating a path to the Bellarine Peninsula.

Peter moved on to nearby Rockgrove. He said it now belonged to Daryl Clark, who was running sheep there, but Peter remembered it in an earlier incarnation. 'It was owned by Peter Cotter. On the day of the big bushfire in 1977, when Streatham was burnt, he drove in to see me in Mortlake. He wanted to talk about buying another property. We walked out into a howling gale. My car was filled with cinders and ash. Fire was everywhere to the north of us. He left immediately and fought the fire all day, and at about five o'clock went home to feed the dogs. They found him dead. He had suffered a massive heart attack, stressed from fire fighting.'

On the way into Mortlake, we drove through an avenue of pines honouring the veterans of two world wars. I thought about how the trees acted as silent reminders for a generation that has lost touch with wartime sacrifice. On a hot day, they provide shade and a visual sanctuary, standing guard below Mount Shadwell, which last breathed fire and stone a mere 5000 years ago. The whole landscape here was interrupted by odd-shaped hills, flat-roofed mounds of earth, the fiery eruption points that laid down the third-biggest basalt plain in the world.

Mortlake was at the centre of the Western District road system, and was once a crucial staging post on the Warrnambool–Ballarat goldfields road. I thought of it as the quintessential Western District town, with its perfectly preserved stone buildings, impossibly wide main street, and 'For Lease' signs that betray a stagnant economy.

Today, though, the town appeared relatively busy. A team of workmen were restoring the main street, and shops were trading with a flourish I hadn't seen in some time. But to dig deeper was to find the stagnation that is widespread across the region. As one old-timer told us, 'The place is treading water.'

Peter personally drove much of Mortlake's wool-broking, stock and station business in the 1970s and 1980s, building a set of sale yards that have now grown rusty with inaction. 'When I started here, we had a sale of 800 head of cattle. Eighteen years later we sold 3500 weaner cattle in one sale. We had a tremendous business here, even if I say it myself.'

Peter worked for Dennys Lascelles, the firm that pioneered Australian wool sales during the 1850s. It became a public company and eventually grew into a big business, until it was swallowed by John Elliott's Elders. 'We all know what happened then,' Peter ended abruptly. Dennys Lascelles lost its identity and with it their core business.

As we left Mortlake and drove towards Hamilton my own personal gloom approached, the sight of Hexham Park covered in its pox of pines. Hexham township a few miles down the road was yet another derelict place. As I remembered it, it had never been bustling, but it did have a pub and a post office, and was home to proud people engaged in their landscape, working the large properties around here. Occasionally it was quite posh, with polo, parties and the odd impropriety.

Peter explained that what kept the village going in those days was the Manifolds' property, Boortkoi, which adjoined the town. They owned six or seven cottages for the workers and their families, and this was the basis of the Hexham population. Then half the property was resumed for soldier settlement, taking it down to 10,000 acres. The Manifold brothers, Andrew and Clive, had run the place together, but then decided to split and took 5000 acres each.

There are still Manifolds at Boortkoi, Peter said. 'Andrew, being the older brother, got the homestead, and Clive built his own house and sheds before he later sold it to a Scotsman. Boortkoi is probably back to 7000 acres after acquiring three of the soldier settler blocks back into the fold, and it has one of the most beautiful homes in the Western District.'

I remembered that house, especially the Edna Walling garden with its long walk, a series of white rubble columns covered with a framework of wisterias. Fellow gardener Helen Proudfoot once described it as a statement of 'restfulness and the rule of taste'. This was the soul of Western District ritual, so connected with the past for me, and with its own stamp of romantic nostalgia.

Peter continued mapping the country, reciting its genealogy, painting its past in words. 'This is Gubbins country on the right, Skermer on the left. Arthur Gubbins bought Coolana when it was considered one of the worst properties in the Western District and turned it into one of the best.'

He spoke of Arthur Gubbins with respect. 'He was a bit of a snob, Arthur, but he could do anything on the land. I went there one day and I couldn't find him, but there he was up the chimney, cleaning it. How many of his ilk would do that?' One of his daughters, Sue, married Andrew Manifold and moved up the road to Boortkoi.

We pressed on to Chatsworth House and into the main drive for a sneak look at the homestead. Peter told me the place had had six owners over the last twenty years. 'The Moffatts, who established the place, employed a manager until the early 1960s – big David McCullough, who had six men working for him. Every morning the men would line up at the stables and Dave would give them their instructions. Dave liked a drink, and if he had had a big night, he could be a bit peppery in the morning. He often sacked one or two of them only to reinstate them an hour or so later.'

The drive back towards Ballarat took us past Carngham, once owned by the pioneering Russell family. It had been a family jewel with a grand gatehouse, cavernous 45-room manor and wild acres of infinite promise. Its sorrow was stark today. The homestead was burnt out in 2013, and I could see nothing but burnt plantations and black, bare paddocks, with only the restored gatehouse as a sign of its glory days. James, the last Russell to own Carngham, sold it a decade ago. As we passed over the ridge and across the flats, a cold shadow seemed to lie over the place. Carngham was the quintessential forsaken land, stripped naked in the gathering dusk.

Peter and I drove on to his home and a well-earned whisky. The songline had finished without a glance at the trip meter. And today I had seen how the margin between failure and success on the land can be thin as piano wire.

The struggle is mostly over now. So many people have gone, beaten or triumphant. Like the ocean, the unforgiving plains are bounded only by the horizon, clad always in soft pastels, and in the distance in good seasons the purple haze of not-so-gentle rain.

4
The Scots

Of all the small nations on earth, perhaps only the ancient Greeks surpass the Scots in their influence on mankind.

Winston Churchill

The Scots who came to Australia were largely free men. In the years of convict transportation, English and Irish magistrates willingly used the courts to purvey one-way tickets to the colony and dispose of excess population, but Scottish judges regarded transportation as a heinous punishment and invoked it only for the most hardened recidivists. According to T.M. Devine in his book *Scotland's Empire*, this judicial subtlety boosted the numbers of English and Irish convicts sent out in the penal colony's first forty years. When the Scots began to flee their homeland in significant numbers during the 1830s, it was as free men responding to home-grown factors. The Highland clearances were entering their brutal nineteenth-century phase, which saw tenant farmers evicted by landlords intent on fencing off the old common lands and replacing traditional farming methods with modern broad-acre grazing and cultivation. Famine and the breakdown of the clans brought many former Highlanders to the shoreline, desperately seeking escape.

The difficulties in the western Highlands and the Scottish islands grew more acute after potato blight struck the region in 1846. Several well-connected philanthropists became convinced that large-scale emigration to the pastoral regions of Australia was the only way to deal with the potato crisis. They formed a London-based Highland

A typical volcanic formation

and Island Emigration Society, which mobilised funds to support the emigration of Highlanders, unusually insisting that they emigrate as family groups. Through this society alone, English aristocrats, Scottish landlords and Australian colonial governments between them provided assisted passage for 5000 displaced Highlanders in the 1850s. Some of these emigrants brought small amounts of capital, which was all that was needed to set up a rudimentary pastoral run, as the colonial authorities made land available for a token payment. Many Scots saw in the treeless savannah a similarity to the Highland moors and sweeter lowlands at home, with the advantage of superior fertility, softer weather and, best of all, freedom of choice.

The Scots focused their attentions on the fecund volcanic plain stretching from Werribee on the western shores of Port Phillip to the South Australian border. Some moved west from Port Phillip, while others beached first in the whaling settlement at Portland, then moved inland.

They lived in logs and under drays, scrounging a life in harsh conditions, gradually learning to understand the new frontier. There was little to impede them from moving into new territory. There were no fences, but they left about seven miles between their properties, with a furrow in the ground to mark a rough boundary.

The whole area was beyond the reach of law, with practically no police presence. The result was that the squatters dispossessed the local Indigenous peoples of an area bigger than England in just six years after 1836. It was a land grab of enormous scale by men who fast became a law unto themselves, riding roughshod over anyone who opposed them. There were more Aborigines than white settlers in Australia until the mid-1840s, but after that the balance was reversed. This was partly because white migration increased, partly because Indigenous people succumbed to hidden killers such as smallpox, and partly because so many acts of violence against them went unpunished. The courts refused to admit evidence from Aboriginal witnesses to crimes, so even some of the worst perpetrators escaped without penalty.

Even so, not all the encounters were violent. In James Ritchie's diary of an expedition through western Victoria in 1841, for example, he observed that black and white lived at 'perfect peace' around Mount Elephant. There were also Scots in the Western District who attempted to develop a sphere of peaceful co-existence and mutual acceptance between Indigenous people and settlers. James Dawson, born in West Lothian, came to Port Phillip in 1840 and established his base in the Western District a few years later. He and his daughter Isabella recorded the languages and customs of the surviving people around Framlingham and Camperdown, where Dawson had an impressive monument erected in the local cemetery to mark the death of Wombeetch Puyuun, the last surviving member of the local clan. Dawson also made many recommendations to humanise government Aboriginal policies. Presbyterian though he was, he opposed the idea of imposing Christianity and the English language on Aboriginal people.

In the early stages of the settlers' movement into the western plains, the squatters had no security of tenure, just a pre-emptive right to graze stock on the land, which was classified as unoccupied Crown land. Conditions could hardly have been more basic. A shepherd would look after his flock during the day, and then move them into a rough fold to protect them from predators at night while he snatched some sleep in a makeshift hut.

In 1847, however, a new Order-in-Council was proclaimed giving the squatters longer-term occupation rights. The colonies were divided into settled, intermediate and unsettled districts, and the Western District was included in the settled area. This meant that squatters could apply for long-term leases once the land was surveyed. They were also allowed to buy freehold title to land around their houses and outbuildings. As one critic put it, the new regulations meant that the land would be 'a sheepwalk for ever', because the established squatters could secure control for a minimum rent, then consolidate their ownership by making strategic purchases, so that they would never have to purchase their land on an open market.

There was something of a building rush as the landholders took advantage of the new regulations to build substantial stone houses for themselves. Among them were Scottish immigrants Niel Black and George Russell, who were supported by syndicates of investors back in Scotland. The impressive profits from Western District stations, which reliably returned 20 per cent a year or more, also attracted investment from Scottish banks and even widows' mutual funds.

And over the hill near Ballarat, gold was found in 1851, just as the colony of Victoria succeeded in separating from New South Wales. It wasn't the gold that interested the Western District squatters but the resulting population explosion. Between 1851 and 1861, Victoria's population grew from 77,343 to a staggering 546,388, and all of them had to be fed and clothed. The downside was that there was a mass desertion of farm workers for the goldfields, but many of them were soon discouraged. In the meantime, squatters such as the Manifolds at Purrumbete took on more Aboriginal workers, while others brought in shepherds from Van Diemen's Land. Profiting first from the demand for food created by the gold rush and then from the large-scale export of wool to English industry, the Scots made the Western District a cradle of unprecedented wealth. Already by the 1870s, the second and third generations on the squatting runs were growing up in bluestone mansions with manservants and maids.

Their social and political power far exceeded their numbers. In the late 1850s, just 240 wealthy squatters held all the pastoral licenses issued in Victoria, and the generous provisions of the 1847 Order-in-Council meant that they had been able to build up an effective land monopoly without paying for extensive purchases. Now, however, with the population boosted by former diggers and other new immigrants, a new coalition of political forces was ranged against them, from frustrated would-be farmers to middle-class reformers who feared that Victoria was sliding into a radically unequal society like that of its motherland. The squatters' opponents mounted a campaign under the slogan 'Unlock the Lands', which eventually led to the passage of the *Duffy Land Act* of 1862. The Act threw open 10 million acres of land for purchase in small blocks, which the reformers hoped would allow Victoria to establish a new class of small farmers.

It was a political disaster. By the time the Act was passed, the squatters had accumulated sufficient wealth to purchase the land for themselves. Stock agent Jim Hay told me the story of how the Act's intentions were thwarted. 'The squatters paid dummy bidders to buy the land, and then paid the bidders a small fee. That is how they accumulated the huge estates. John Moffatt of Chatsworth House was famous for that. He was lambasted in the Victorian Upper House for the skinflint mongrel he was.'

The main effect of the Act was to increase the amount of land the squatters owned outright. Within two years of the Duffy legislation, a million acres of land had been sold, and two-thirds of that area was owned by 100 Western District squatters. The measure intended to unlock the lands had actually locked them up by exactly the class of owners the reformers had hoped to dislodge. Thirty years after they were sleeping under logs and grazing their sheep on Crown land under annual licences, the Scottish squatters had become an economic, political and cultural force to be reckoned with.

In following generations, hardness and thrift were softened by a cocoon of success. Tales of excess: it was said that more than 80 per cent of the Scotch whisky imported into Australia in the late nineteenth century was consumed in the Western District. Then there was the Western District squatter who decided to celebrate his enormous wool cheques in the early 1950s by setting out on his own grand tour of Europe. He based himself at the Savoy Hotel in London, where he took a permanent suite for six months. All the while, however, things were sinking back home. Wool prices had plummeted, making a hole in his earnings. When a cable reached him with the bad news, the squatter fired back the best shot in his locker. 'Shear again!' But if the austerity associated with Calvinism had weakened before my family moved to the Western District, there was no missing the district's Scottish heritage, and especially that of Hamilton.

I am eight years old, waiting for my parents in an alcove of St Andrews Presbyterian Church, the dominant spire at the top of Hamilton's Gray Street, overshadowing the Anglicans opposite. Because of the hot day, the large, wood-panelled door to the inner sanctum has been left ajar, and through it comes the voice of the minister, getting louder and, for me, more and more threatening.

I back out into the sunlight, but the voice follows. From the great gusts of Scottish brogue I know the voice is not pleased. This is no pleasant Sunday morning sermon. Everyone inside must be feeling the heat. And the fire is not just from the sun burning on my neck above the starched collar and tie.

The voice is reaching a crescendo as the fists pound the lectern. No one is in doubt that they are sinners, incapable of true faith and at the mercy of God. As the towering gothic arches shake, so do I.

The voice has no need for clever phrases. His religious certainty rings out as loud as the bells of his church every Sunday, God's day. In his world, you're permitted to prepare a fire in the hearth at home on Saturday and light it on Sunday, but to do both on the Sabbath is blasphemy.

The voice is that of Rev. Neil McLeod, a follower of the fiery Calvinist John Knox. McLeod was steeped in the strict moral code of Knox's Scottish church. It was said that he once ordered his teenage daughter to return some presents she'd received. She hadn't earned them, he said, and should give them back before her soul was corrupted by the weakness of the flesh.

Yet I don't remember Neil McLeod as a monster. I was fascinated by his northern European parchment-white skin and ruffled grey hair. He had the ample figure of a man who rarely missed lunch. He was not big, but he cast a huge shadow in Hamilton.

He was convinced God had the power of salvation. Unlike other humans, who were enslaved by sin and incapable of repenting, the true believer was one of the predestined lucky few. I suspect this fortunate group included many of those assembled piously at St Andrews. Not that I knew these subtleties then, but I remain in awe of the way these good burghers crammed into the kirk each Sunday to be given the rounds of the Presbyterian kitchen.

When the collection bowl came around, it was laden with pound notes and sealed envelopes with money promised under a financial plan agreed in private. I imagined untold wealth enclosed in these secret packets, and I was probably right. The donation each Sunday was a down payment on getting through the pearly gates, or at least a credit against going the other way. There was a whiff of guilt in the air, detectable even to me as a young boy.

It seemed to me that the church was having two bob each way. The rich graziers and successful town businessmen were berated as sinners who could not buy their way into heaven, but they could do it by thrift and hard work. If they made a fortune on the journey, they could come this way and spread their wealth. Calvinism was capitalist-friendly and situated the minister as the personal guide to a parishioner's individual faith and destiny. That is what Neil McLeod's life as a Presbyterian minister was about, and he practised it with gusto.

St Andrews today remains true to the cause. While the Uniting Church gobbled up most of the Presbyterians, Methodists and Congregationalists under one roof in 1977, St Andrews refused to take part in the merger. Hamilton College joined the Uniting fold and has since become largely disconnected with St Andrews. David Schulz, the minister there, knows he has the job in front of him to stoke the fires that stirred McLeod's devotees.

About 80 parishioners now make their way up the hill each Sunday, as opposed to 800 in McLeod's time. I wonder if the egos of today would appreciate the searching, uncomfortable question McLeod used to ask: 'Does your life adequately reflect your calling as a Christian?' It doesn't leave much room for manoeuvre, and there wasn't much time for sophistry in McLeod's Hamilton then.

My father often travelled to visit Scottish squatters around the Western District in McLeod's big black American car, raising donations to keep the doors of Hamilton College open. Fortunately for them, the Scots have long believed education was sacrosanct. If you can't read, then the scriptures won't be read.

The two made a great combination. Dad's gentlemanly tact was a perfect foil to McLeod's forthright threat that man cannot save himself without acts of goodwill – and donating to the school was in that category.

But McLeod was far more skilled at receiving pound notes than he was at driving. My father would often arrive back from these fundraising trips ashen-faced after the preacher had run off the road at speed, skittling saplings and even flattening fence posts, then pulled back onto the country track with never a mention of their near-death experience. I assume McLeod trusted that doing God's work made them immune.

5

The Wool Boom

When I arrived in Hamilton, the 10,000-strong citadel of Scottish heritage was walking on air. It was a time of propitious wealth for the sheep capital of the world. My schoolmates confidently told me that a wool producer was never in danger of getting too big for his boots. His wealth was measured in Rolls-Royces, his carefree fortune bred by faraway politics and war.

A tense world had ignited in 1950. North Korea, backed by China and the Soviet Union, had marched against its brothers in South Korea, and the USA, inflamed by the 'red menace', retaliated by going to war. The immediate effect in Australia was a stampede of buyers to the wool auctions, seeking wool to clothe the Western alliance's soldiers in that freezing quagmire. The wool price rocketed to the proverbial 'pound a pound'. The Western District had never seen its like before.

Jim Hay, a retired stock agent, tells me that the equivalent in today's money would be 13,000 cents a kilo. 'Instead, it's 1100 or 1200 cents, and we reckon that's all right. So people were unbelievably wealthy. Their 1000 sheep, instead of being worth £2000, were now worth £35,000 or £45,000.'

My father Harry told me that in June 1953 he took a phone call from his friend Hal Laidlaw, who owned Toora station and was chairman of the Hamilton College council.

The gates at Toora are now rusting

'Harry, I've just bought a bottle of Scotch, and I'm coming up to see you.'
'Yes,' said Dad. 'What's the celebration?'
'I've just been to the Post Office and picked up my wool cheque.'
'Is it a good one?'
'Yes,' said Hal. 'One million pounds!'

My memory of Mr Laidlaw's visits may not include that particular celebration, but I remember the smell of cigar smoke and a man in tailored tweed emerging from Dad's study to disappear down our drive at sunset in the largest Rolls-Royce I'd ever seen. Ironically, I later discovered that Mr Laidlaw already drove a Roller, purchased the year before the million-pound cheque arrived.

The Laidlaw income that year was roughly equivalent to $34 million in purchasing power today. Costs were minimal. At the Mackinnons' Mooramong, a station of similar size, the ledgers show in September 1947 £4,800 for 25 staff for the month. Allowing for inflation in the early 1950s, wages might have been just under £60,000 annually, when the wool cheque was about a million pounds, and shearing would probably cost about twice as much again. So, about £120,000 spent to make a million. These were the maths underpinning that extraordinary age.

Hamilton was now not only the centre of the Western District, but in many minds the axis of the universe. A sense of overexcited self-importance gripped the town. There were dazzling balls, house and garden parties.

Stewart McArthur is a scion of the landed gentry whose family seat is Meningoort near Camperdown, at the other end of the Western District. When I asked him how he'd characterise Hamilton, he replied, 'Hamilton is not near Adelaide, nor is it near Melbourne, so it is near Hamilton. The people have always been a bit insular.'

But the Hamiltonians of the 1950s could afford to be insular. The town revelled in reflected glory from the graziers' new wealth and the growing political and social potency of its own Hamilton Club.

Winners please themselves. That brief 'belle époque' built on sudden wealth had created in Hamilton a distinct social order in a perpetual state of being pleased with itself. My mother Joan felt it immediately when she came to Hamilton. In Brighton, her home, she was recognised as a member of a well-to-do family, but in Hamilton she was merely the headmaster's wife and was invited to some houses but not others. Her social place depended on her husband's occupation, in a hierarchy set in stone.

Down in the village, it was the working men who glowed. The shearers were celebrating the fact that their piece rates had more than doubled – in the midst of the boom, 39/6 for a hundred sheep became £5. In the pub, the union organiser beamed. The Bluestone Arms was open, rollicking and roistering. The crowd grew, with thirsty soldier settlers boosting the number of patrons. There were nice nights of cards and rum, the footy club and beer, the locals pitching in after work, gratified by their jobs.

Along the bar were ranged the village's collection of essential workers: the mechanic, the bloke who could weld, the postman, the butcher, the baker, a railway worker. There were shandies for their families before they headed home for tea. Kids played in the car park in summer, and in the dark shadows of winter they waited for Dad, playing hidey with the town kids under the sparse street lights. The pub was a place of talk, stories, tales around a red-gum fire in the language of community.

There were pretty teachers and dances in the Mechanics Institute on Saturday night and movies in the hall, pictures of passion and film stars in the barber-shop magazines. There was gossip – and local people to gossip about.

But squatters rarely ventured into the pub. Some even made avoiding the place a job condition for workers: don't be seen in the town watering hole. The squatters were averse to having their secrets spilled over the bar, and they drew the line at drinking with querulous employees. Self-preservation, they called it as they stayed away.

Some had a staff rule that you could not drink in the local hotel, but Ian Armstrong ran Hexham Park according to different rules. He drank at the Hexham Hotel each week night with the locals, including his best friend, shearer Ken Hamilton.

The squatters might sometimes indulge themselves after a good sheep or cattle sale, but as a rule they drank elsewhere. Sure of their superiority, dismissing the risks of drink-driving, they would travel the long, dangerous miles into clubs in Hamilton, Ballarat or Warrnambool. Integration with the locals came later, if at all.

For the young men who had come into sudden wealth during the boom, everything had a season, a reason – polo, racing, hunting, shooting, fishing, tennis and croquet on the lawn, high teas and low heels kicked off at five for cocktails before the proper party began. Swell balls for daughters coming out and sons coming home.

There didn't really have to be a reason. The bank was paid, the war over, the future good, and everyone was tipsy with joy. It was party time on the plains. Dennis Farrington's band would play on, the tinkling piano merging with the magpies' song in the morning, phonograms and discarded suits decking the woolshed floor, and bleary eyes barely registering a hangover breakfast of mutton and eggs cooked on a wood stove smelling of lanolin.

Underneath all this, young men back from the Second World War now had money and time. They drank and stayed at the Windsor in Melbourne. Melbourne Cup week was a fortnight and the Royal Show a month. They had trouble settling, going back to the farm – soldiers succumbing to phobias had always been a problem, but never like this.

Alcohol was everywhere. There were jokes about who opened the homestead bar earliest, and late closing was never mentioned. The best Scotch was the one before breakfast. There's a famous story of a grazier, said to be Rod Calvert, turning up at Tom Austin's property at 8.30 am with the opening remark 'Your shout.' Fortunes were squandered and bad habits formed. The party circuit grew an appetite that could never be sated, a craving especially prevalent among those who had served their country. Returning to a commodities boom was a lethal, head-turning mix. For many scions of the pastoral families, the work ethic disappeared and just simply ran out of steam.

Neat Scotch fuelled the lonely pampas as the gilded invitations flowed. Guests rated the gatherings as one, three or five-pole parties, numbering the uprights in the marquee as a sign of the host's benevolence.

On the coast, Shipley homestead on the bank of the Hopkins River near Warrnambool became the focus of a glamorous social whirl involving bachelor and spinster balls, trap-shooting, golf and racing, especially meetings of the Warrnambool Racing Club. The city press ran reports of these parties, with guests representing the great squatting families of the Western District as well as metropolitan and interstate visitors. The newspapers sent their social editors down from Melbourne. As the *Argus* described the scene:

> On the sloping terraced lawns, old English wrought-iron lamps glowed among the trees. Beyond a thicket of cypresses, black in the moonlight, picturesque glimpses were obtained of the tree-fringed river winding among the hills. Autumn-tinted foliage decorated the ballroom, with festooned streamers and hanging Chinese lanterns making a gay colour scheme. Bronze and amber chrysanthemums were set in the lounge, and in the dining-room, where a buffet supper was served, were jars of orange and yellow poppies.

These occasions weren't always so couth. In the 1960s, I remember the social writer at the *Age*, the indomitable Meredith Dawson, stripped off on the circular bar of the Lady Bay Hotel after a hard day's racing during an overheated and socially reprehensible May racing carnival.

One of those who, in his own words, 'careered' through those parties was James Kimpton, who is connected to the squattocracy through his mother, a member of the Creswick family. During the wool boom, he was a Melbourne-based adolescent, and he may have approached the social life of the district with less reticence than the locals. 'I was a boarder at Melbourne Grammar,' he explained, 'although I lived within a tram ride. The fees were tax-deductible. I think my parents, who had lived through the war, felt they had some catching up to do and tried to live the life they had been deprived of. The same applied to many of the returning soldiers to the Western District.'

James's mother had been schooled at Clyde, a prestigious private girls school, and had strong connections to the Western District through her school friends. His father was Oxford-educated and had fought in the Air Force, so he also had an entree. James remembers attending parties out there to mark boys' twenty-first birthdays and girls' coming out as debutantes. Gilt-edged invitations would summon the family from Melbourne, and black tie was de rigueur.

'Starting time was 8 pm. Finishing time was often not until the sun came up next morning, and was often accompanied by some sort of breakfast. The parties were far larger and far more meaningful than we ever had in the city.'

James remembered passing sheep grazing, but he rarely saw much of the farms. 'You were conscious that there was history and heritage and a multiplicity of generations, people following in Father's or Grandfather's footsteps. You arrived on your own and tended to be with your own age group. You would stand around and talk. If it was a programmed dance, you would make an effort to fill in the dances, and if it wasn't you would chat to the various girls you knew.'

The place he stayed most often was the Afflecks' Minjah, because some friends of his, the Carter family, knew the Afflecks, and he was invited there on their coattails. 'The Affleck household was not uninteresting,' he said, 'because the children had been orphaned and they were in a sense in charge.'

Later, James saw the breaking up of family properties, including some of those owned by his mother's family in the Riverina. He said, 'As so often happens with families, it was easier with these big properties to put them on the market than split them up. I felt the squattocracy was being edged out.'

James mused about the squatters' political power at that time. 'If you define political power broadly, then they were powerful. They were club members, Melbourne Club particularly. They had prestige, influence and importance. They had been to the good private schools; some had gone to Oxford or Cambridge.'

He also stood up for their practical skills. 'To do what they did took a certain amount of skill, a practical knowledge and an ability to manage men. You didn't do the fencing or worming of sheep or shearing yourself – you got others to do it – but you had to know whether or not they were doing it the right or wrong way. You also had to know how to deal with your bank manager or stockbroker, to have a feel for the financial performance. My feeling is also that your place of residence was the land. You may have a city pad for social things and business meetings, but if you were serious, your property was your home.'

The apparently unstoppable wool boom was nowhere more celebrated than at the salon Le Louvre, an oasis of ersatz gilt, huge mirrors and soft leopard skins in Collins Street. This opulent boutique, which demanded an appointment to visit, became the ultimate destination for cashed-up Western District wives and daughters with a devil-may-care attitude to price tags.

Its founder, Lil Wightman, was a Ballarat girl who found fame and fortune in the Melbourne world of couture, taking advantage of munificent wool cheques. The salon's name was chosen because 'it just sounded French' says Georgina Weir, her daughter, but the name and the reputation obviously had an air of authority.

Georgina remembers the halcyon years of that ultimate Collins Street frock shop. 'There was a flock of wives of wealthy graziers that shopped at Le Louvre. They didn't go anywhere else. They came down from the Western District and stayed at the Alexandra Club opposite.' Lillian Wightman frocked them up, made their bridal trousseaus and produced the equally complex trousseau of clothes required for them to attend private girls' schools.

Lillian Wightman in 1981 with Amelia Coote,
who is now the head buyer for Le Louvre

The new Le Louvre, now located in South Yarra

'Mum was a hard worker,' says Georgina. 'She didn't keep lady hours. She loved that shop and she spent her whole lifetime there. Women would make appointments to see her. They would come in for maybe three hours, have cups of tea and, as my mother would say, 'buy their summer trousseau'. It was one-stop shop. Mum and Thomas Harrison the milliner would also go across to Adelaide on the train twice a year and do the same thing there.'

The trade was at its height when wool was fetching record prices. 'At the peak of the wool boom, they would come in and buy 15 dresses at a time. They needed them because life revolved around the races, and they needed those clothes to wear to the various parties attached to the races, like the Melbourne Club cup eve party, balls, and you couldn't be seen in the same clothes twice. Trevor Clarke used to come into the shop, a huge man with quite a presence. Sir Robert Law-Smith also loved coming in. My mother was good with those old blokes – she'd chat away about cattle or whatever.'

Georgina tells me that her mother would have dinner with clients at the Windsor, but she didn't make great friends of them, 'always saying if you did so, you would regret it. The shop was like a salon in the true sense. The Europeans would gather there because it was like a piece of home – artists like Louis Kahan and others. She was pretty straight-laced, not bohemian.'

Georgina belongs to the next generation and says the daughters of her mother's customers are now her friends. Many of them would never shop anywhere else.

Like her mother, Georgina will go to Paris to buy dresses with particular clients in mind. She says, 'I know what they want to wear, and I'm usually right.'

The business has been going for 90 years. When Lil first came down from Ballarat in 1923, she took a little shop in Howey Court, but then she moved up to Collins Street. 'There were a lot of doctors up there, and they had money and wives.'

Lil died in 1993, leaving a mass of mourners unsatisfied. Before she died, Georgina says, she announced her preferred way of going. 'Darling, I don't want any rubbish about coffins and funerals. I just want to float down Collins Street like one of those giant leaves in autumn.'

Reflecting on it, Georgina says, 'She virtually did, really.'

Some years after Lil's death, Georgina sold the shop. The site was to be redeveloped, but the developers were told they had to save the shop façade.

'There would be a terrible hue and cry if they tore the shop down,' Georgina says. 'I still have people come up to me and say, "How could you have sold?" But I couldn't refuse the offer.'

Georgina mainly remembers the Western District after the wool boom had begun to fade. She's an acute and acid commentator.

'The blood's got pretty thin out there,' she says. 'I remember the old, unmanageable houses – wife killers. There would be buckets around the floors, because there had been rain and the roof leaked, and nobody had the money to fix it. My mother used to talk about country houses as the great Australian loneliness with the blowfly jazz band playing on the window.'

Georgina was struck by how few luxuries the squatting families enjoyed. 'Many of those people lived in a very austere way,' she said. 'Yes, they did have parties, but by our standards today they were pretty prim and proper. They were mostly old Scots, and they wouldn't be spending money. They may have bought their clothes from my mother, but they lived in a sort of genteel poverty. When I visited their homes, I couldn't believe the sheets – I would have given them to the op shop years ago. That's how they lived. Things might be worn out, but it's OK, one of the great-aunts left it to them. I don't live like that. It would be on the bonfire. I don't want memories of great-aunts.'

Georgina also found the ever-present smell of dogs hard to handle. 'It was like living in a kennel, the stench. I love dogs, but outside. I don't sleep with them on my bed.'

She marvelled that the families who had so much money have none today. 'The big houses just sent them broke,' she said. 'They sold them and were glad to get rid of them. The Baillieus have sold half of the housing land they have at Melton. That's how they can afford the Western District property at Yarram Park.'

She was critical of the assumption that the eldest son would take over the property. 'Was he trained for it? Did he want to do it? Never sent to the right schools to educate him for the job. Came home and just got on the tractor and grew into a dunderhead.'

She asked a penetrating question. 'Is there any great art in the Western District? Where are the great artworks, good collections of furniture? Lil gave the wife style, and through that the couple had some style. But that was it. They could have gone to Europe to buy the best furniture, the best paintings, but nobody did it. If the money is just coming out of the land, it will dry up.'

And dry up it did, in a way that caught many of the squatters off balance. Agent Jim Hay gives his version of what happened. 'It was fantastic until the accountants said to the wool men, "You are going to have a huge tax bill. You had better go and spend some money." So they went out into the market and bought sheep at these inflated prices. Then the Korean War came to an end, wool prices collapsed, they had a huge tax bill and sheep worth only a third of what they had paid for them. That was the sting in the tail.'

6

In the Limelight

Time passes in Barwon Heads or Port Fairy, dragging the people with it. The belle époque of the 1950s is denied, stranded in its own limelight. Those who lived through the Western District experience hide more than they reveal. The belle époque also seems to have brought a doctrinal backlash among the most faithful. While most townspeople were happy to accommodate the dramatic influx of wealth, Hamilton's God-fearing Calvinists often refused to countenance anything that involved succumbing to Mammon. As far as I could see, this involved a denial of the district's social history, as became evident when I ventured to ask about the conspicuous consumption and general shenanigans associated with the wool boom. Many of those who lived through that era would have me believe it was a figment of my imagination.

Among the remaining rump of the squattocracy – a 'tribe', in the words of Eda Ritchie, who is descended from it and married into it – there is little recognition of la belle époque, even denial of its existence. Eda Ritchie sees it as part of a mirage created by player pastoralists and their party wives. In her eyes, the Western District was just a rich vein of soil that struck it lucky twice, supplying meat to the Ballarat goldfields in the 1850s and wool to US soldiers in Korea a century later. And during that second boom period, she says, the Western District squatters were more than fully occupied contending against the forces of the market, the rabbits, government measures that penalised wealth, and the demands of siblings with their hands out.

She suggests that I have misremembered the period because I was a romantic, impressionable youngster overwhelmed by a fantasy. But I venture that it is she who has mislaid her memory. Earlier, Eda had mentioned how her mother wore smart suits into Hamilton to grocery shop and drove there in a Daimler as if this had been common practice in the austere 1950s.

Another who questioned my version of the 1950s flamboyance was Fleur Gibbs (née Mein), a widow who has a huge, elegant apartment high above St Kilda Road and also retains the 6000-acre family estate of Toolang near Hamilton. Fleur denied that anything special had happened to her in the wool boom. I did observe, though, that she talked of her finishing school in England with matter-of-fact fondness.

'My mother took me aboard the *Orcades* to Winkfield, near Ascot, where I still go each year to the first day of the Royal meeting. My mother went off to Paris to brush up on her French with a six-month course at the Sorbonne.'

Fleur describes Winkfield as 'a finishing school for cooks or secretaries'. She learnt cordon bleu cooking, but she says, 'While they were intent on polishing my culinary art, the school taught me nothing about being a lady.'

As it turned out, Fleur did not become a professional cook or secretary, but went on to enjoy a life between the Western District and Melbourne, with extended visits to London as well. When she was in the Western District, there were black-tie dinners with the Ritchies at Blackwood or the Clarkes at Devon Park.

In 1965, Fleur married the Anglo-Australian businessman David Gibbs of Gibbs Bright and Co, a large international trading company.

They had a lavish five-pole Western District wedding on the family property at Toolang. The shining couple spent time in Australia and England, travelling between London and Melbourne with the smallest of suitcases, evidence that they retained complete wardrobes in both cities. David Gibbs, whose family had owned farming country in southern England for five centuries, retained a graceful authenticity. Gibbs built a reputation as a 'businessman of rare goodness', and on his death in 2009, the *Sydney Morning Herald* described him as 'not so much preaching the gospel as living it'.

But Western District pastoralism, Fleur asserts, was a difficult business. 'There was nothing exotic about it at all. My impression is that farming is hard. Always has been, and it was no different in the 1950s, apart from a brief respite.'

Those images of smart suits, Daimlers, five-pole weddings and English finishing schools are uncommon in the normal Australian experience of the 1950s, but these two ladies are intent on expunging any idea that the wool boom brought a 'wild old time in the WD', something they insist is of my own making.

Catharine Winter Cooke of Murndal is equally muted, although she didn't arrive until 1960 as a young bride from England. 'I would say on Murndal we have had 30 good years, and the first buildings were erected there in 1837. Those good years would have been from the 1930s to 1960, so you can see it hasn't always been high times,' she says. The 1950s wool boom, however, fits into that span of years.

Then there are those whose wealth allowed them to ride safely through challenging circumstances. Patricia McKenzie (née Mackinnon) was raised on Langi Willi at Linton, which was owned by her mother's family. She remembers asking her mother what had happened in the Depression. 'Darling, I have no idea,' her mother replied. Patricia tells me she has no memory of the wool boom. 'It was just life as normal. I have had a privileged life. We had staff. I went off to school. I don't remember any boom or busts.'

Like many Western District squatting families, the Mackinnons drew a large part of their wealth from off farm. Patricia's father Dan was a part-time grazier and Liberal MHR for Corangamite. His wife was connected to the Miller family, who had a history of investing in Melbourne land, and that inheritance smoothed the ups and downs. The Mackinnons still share in the ownership of Langi Willi and lease Mooramong from the National Trust.

The Western District withholds its legends. No writers venture here. There is not much sentiment, no drama, no love songs. Somehow the pale yellow paddocks have absorbed the tales of that epic epoch. No forbidden secrets emerge from the silent figures in the landscape, hamstrung by the fear of appearing to have enjoyed themselves.

7

Landmarks

Thinking about why this land has so much meaning for me, I realise that it's because I learnt its landmarks. Travelling on narrow bitumen roads, I'd look out for familiar hills, front gates, mailboxes and hidden homesteads glowing in the evening light. Those hidden houses gradually became places I'd visited, and where I'd met people I knew. It was then that the lonely spaces became more welcoming.

Now I'm travelling to Hamilton, with its tree-shaded hills and leafy glades – Scotland's Perthshire meets its colonial cousin in an embrace of rural splendour.

The novelist Martin Boyd once wrote that we romanticise anything we are interested in. I've been romantic about the Western District since I was a child. My idealising began in the 1950s, between the ages of 8 and 15. Hamilton was my city of reverie, the farms around it the parklands of my soul.

I was a boarder in a school for farmers' sons whose live-in headmaster was my father. While he ran the school, it could be said that I had the run of it. My boundaries were my decision; at night, I could either sleep at home or go through a connecting door to the boarding house and the dormitory with my friends. I could decide my daily bread, eating home-cooked meals or going to the school's dining room. Mostly I preferred to be with my friends, but the fact that I had a choice made me the envy of my schoolmates. Many of them came from faraway homes that they only visited at the end of term. For some, particularly the boarders as young as five, a term was an interminable twelve-week stretch.

Undisturbed by pangs of homesickness, I spent my time playing on the school oval and daily falling in prepubescent love. On holidays, I'd walk the burnished plains hunting rabbits or foxes with a pack of sixteen dogs. I was unfettered and free in a time of optimism and unimagined fortune.

My friends' fathers drove battered utes one week and Rolls-Royces the next. Some of them had two Rollers, one for town and the other for the farm. They lived in fine houses built by fine wool. At night, a friend and I sometimes stole down the deserted passages of his house and fetched Coca Cola from the homestead's own vending machine. I told my mother about it on returning home, while she did her best to stem the desire in me.

While workers and small landholders celebrated in town, the squatters caroused at house parties that lasted for days. I spent nights in homestead lying in silk sheets listening to the muffled resonance of dance bands and the squeals of adults pursuing each other. From what I heard, they were delighted to be chased – and caught.

The Western District's essential point of difference is the class who rose there in the nineteenth century to become the richest people in the richest country in the world. A lot of that wealth was celebrated here in Hamilton by squatters who lived within striking distance of the town. And when they came to Hamilton, they could enjoy their very own retreat in the Hamilton Club, an exclusive institution that allowed them to drink Scotch to their hearts' content with no risk of being seen by prying eyes.

The Hamilton Club – 'neck ties required for gentlemen'

Behind its Doric façade, the Hamilton Club in the past sported a notice: 'Gentlemen are required to wear ties after 5 pm'. Ironically, one of its founders was the son of the Victorian novelist Charles Dickens, a great foe of conservatism.

The first thing I see is the impressively named Alfred D'Orsay Tennyson Dickens Library, which specialises in Western District pastoral history. I'm rather puzzled by the name. Was the library named after a bunch of influential nineteenth-century writers?

In a way, it was. Charles Dickens named his fourth son after his godfathers, his father's friends Lord Tennyson and Count d'Orsay. Young Alfred probably bore the moniker with some embarrassment during his sojourn in Hamilton, where he arrived in 1874.

Alfred had come to Australia as a 20-year-old emigrant with the best wishes of his father, who was a great supporter of the idea of Australia but never visited. The young man initially bought a grazing property at Forbes in central New South Wales, but then, without much explanation, found his way to Hamilton, where he became the first secretary of the Hamilton Club. Not long afterwards, though, Alfred left Hamilton after his wife Jessie was thrown out of her carriage and killed. He died in New York in 1912 while touring America speaking about his father.

Tyrrell Evans remembered the Hamilton Club as the squatters' exclusive power base. 'In the early days, people were blackballed from the Hamilton Club because they were businessmen,' he told me. 'The membership were pretty much all squatters. One or two soldier-settler farmers managed to get in because they had good pedigrees and good war records. Jim McConachie managed to get in – he was a fighter pilot and old Geelong Grammar boy who got a block.' There were very few Catholics, though one of them, Reg Toomey of Kinonvie, became club president. The club also now admits local business people.

The club has been a hardy survivor. While equivalent clubs in Ballarat, Mount Gambier and Warrnambool have wilted, the Hamilton Club has miraculously kept its doors open. Although membership has risen and fallen with commodity prices, the club continues to prosper. It currently has 380 members and organises masked balls, restaurant nights, wine tastings, library dinners and over-60s luncheons.

The honour roll of past presidents is like an index to the old squatting families – McKellar, Learmonth, Winter-Cooke, Rippon, Armytage and so on feature. More recently there has been an influx of local businessmen like accountant Tony Gurry and builder Noel Gunn.

The general decline of the Western District squattocracy's political and social power is visible at the club. As Evans described it, 'The Hamilton Club has become a wine-tasting and dinner society, mostly town-based members, with not one grazier on the committee.' For the members to exert political muscle now is as unlikely as having one of them light up a cigar inside its hallowed walls.

In Hamilton today, education and health are the heroes, as trade slips. Reg Ansett's old bus garage is deserted in Gray Street, and the pub opposite is sullenly shut for refurbishment. There isn't a Rolls-Royce in sight. I'm reminded of the old joke about the town: 'Hamilton in the 1950s had more Rolls-Royces per head than anywhere else in Australia. They still have them now, but they're the same Rolls-Royces.'

One of the clearest signs of change is the role reversal of Warrnambool and Hamilton, the district's two biggest towns. Boosted by massive pastoral profits, Hamilton had a leading edge over its rival into the 1980s, especially after the closure of Fletcher Jones, once Warrnambool's largest employer and a rock of support for the town. In those days, Hamilton didn't hesitate to remind its coastal competitor of its ascendancy.

The rivalry began in sectarian snobbery. 'We shop in Warrnambool and have our social life in Hamilton,' was the cry of the squattocracy. According to Gordon Forth, author of the modern history of Warrnambool, Hamilton people who retire go to Robe or Port Fairy. They 'would rather have their fingers cut off than go to Warrnambool, where people with Catholic names walk around with greyhounds wearing cloth caps'.

But those who turned their noses up are increasingly sidelined. Warrnambool and Port Fairy now have 40 per cent of the district's population. Forth says provocatively, 'Hamilton has become a satellite city to Warrnambool.' While Warrnambool's service and professional industries have grown, Hamilton's struggling pastoral base has held it back.

There are signs of change in Hamilton, though, many of them due to members of the Murdoch family. Rupert Murdoch's late sister Helen Handbury and their younger sibling Anne Kantor each

Geoff Handbury

received a third share of $600 million when their brother bought out the three sisters' share in News Limited in the 1990s. Some of the proceeds were used to buy properties around Hamilton and further north, but the sisters and their families have also dispensed philanthropy to the town's schools, particularly Hamilton College and Monivae, the Catholic boarding school, as well as the Hamilton hospital.

The most visible member of the family is Geoff Handbury, husband of Helen, who has farmed in the area for years. Now domiciled quietly in Hamilton, he watches his Ace Radio empire expand under the chairmanship of his son-in-law and partner, Rowly Paterson, and his daughter Judy. At last count, Ace Radio owned a Victoria-wide network of 13 FM and 7 AM stations, the Melbourne Radio School and the *Weekly Advertiser*.

Rowly Paterson is very much a straight-backed farmer when you meet him. He seems a most unlikely media tycoon. In the Western

Allan Myers

District, he has a reputation as an efficient operator of broadacre cropping and is developing a major operation from his property Wirrincourt, near Willaura.

The Handburys first came to rural prominence in 1995, when Geoff's son Paddy purchased Collinsville, a legendary South Australian Merino stud, after the 145,000-acre station had been placed in receivership. Handbury sold the property in 2014 but retains The Rises at Balmoral in the Western District and various other properties in South Australia.

The effects of the family's patronage are evident all around Hamilton, from a luscious red sculpture in Gray Street to the refurbishment of Hamilton College.

When I discussed Geoff Handbury's contribution with Allan Myers, he pointed out that Handbury's generosity wasn't limited by sectarianism. 'He doesn't only support the schools his children and grandchildren attend. He gave $3 million to Monivae in 2013.'

Myers is certain that education is the key to Hamilton's future. 'The schools in Hamilton will be improved and draw pupils from all over the place, including abroad. Warrnambool and Horsham will be the two towns where Government activity is centred. There will be depopulation, and the occupations offered to people will be different, but I can see education having a role.'

Before leaving Hamilton, I look for public structures heralding the 1950s boom, as there were in the good times of the 1870s.

There's nothing. The boom was over quickly and came on the back of war and straitened times. No one felt like leaving a reminder.

There isn't a great deal of festive emotion along the Glenelg Highway either. I head for the South Australian border through the dwindling roadside town of Coleraine. Between Coleraine and Casterton, the plunging valleys and long views take me back to a schoolboy visit nearby at Wando Vale, where the homestead I stayed in had windows facing a luscious view of rolling hills and mystical gullies, but was blindfolded, covered by gloomy curtains the entire weekend. I came to the conclusion that the pressures of daily life in the Western District were preventing people from enjoying its compelling good looks – or even noticing them at all.

It goes deeper. I am certain the unnoticed landscape has played a destructive role in the lives of that fading ruling class. The huge dimensions of the countryside have dwarfed the inhabitants and broken many lives, especially those of the squatters' descendants. Their industrious forebears worked without a sense of class superiority. It was the later generations who embraced it with conceit. Their prosperity and social prominence also masked other pressures, like the feudal expectation that son would follow father on the land.

Walt Whitman, the American working-class poet, wrote in

A wedding party in Hamilton, 1995

Leaves of Grass that his own 'lack of pedigree allowed him to become the person he wanted to be'. In a contrary way, his observation would resonate with many squatters' sons who were pressured into following their fathers and grandfathers into roles that neither suited nor attracted them. It's a familiar story in the Western District, and one that rarely has a happy ending.

I turn from the plunging valleys and head back along the Glenelg Highway to a safe and familiar haven.

8
The Middle Ground

John Ruskin said the Scottish Grampians 'cause the most thoughtless to admire the glory of a supreme being'. Their Western District namesakes, viewed from afar, are a magical bulwark, a sandstone ridge of blue-green that must have been a friendly sentinel to Highland farmers alarmed by the lonely, flat lands of this great expanse.

At the southern end, the town of Dunkeld sits beneath the pointed peaks of Mount Abrupt and Mount Sturgeon, joined at the hip and vying for the tourist attention that now defines the Grampians as the Western District's 'go-to' precinct. But long before the makeover of Dunkeld, with its degustation restaurant, couth bookshop and underground electricity, there were other transformations that had nothing to do with men, just the movements of the earth's crust.

The Grampians fill the middle ground between two soil types, lava and loam, the latter nursing the picture-book red-gum woodlands around Dunkeld. There is a vivid illustration of the soil transition just off the road from Dunkeld to Melbourne. If you turn right onto Penshurst Road, a few minutes later you can see the soil change. Here, the open grasslands of the basalt plains, spreading for endless miles, take over from the parklands of the Grampians. No burning could have achieved this dramatic demarcation. The change to the plains from woodlands comes from the soil, and terra firma out here is not man-made.

Mount Sturgeon today, and as painted by Arthur Streeton

The farmers have adapted to the variation in soil and vegetation by alternating sheep and cattle, using different grazing rates. A minute up the road, near the discreet bluestone mailbox of Devon Park, I can see across to Mount Rouse at Penshurst. The landscape here is interrupted only by the homestead of Blackwood station. Perched on a volcanic mound, the rambling red Tudor pile is controlled by Chinese owners after 170 years in the hands of the Ritchie family, reminding me of the dramatic changes taking place as this ancient landscape adjusts to new owners.

A motorist stops alongside me. A commercial traveller, he says he can always tell where he is in the Western District by the location of the extinct volcanoes. He would have no use for a map even if there was one.

North-east of Dunkeld is the country where the artist Sir Arthur Streeton orchestrated his famous painting 'Land of the Golden Fleece', grappling with the heroic rocky range where Mount William rises from the plains. Streeton painted the same scene twice, capturing the quixotic light and incalculable dimensions that defied so many of his colleagues. For many, the Western District is a difficult mix of the obvious and the covert, of chocolate-box prettiness and the mystery of marginal wilderness. Sir Arthur got it. Born at Mount Duneed near Geelong, he had lived with the contradiction all his life.

Over breakfast in Dunkeld this morning, I was reading Gib Wettenhall's *Gariwerd: Reflections of the Grampians* when I came across the sucker-punch sentence: 'Sheep were only the first of many introduced pest species.' I'm now meandering north, thinking about what he said. The notion of sheep as an 'introduced pest species' certainly has no reality for me in understanding these kindly wooded grasslands or the people who have lived in and shaped the landscape.

Dunkeld, Scotland

The Western District identity is already darkened by blame, the squatters sorted as despoilers and dispossessors, their descendants' dispersal ignored. I fear that to moralise the colonial story in ecological terms will make the lost white tribe even more likely to jettison their stories of the past.

Robert Hughes in *The Fatal Shore* says Australians have ignored our history because we were settled 'in a jail of infinite space'. This contrasts with the USA, where Hughes spent most of his creative life. Hughes wrote, 'Space, in America, had always been optimistic; the more of it you faced, the freer you were. "Go West, young man!" In Australian terms, to go west was to die, and space itself was the jail.' Our aim was to forget our past and drive it down into 'unconsulted recesses', and this in turn affected our feelings about the landscape itself.

The Western District descendants in pastoral lands are in the front line of forgetfulness. Here, past and present are strikingly together. The people rub shoulders with history without wanting to disturb it. Historical societies flourish, and local happy stories are published. Introspection is the enemy of what historians call 'heritage from below', local stories documented by people who feel they belong, a process that in turn establishes and maintains identity.

There seems to be a particular shortage of written or oral testimony about the realities of rural life in general and soldier settlement in

Scotland's Dunkeld district; no wonder the squatters felt so at home

particular after the Second World War. Although Marilyn Lake's *The Limits of Hope* offers a searing account of closer settlement after the First World War, there is no similarly close-up examination of the next generation of soldier settlers. Could the people who lived through those years be inhibited partly by the new historians' heavy focus on indigenous occupation at the expense of their own? Reformist academic Sarah Madison says collective guilt about settlement crimes leaves non-indigenous Australians 'unsettled' and profoundly threatens 'our sense of who we are and the values we cherish'.

Two tribes have lived here. One was displaced, and the other is leaving. The romantic in me wishes this Grampians country could talk, whether in Gunditjmara or English, in words free of cant that can take us to an understanding of what shimmers below the superlative surface. I want to look beneath the cadences and clichés to open our human heart. History shapes people, and we need to get inside the emotion and texture of the settlers' time here.

As a reporter, I spent two days on the Baillieus' Yarram Park, one of Victoria's largest sheep and cattle stations, which is a few kilometres from where I am now across a swathe of bending grass and twisted eucalypts. My host was their cautious manager, but there was many things I couldn't learn or ask. Later, I talked to Antony Baillieu about his late father John, a scion of one of Australia's most famous financial dynasties who became an influential stockbroker and land boomer in his own right. Though he was such a large contributor, a creator of city and rural wealth, he chose as his headstone a small bluestone slab below a garden gum at Yarram Park, simply giving his name and his dates of birth and death. When I asked Antony whether a biography was planned, he explained 'He wasn't like that – he wouldn't have encouraged a biographer.' As a result, John Baillieu's insights remain unexplored.

But what led him to get into his car in Melbourne in 1948 and drive the long four hours to Yarram Park so he could buy a vast sheep station infested with rabbits? It may not have been a plunge into the unknown for a hard-headed financier with agricultural blood in his veins, having already been a partner in nearby Woodhouse, but it still had a touch of the Wild West about it. And did he view the land as more than a mercantile resource? Did it fill a need within him?

I stop at the entrance of once grand Toora, where all those years ago after drinking whisky with my father, Hal Laidlaw drove his Rolls-Royce through this opening, his million pound wool cheque tucked safely in the velvet-lined glove box. Rust is spreading into the gateway's white rails, and I wonder what Hal would have made of this tired entrance. He was a fastidious man who employed a full-time painter. And what would he have thought of Wettenhall's judgement? I can imagine Hal saying, 'Some pests those sheep on Toora! Perhaps the kelpie should have been next on the nuisance list – they can be a pain in the arse too.'

Cutting through lanes lined with red gums, I reach Willaura,

The Willaura Bakery, and its baker, Gary Jaensch

Yarram Park's local town, which has been degraded by time. It has that overwhelming feeling of something lost or disappearing, a Western railway town from Hollywood where the train never arrives. The steel rail line, dominated by a wheat silo, runs along one side of the main street. The derelict station is surrounded by temporary fencing, and there's a desultory assortment of paint-peeled shops on the other side. A red-brick barn of a pub is bedecked with signs telling you when you *can't* enjoy its hospitality. It stretches down the street, its size emphasising that there was once a much greater need to handle a crowd. The ennui walking this Willaura footpath of failed commerce is tangible.

At the western end of the main street is the Willaura bakery. It's open, a mother and two kids sit at a table eating buns in the shade of the veranda. I sit for a moment at a second table while workingmen in hi-vis jackets and wool-rubbed overalls arrive in their utes for their lunchtime pie and sauce.

There is a trickle of life through the old wire door, and a friendly grin from the baker, who tells me he bakes everything in house. Gary Jaensch is an import who fled a bakery at seaside Portsea in search of a quieter inner and inland life for his wife and two kids. That was eighteen years ago, and he's just had his best year ever. He is infectiously optimistic.

A young woman in her thirties bustles in, also cheerfully positive about Willaura, but with no obvious reason. She has been made redundant by a city-owned piggery down the road where, according to Jaensch, she basically ran the place. While waiting for her lunch to heat, she overhears my conversation with the baker. I'm a couple of dollars short in paying for my order of a chicken sandwich, a cup of tea and a late decision, a vanilla slice, which is now beyond my cash in hand. The bakery deals only in hard currency, no cards, so I have to forgo the vanilla slice. Then suddenly it reappears in its paper bag beside me. The woman from the piggery has shouted me the treat. I can still taste the random kindness.

Willaura, locals say, is named after the unanswered puzzle 'Will Laura?' which seems to suit the enigmatic nature of its future. This dejected town so close to the Baillieus' splendid Yarram Park illuminates the economic divide between town and country. They have never been so starkly apart.

The grandeur of the landscape around me remains heroically intact. It's the inhabitants, the figures in the landscape, who have been rearranged willy-nilly.

Farmer numbers in the district have dropped 40 per cent in the last 30 years. The withdrawal has been dramatic, the public upheaval intense, especially in the large soldier-settlement areas of Balmoral, Casterton, Hawkesdale, Mortlake, Caramut, Skipton and Terang. Most of the soldier settlers and their sons have succumbed, and with them has gone the temporary flush of population that filled the postwar pubs and general stores.

While the exodus from the farms was going on, there was a parallel flight from the towns. Here, the leaving was just as painful. People linked by kinship were prised from their hamlets and villages by economic rationalists who decided that time had run out for the wool towns.

In terms of numbers, they were right. The population of Victoria's Western Statistical Division, which begins 25 kilometres west of Geelong and extends to the South Australian border, was 198,000 in 1961; by 1996, it had fallen to 135,000, a drop of more than 30 per cent.

The underbelly of population drift is that the deserted communities suffer from desperately low house prices and giveaway rents, which attract those who can't afford to live elsewhere and create social problems of their own.

In the Shire of Minhamite, the number of schools has fallen from 43 to just two, the combined result of population decline and a policy decision to bus children to school. It's a classic symptom of degeneration when a town becomes too small to support a school, and it has negative effects for community life.

The decline of sporting clubs is another sign. Here, successful clubs were often built around a few families, and when they left, the clubs could no longer muster a team. The highly successful Bessiebelle football team, for example, often consisted of sixteen Sharrocks, all related to Geelong premiership player John Sharrock, but it eventually succumbed to population drift and family fragmentation.

Further north, the Hexham cricket team would field nine Jubbs and two Armstrongs, both of whose families have left. And at Orford, professional athletes from all over Australia used to compete at the town's athletics carnival, but both the oval and most of the town's population have now disappeared from view.

Glenthompson, Willaura, Hexham, Derrinallum, Cressy, Skipton and Streatham, all romantic names, were the proud home addresses of my schoolmates and their favourite football teams. No influence of the big league here. The home-grown team was listed in a pre-eminent spot on the milk-bar door, and reading the list was a winter ritual for the busy farming folk. In the street, people talked about the game. On Saturday they honked their horns, and on Sunday they gave thanks for the harvest – or a win. On weekdays, the dusty streets were alive to the cries of children after school and the labours of machine shops and engineering sheds, making the things that powered the place.

Now they echo emptiness as the abandoned wool towns of the Western District return to dust. Life has been grim in the rural towns. The pub was the last to shut, the post office just before, the shop that sold tomatoes and a reel of cotton, the newsagent a distant memory. No banks or doctors or undertakers. Time has gone by, taking everyone.

When I asked Hugh Beggs about the decline of the towns, he was philosophical. 'I think it's inevitable,' he said. 'A lot of these towns were so close together purely because of horse transport.' He argues that some of the bigger towns are doing all right; it's the little ones that barely survive. He said, 'Chatsworth never really had anything, for example. Miss Cross had a store with faded Smarties in the window. Our roads have improved, and we can transport ourselves around, so there is no need for smaller towns. Now it's half an hour into Hamilton, where it used to be an hour, and you wrecked your car.'

But there are costs in all of this. As the Western District is rationalised, bush workers and townspeople alike are pushed out, their skills not wanted or afforded. Many of the squatters still on their farms are like stranded whales hiding in the three rooms of their huge homesteads that remain liveable.

The big silence is deafening. The mute plains make no judgement on the disappearing occupants. Judged against history, the squatters came and went in the blink of an eye. Their imprint is vanishing. The silence unsettles the newcomer as a new age of working managers and contractors dawns. They are light years from their dynastic predecessors. Backed neither by family blood nor by religious certainty, they are the new, untried plainsmen.

9

Up in Smoke

> *For thousands of years this volcanic country had been like a park, for the grasslands were created by the regular and systematic burning practised by the Aborigines.*
>
> **Geoffrey Blainey**

The idea that the Australian landscape was shaped by Aboriginal burning has been gaining traction for almost fifty years. Archaeologist Rhys Jones coined the term 'firestick farming' in 1969 to describe the role of fire in pre-colonial Tasmania and challenge the notion that the continent was uncultivated before Europeans put it under the plough. In 1992, Tim Flannery's *The Future Eaters* emphasised how the use of fire had kept the forests open and promoted the growth of gum trees at the expense of more fire-sensitive species such as the Antarctic beech. A more recent contribution is Bill Gammage's 2011 book *The Biggest Estate on Earth: How Aborigines Made Australia*, which has helped bring this discussion to a wider audience, promoting the notion that the use of fire by Indigenous people had created a park-like estate across much of Australia before colonisation. The idea has been adopted by writers of widely differing views, including Geoffrey Blainey, George Megalogenis and Don Watson.

Gammage argues that the Indigenous people who were the continent's first settlers used a mosaic of judicious burning to create 'a great estate', a park-like food bowl, through which they ranged as 'free gentry', evoking images of English gentlemen gambolling in idyllic pastures. Gammage's theory reinforced the view of Australian settlement as invasion. Eastern Australia before the advent of stock was viewed as a nirvana for grazing animals, which browsed fenceless cool-burnt paddocks and were celebrated in stories and rituals the people's efficient land management gave them unlimited time to enjoy.

George Megalogenis ventures further in his *Australia's Second Chance* (2015), suggesting that Aboriginal 'cultivation by fire' had unwittingly prepared 'the land for a wool boom'. Watson's *Caledonia Australis* agreed that Indigenous people 'farmed with fire' and his *The Bush* (2014) excoriated the squatters for brutalising the fragile rangelands, introducing salinity, erosion and destructive hard-hooved animals. Watson's view of the changing landscape suggests we should recognise the spiritual superiority of Indigenous cultures over that of the Calvinist despoilers. He writes: 'Aboriginal religion demanded more respect for creation than the religion which held that God was the creator of all things'.

Similarly, Gammage argues that Indigenous culture is founded on two key principles: that people should obey the law and leave the land as they found it. These are surely the basis of a useful life, and not too distant from the faith of the white settlers, whether Calvinist or Catholic, who would have been astounded by the locals' discernment if they had known. Gammage uses the meticulous paintings by Eugene von Guérard, Joseph Lycett and Robert Hoddle of man-managed colonial Australia as evidence that Aboriginal people were superior farmers who understood land care and made a mockery of the white émigrés as land managers and conservationists.

But from the 'old history' – written by those Paul Keating would describe as suffering 'a failure of imagination' – come tales of a very different place, of thin soil and deep loneliness with no sign of Arcadian England. Australia, wrote Charles Darwin, was the creation of an inferior God. The gentleman botanist became disenchanted with each step of his ride west from Sydney to Bathurst in January 1836, questioning whether this agricultural wasteland would ever feed a soul. A few miles away near Orange, his friend Major Thomas Mitchell, a rakish officer and Crown surveyor on half pay, was preparing to press south. Later that year, Mitchell traversed the country west of Port Phillip, increasingly excited to observe the gold that grew out of the earth. He wrote:

> The land is open and available in its present state, for all the purposes of civilised men … In returning over flowery plains and green hills, fanned by the breezes of early Spring, I named this region Australia Felix.

In the style of a real-estate agent, Mitchell was the first to advertise the Western District under the sales tag 'Australia Felix' – 'fortunate Australia'. Ten years later, John Dunmore Lang toured the Western District and described the tag as 'rather a poetical designation than a proper name'.

The rest of the colonies were reporting mixed results for pastoralism and agriculture. Some of the densely forested areas became agricultural gulags where fortune hunters and ex-convicts simply hacked at the bush in all directions, their only plans to survive till next day. They had no time in a timeless land, with no knowledge of any Aboriginal universe nor desire to find it. Their sole claim to storybook glory was that they were pioneers. When they faced floods, fires and drought, they had no option but to stay there and fight.

But the land was different west of Port Phillip and north of the whaling outpost at Portland, where stockmen drove their sheep towards the 'weird horizon', where they found juicy grasses and a kind climate. The squatters said this felicitous land reduced the cost of producing wool because of the open character of the country and the sweet pastures, which were superior in every way to cold, sour-grassed burnt Tasmania. Fertile soils raised sheep that matured early and lived long, productive lives.

While stock thrived, the Aboriginal population declined; Lang estimated it had already halved in 1846. He visited a mission station near Colac, where children had been taught to read and write. The austere Calvinist lamented the Aboriginal plight, 'their pleasant land seized by strangers ... becoming a band of outcasts among their father's graves'. At no point, however, did the perspicacious Lang mention Aboriginal shaping of the landscape. In his 1847 tome *Phillipsland – A Highly Eligible Field for Emigration*, Lang conducted detailed conversations with geologists about the plains, but tantalisingly reached no conclusion. He wrote leaving the 'untold story of surpassing interest, the past mutations of the soil surface in this part of Australia, to those who have the science and perseverance to extract it'.

In Gammage's colonial Australia, the lush Western District must have been a living larder, yet *The Biggest Estate on Earth* barely mentions it. So what was the Aboriginal influence on the grasslands, which according to Blainey had been 'created by the regular and systematic burning practised by the Aborigines'? I decided to ask Bill Gammage by email. I asked him what he thought was the Aboriginal influence on the plains of western Victoria. Could Aboriginal people have been responsible for the lack of trees. I also raised the possibility, 'Did they burn mosaics in the great expanse after the explosive age of volcanic eruptions?'

My question was answered later that day. Speaking of the volcanic plain, Bill Gammage wrote:

> It's very commonly assumed to be natural isn't it?
>
> But trees grow there now, and that needs explaining. I suspect that it is not especially easy country for trees to grow, as they don't seem to have come back especially quickly. But it may have been grassland so long that there are no tree seeds left in the soil, so you get edge invasion at best.
>
> Certainly the grassland was open and extensive in 1835

and I think Aborigines had a hand in this. The question is why so open, given the fine-grained mosaic burning that was their specialty. On the face of it, such extensive grasslands hardly fit that.

Bill went on to suggest several possible explanations:

> They over-burnt while learning to burn properly. This doesn't really make sense, as in many places it is clear that they could let trees grow – that's not hard.
>
> They were protecting the grasslands from grazing. The plains from Melbourne to Mount Gambier, broadly speaking of course, were once yellow with *murnong flowers* – yam daisy. *Microseris scapigera*. Kangaroos and other grazers love yam daisy, but grey kangaroos graze out from shelter. Perhaps people kept the plains so open to protect the daisy from the roos. That would make sense. I was led to this possibility by puzzling at how people would keep animals away from favoured food plants.

Gammage's hesitancy is at odds with Geoffrey Blainey's confident statement about the grasslands' debt to Aboriginal burning. If, as Gammage speculates, 'It may have been grassland so long that there are no tree seeds left', then fire would have had little influence, because seeds need to be there before it can trigger their release. The history of vegetation in the Western District since colonial times also teaches us that the bulk of the local foliage isn't suited to fire. In fact, much of the 'stones vegetation' on the plains needs protection from burning to thrive. In the Grampians too, many ancient plants only survive without fire.

Locals are sure that the grasslands were established when trees were buried by multiple layers of lava. A farmer in the district, David Barry, told me that when he drilled bores on Bolac Plains near

Skipton, he found 'petrified wood, 30 feet underground, buried by the lava flow'. David was sure that the seeds had been smothered by the lava, leaving the open grasslands to flourish. David pointed to other effects as well. 'Waterways are also buried. The Western District is drained underground. That is why we have few creeks and rivers.'

Similarly, an academic study of sediment cores 70,000 years old has revealed that fire frequency in the district actually increased fifty-fold with the arrival of Europeans. This is reinforced by eyewitness reports from the 1840s, which talk about 'blackened plains' and the squatters lighting fires that spread 'as far as the eye could see'. This practice was later discontinued when it was found that fire soured rather than sweetened pasture, as it had done in Tasmania.

David Horton, editor of *The Aboriginal Encyclopaedia*, has argued that the 'use of fire had little impact on the environment'. As he sees it, the environment 'has been altered by climate change, not by the fire stick'. Phil Zylstra, a fire researcher who has spent a decade studying the Ngarigo people of the Snowy Mountains, says small areas were occasionally burnt for specific goals like 'reviving a declining possum population or eliminating a stand of parasite-infected trees', but it didn't happen very often.

Dr Scott Mooney of the University of NSW has adopted a similar view. He says, 'People have imagined the past. They have imagined the Aboriginals were using fire very frequently and very extensively in the landscape. I personally think they were using fire much more selectively around their campsites and when it worked for them on a local scale.'

Professor Blainey also made far more modest claims in his 1984 book *The Story of Victoria*, where he wrote: 'Aboriginals probably used fire to encourage green shoots of fresh grass, which in turn attracted grazing kangaroos.' In any event, the mosaic pattern of restricted burning Gammage has described couldn't possibly have created grasslands on such a scale. Victoria's government geologists remain solidly behind the theory that 'the western plains are the result of the spread of sheets of viscous basalt lava'.

The only reference to the impact of fire on the open grasslands is where it occurred as a result of volcanic eruptions. Neville Rosengren from La Trobe University has suggested that 'Volcanic activity may have triggered fires and local ash fallout that impacted vegetation and provided a mosaic of landforms and soils of different ages.' He has also observed that soil erosion had occurred as a result of 'long periods of weathering' thousands of years before European arrival.

Of course, Aboriginal people and fire were inseparable. Fire was used as a signal of arrival and illuminated their nights. They were 'peripatetic pyromaniacs' who burned any time it wasn't raining. The first thing James Cook saw on sailing into Botany Bay was smoke.

Moving closer to the Western District, there is no doubt that Aboriginal people used fire for land management in the heavily timbered Otway Ranges, for example, but as you move west there is little conclusive proof that firestick burning created the dreaming grasslands. Gammage's question, 'Why so open?' is unanswered in clear air. As always, it is dangerous to typecast the Western District or to assume it is covered by a general rule.

I am not building some reactionary thesis here, but would simply argue that the Western District's unique topography and geological history are not for burning. The plains vegetation wouldn't have suited a mosaic pattern of cool burning, and the fact that there was no regrowth when Western settlers intervened makes the assertion of Indigenous agency problematic. It is a romantic notion to explain the park-like plains as resulting from human effort, but as the facts stand, it remains just that – romantic.

10
Coming in from the Cold

Hamilton's Melville Oval is the mystical home of my football spirit. It was on this hallowed turf that I first experienced the highs and lows of supporting a football team. I spent a great deal of my youth watching football as a one-eyed supporter, the seeds from which have made me an old-age fanatic.

After playing in the local Hamilton competition on Saturday mornings, we trekked down to Melville Oval at the centre of town and watched one of the city's two teams, Hamilton and Hamilton Imperials, play against other towns in the Western District Football League.

Their best opposition was Heywood, a small town south of Hamilton that had won the district grand finals in 1953 and 1954, first by beating the Imperials and a year later by defeating Hamilton. They won with the help of two brilliant Indigenous footballers, Jack and Wally Lovett. It was my first view of their sublime athleticism and freakish skills, and my first contact with the family name.

Heywood always had a Lovett playing, and they were always impossible to stop. Their impact was such that on Thursday nights we'd stay up in our dormitories to listen on crystal sets to radio 3HA to hear the district's teams read out, always hoping not to hear the Lovett name, especially if they were playing one of the Hamilton teams.

The Lovetts hail from Lake Condah, a tiny village halfway between Hamilton and Heywood that was the site of one of Victoria's last Aboriginal missions. They are much more than champion footballers. Their experiences as a family are an inseparable part of the district's history and an abhorrent reminder of its past.

Tony Wright of the *Age*, a Heywood native, tells us that 42 men marched from Lake Condah to join the army at the outbreak of the First World War. Fourteen were Aboriginal men, and five of them were Lovetts. Later, four of those Lovett men re-enlisted in the Second World War. In all, 23 of Lake Condah's indigenous people have served in the armed forces, taking part in every Australian conflict up to the war in Afghanistan. Not one of these men received a single square inch of land as returned soldiers, although they made successive applications to the settlement bureaucrats who administered the Western District.

Years later, in 2007, the Federal Court finally granted the Gunditjmara people of Lake Condah access to 130,000 hectares of vacant Crown land, rivers and national park reserves for a new generation to administer. This land had been given and taken repeatedly over previous years. While the move did represent some compensation, it did nothing for the generations of Gunditjmara war veterans who had been rejected on the basis of their skin colour.

The Lovetts' football fame has drawn attention to their family's rejection, but their prowess has also extended down the generations. In 1982, Wally Lovett, a son of the Wally I watched at Hamilton, became the first Indigenous player signed by Collingwood, an AFL team that had previously been slow to recognise Indigenous players' potential. Later, Andrew Lovett and Nathan Lovett-Murray both had careers at Essendon, where the forward-thinking Kevin Sheedy encouraged Indigenous footballers to play for the club.

Back in Hamilton, I became an Imps supporter, as the Imperials were called, purely because of their captain-coach, Reg 'Bomber'

Murray. As wide as he was high, with a massive hairy chest and hands as big as dinner plates, Reg had played proudly in the famous working-class football team of Port Melbourne, where he had established a name as a strongman.

These were the days when local football was the focus of community fascination and central to its pride. Bomber soon became an inspirational leader of the Imps, refusing to be cowed by the notion that Hamilton, the elder club, should enjoy any special status. I would squeeze into the rooms before a game among tall men in long coats and hats, their ever-present smokes creating a grey haze above the excited supporters and the smell of liniment.

No one would say a word when Bomber spoke. He would growl, then boom and work his way up into a guttural war cry like that of his Scottish ancestors, the Murray highlanders, who followed William Wallace to glory or death. He was at his best when the hour was darkest and the club was about to meet its arch-enemy, Hamilton, getting ready in the adjacent room.

The match between the two local teams was the anticipated clash of the year – it never let us down. The Imps were always the underdogs, the smaller, less well-bred poor relations. This was the food of Bomber's feast, the stuff of the inspiration he poured into the players as they sat with their heads down, staring at the sea-grass matting beneath their studded boots.

After Bomber's speech, everyone in the packed room would give a roar of support, intimidating the Hamilton men next door with the message that they were in for a doomed afternoon. And so the civil war began – workmate against workmate, brother against brother and friend against friend. The battle rolled up and down the ground, all described on local radio 3HA by a man with a thin, reedy voice, whom I imagined to be older than time itself and always biased against us.

Normally we lost, but one special day, Bomber scythed his way through the entire Hamilton defence, putting a couple of them on stretchers. At the end of the game, we'd won. The Imps supporters, determined to savour all the joy, lingered long after the game had ended. I remember Bomber leaving the changing rooms and walking through a cheering honour guard to where his ute was parked at the back of the grandstand. He was grinning the victor's grin and looking a lot less fierce with his teeth in, wearing workman's overalls and gently holding his baby daughter.

If Bomber was a fierce, uncompromising footballer of Scottish heritage, so was the Aboriginal activist Geoff Clark, who was a veteran of many skirmishes in various local teams around Warrnambool and Mortlake. They played in different eras and different teams, but a clash between them would have been nuclear.

I last saw Geoff Clark at the races in Warrnambool. It was Warrnambool Cup day, but it was 6 pm and icy. I was at the entrance to a race club marquee, where the local grandees were entertaining Victorian racing officials as a postscript to this most important day in the town's calendar.

Geoff Clark, who lived just outside town, approached just as the security staff gave me clearance to enter. He stopped behind me and asked to go in. I wasn't sure he had tickets. He was dressed in the standard member's garb, a baggy suit and tie, as were his two mates. I stepped aside to watch, drawn by a circling sense of threat.

The security man sent inside for advice. I suspected he knew Clark's reputation as a professional pug and ruthless combatant on the football field, where he played in the South and Western Australian leagues as well as for Western District clubs. Now the fighting man was carrying the extra weight of financial scandal and rape accusations after being sidelined as the head of the Aboriginal and Torres Strait Islander Commission.

Though diminished on the national political stage, he still had a profile in his hometown. Defending himself when rape allegations were aired in 2000, Clark said, 'My only crime is that I am an Aboriginal and I have had the audacity to question the legitimacy of this country, to question the treatment of Aboriginal people ... and I have called for a treaty to settle our differences.'

Outside the Warrnambool race tent, the message came back: 'Let Mr Clark and his friends in.' Clark entered the cocktail party, which was now starting to gather some noise. He was listless, didn't stay long and left without fuss. A victory for both sides.

On reflection, I cannot help but see the irony in Geoff Clark. His aggression is stereotypical of the dispossessed. He is the product of an Aboriginal mother and a white father of Scottish ancestry. His ancestors have been the targets of ethnic cleansing on two sides of the world, here and in Scotland.

Who is to say which of his antecedents was more grievously wronged in their native land? It was an act of economic terrorism when the Scots were driven from their tenant farms during the Highland clearances, starved of food and denied the opportunity to practise clan tradition. When they could stand the degradation no more, they boarded boats bound for the bottom of a universe, to a foreign land of which they had no conception.

Then it was Aboriginal people's turn for forced removal and the destruction of their way of life. Nowhere was it more ruthless than in the Western District. The secret was well kept for generations, but is awakened now in young Indigenous people, who rise in anger at its injustice. Yet there is also a deeper response; with the help of historians like Bill Gammage, there is hope that white and black society can piece together the remnants of a civilisation that had learnt to live with this land.

Still, the majority of the recent settlers turn a baleful eye towards Indigenous people, feeling locked out of any connection with their cultural past. Some, failing to understand Aboriginal people's difference, accuse them of failing to adapt. Clark was raised by his

Aboriginal grandmother Alice at Framlingham, a hamlet outside Warrnambool that became a settlement of fringe dwellers after the local people refused to obey when the reserve managers ordered them to leave. He has stormed about it all his life, and what was once a brilliant career has since been cut down.

It was in Clark's lifetime that black anger rose above the surface and governments tried to abate it with billions in handouts. I remember attending a function in Canberra on the day Prime Minister John Howard was called a racist in Parliament. Howard, whom I knew from my days in the press gallery, told me with pained disbelief, 'And I had just signed off on a bill giving $2.4 billion to Aboriginal welfare.'

They say money speaks all languages, but it hasn't spoken in Indigenous tongues. Nothing will assuage the fury of the dispossessed. I saw it that night after the Warrnambool Cup, when a barely contained furnace could easily have erupted at yet another affront.

Oddly, if you go back a couple of hundred years and place Geoff Clark in Scotland with his blue eyes and ginger hair, he could equally have been waving a cutlass on the Culloden heath, crying 'Freedom' as a brave heart fighting for his birthright.

11
A Lost Land

There is on some properties a palpable sense of life gone by, of loss and a creeping, rural, melancholic paralysis.

Andrew Clark

There is something deeply romantic about the idea of a lost land that once defined its times but is barely remembered today. It evokes images of kingdoms rendered impotent by a bad royal marriage or a king gone mad. European antiquity is littered with these forgotten kingdoms. The Western District can't claim such elevated status, but in 1863 the squatters were bold enough to propose seceding to form a separate state called 'Princeland', which would cover the Western District and south-east South Australia. The move was led by Edward Henty, who had founded the settlement at Portland almost twenty years before. Portland was to be the new colony's port, and its capital would be Mount Gambier.

Arrogant as ever, the squatters were confident that Princeland would prosper because their wealth dwarfed that of the rest of Victoria by a ratio of four to one. They raised 1500 signatures on a petition to the Queen, but it was swiftly rebuffed. To establish the new colony would require agreement from South Australia and Victoria, but both understandably refused to support the move.

Having abandoned the idea of establishing their very own colony, the squatters focused on asserting economic and political power by more conventional means, capitalising on their position as Australia's largest export industry. Charles Massy points out that the large-scale

STATIONS.

NAME OF STATION	OCCUPIERS	AREA	GRAZING CAPABILITIES	NAME OF STATION	OCCUPIERS
Ballangeich (Home)	John Eddington	12,000 acres	3,000 cattle	Linlithgow Plains	P. and G. M'Arthur
Blackwood	D. Ritchie	5,500 ,,	5,500 sheep	Merrang	Area and grazing caps
Burril Burril	Sanderson and Co.	21,000 ,,	21,000 sheep	Minjah	J. Ware
Bushy Creek	F. Beggs	11,700 ,,	11,700 sheep	Muston's Creek, No. 1	J. Ware
Caramut	R. and H. De Little	12,000 ,,	12,000 sheep	Muston's Creek, No. 2	J. Ware
Bryan O'Lynn	D. Wilson	6,800 ,,	860 sheep	Pollockdale	A. M'Kinlay
Drysdale (Home)	J. Eddington and Son	13,800 ,,	3,860 cattle	Purdut	D. Hutton
Dunmore	Hamilton and M'Knight	41,000 ,,	6,150 cattle	Spring Creek	R. Whitehead
Eumeralla E.	Ed. Hurst	10,000 ,,	10,000 sheep	St. Kitts	E. Youl
Gazette (Home)	W. Hutten	21,500 ,,	21,500 sheep	Sturgeon, Mount 3	H. Glass
Glenormald (Home)	J. Hutchinson	24,000 ,,	24,000 sheep	Sturgeon, Mount 4	H. Glass
Grasmere	Wm. Carmichael	15,000 ,,	2,300 cattle	Sturgeon Mount, Plains S.	S. and G. Henty
Greenhills	J. Austin	10,500 ,,	7,875 sheep	Taroome	H. Phillips
Greenhills (Home)	John Ware	18,000 ,,	4,750 cattle	Tea Tree Creek	C. Willis
Harton Hills	Wm. Carmichael	30,000 ,,	18,500 sheep	Woodhouse	S. Ritchie
Hopkin's Hill	J. Moffatt	57,000 ,,	37,000 sheep	Woodlands (Home)	W. Nicholson
Koler	J. Twomey	3,000 ,,	3,000 sheep	Yambuk	W. Hindhaugh
Laurcany	P. and G. M'Arthur	8,260 ,,	9,051 sheep	Vanghar	A. Lang

A listing of stations, their owners, extent and carrying capacity

industrial use of Australian Merino wool in England marked the first time that manufacturers had ever been able to apply mechanised processes to animal fibre. By the 1880s, Britain had the largest wool industry the world had ever seen, concentrated in the industrial cities of Yorkshire and Lancashire. For decades, wool was our most valuable export, and Australia was indeed 'riding on the sheep's back'. Woolgrowers were an elite class with a grip on power far in excess of their electoral numbers. Wealthy and often university-educated, they formed the bedrock of the conservative coalition both in the states and in Canberra.

Governments also played an important role in the wool market, especially during wartime, because wool was strategically important for making the troops' uniforms and blankets. The British government bought the whole Australian clip during both world wars. Now and then, there were murmurs in Australia and Britain about establishing a permanent scheme under which governments would buy the clip. Most woolgrowers resisted the notion, distrusting government intervention in the market, but the idea was floated again after wool prices plummeted at the end of the Korean War.

From the mid-1950s, demand for wool became increasingly fragile. Cheap synthetic fibres had been developed from petrochemicals, and they were being used in blends with cotton, wool's great historical rival, to produce cheap, colourfast, wash-and-wear textiles of consistent quality that grabbed the attention of fashionistas and the merchandising world. Then Britain, long the Western District's emotional and economic hub, began to explore the possibility of joining the European Common Market, as it was then known.

The woolgrowers' response was to panic. Using funds raised from a levy on growers, the Australian Wool Council began lavishing money on expensive public-relations campaigns. These made millionaires of advertising agents, fashion photographers and magazines like *Vogue* but didn't lay a glove on market preference, as wool went out of fashion and the price continued to slip.

The falling wool price galvanised the agrarian socialist element in the Country Party, which had long supported using government intervention to privatise their profits and socialise their losses. The key figures agitating for intervention in the wool industry were the agri-political behemoth Sir William Gunn, a Queensland grazier, and Country Party leader 'Black Jack' McEwen. The two began promoting a scheme to control the stalling wool market by setting a minimum price and establishing an organisation to buy wool that fell short of that level, to be stockpiled until the market recovered.

Gunn and McEwen were victorious in April 1969, when a new body called the Australian Wool Marketing Corporation was established, with power to buy up to 40 per cent of the national wool clip. These powers were put into action in 1971, at a time of historically low wool prices, when the coalition government introduced what it called a Wool Deficiency Payments Scheme, promoted as a temporary measure to provide a safety net for the industry. Introducing the legislation to parliament, the Country Party's Doug Anthony described it as 'filling potholes in the market'. Two years later, the

Whitlam Labor government converted it into a more permanent reserve price scheme.

Sceptics pointed out that there had been comparable price maintenance schemes in the past, but all of them had eventually collapsed, causing massive disruption to markets. Most recently, New Zealand's wool price scheme had collapsed in 1967. It wasn't a good omen. The only price maintenance scheme that had survived was the De Beers diamond cartel. But the promoters of the scheme were scornful of any criticism, and they succeeded in persuading both the coalition and the ALP that intervention could be justified as a measure to achieve stability.

Supporters of the reserve price pointed to the increasing volatility of the market as a reason for intervention. Japan had emerged as Australia's biggest customer for wool, but its purchases came in fits and starts. 'They would buy up vast amounts and then stop suddenly, meaning big fluctuations in the price,' former Wool Corporation chairman Hugh Beggs told me. Sir William Gunn and David Asimus, Gunn's successor at the corporation, both advocated minimising fluctuations by buying wool when Japan was out of the market.

For quite a long time, the reserve price scheme appeared to be working. Trading conditions were stable for much of the 1970s, and wool prices rose gently. But after Labor won government in 1983, the Wool Corporation faced an increasingly risky environment. The Australian dollar was floated in December that year, demolishing the corporation's argument about achieving price stability, which was now an impossible goal. For a time, wool benefited from the dollar float. As the value of the Australian dollar fell in the mid-1980s, international buyers found the price of wool more competitive. Demand picked up and prices with it. Wool prices spiked in 1987 and early 1988 when it emerged that international buyers couldn't obtain enough wool to fulfil the orders they had taken. The atmosphere was reminiscent of the boom during the Korean War.

But it was a temporary flush. In spite of all the corporation's marketing efforts, wool continued to lose out to cotton and synthetics, and its position became less competitive as prices rose, especially when the value of the Australian dollar began to edge up again. David Asimus at the Australian Wool Corporation seemed oblivious to these developing structural problems. In the fevered environment of the 1980s, the corporation set higher and higher reserve prices, lifting them by about 70 per cent in a couple of years. Finally, in 1988, just as Asimus was leaving the industry, the Wool Corporation made the fateful decision to lift the reserve price to 870 cents a kilo. Ignoring warnings from international clients that wool orders were drying up, Asimus insisted that the corporation's skilled marketing had shifted wool onto a 'new price plateau', where it would permanently stay.

At the same time, high wool prices had attracted new growers to the industry. The Australian sheep population began increasing rapidly in the mid-1980s, boosted by a run of good seasons. But just as the size of the clip began to approach record levels, demand for wool fell away. At this fatal point, the corporation began purchasing huge quantities of wool to prop up the reserve price. The corporation spent all its reserves and then borrowed money, eventually building up a vast stockpile of 4.77 million bales of wool and a debt of $2.8 billion.

This put the Labor Minister for Primary Industry, John Kerin, in a quandary. To suspend or cancel the reserve price scheme would send the wool market into a tailspin, exposing the government and the corporation to criticism. He repeatedly put off making a decision, but even as he hesitated, the position became more desperate. The Corporation acted at last in February 1991; the reserve price scheme was suspended immediately and abolished soon after.

A drastic fall in wool prices followed. Wool was soon selling for 430 cents per kilo, less than half the old reserve price.

The effects spread across the globe. Overseas customers who had bought at the old price were saddled with expensive stock that could only be resold at a loss, and they vented their fury on the Australians. In Australia's wool-growing districts too, the value of stock and land fell sharply. Stock and station agent Jim Hay recalled, 'Land I had just bought at $700 an acre was now worth $400. That took fifteen years to get over.'

The massive wool stockpile too was devalued. Wool that had cost the corporation $5.7 billion to purchase was only worth $1.4 billion in March 1991. It was a decade before the last bale was sold, and about the same time before the debt was paid off.

Charles Massy has branded the result the worst corporate collapse in Australian history. In today's terms, he estimates the cost of the disaster at $32 billion, of which $12 billion was paid by woolgrowers and the remaining $20 billion by taxpayers. The loss, he says, eclipsed the excesses of the 1980s entrepreneurs, and the wool industry has never recovered. Twenty-five years after the scheme failed, Australia had lost almost 60 per cent of its sheep population, and annual wool production had fallen to less than a third of its level before the abandonment of the scheme.

Few Western District squatting families were prepared for a crisis of this magnitude, and even fewer could readily adapt to a future in which wool was no longer a ticket to wealth. Bill Wood believes that many of the old dynasties foundered because of their sons' spoilt or wayward lifestyles. 'They would come back from safari in Africa or a life in London expecting to run a sheep station. They just didn't know how, and often it led to clashes with good managers who had run the place in their absence. The managers left, and the sons ran the place into debt with bad decisions.'

Tribal member Russell Chirnside, who was born at Carranballac near Skipton, agrees. 'The sons of families with money wanted to play, not work. Life on the land was too tough for them.'

Watching keenly from a distance, Wally Merriman and Hugh McLachlan both remark on the softness among those who wore the crown. Merriman, a Merino breeder from Yass in southern New South Wales and Chairman of Australian Wool Innovation, says, 'We basically arrived at the same time as the Western District squatters, but their land was much more forgiving. We had droughts and barren hills, more marginal. They had creek systems, built-in water. They were never like us.'

McLachlan, Australia's biggest sheepowner and as hard as Adelaide's water, prefers to link his attitudes to the simplicity of sport. 'We found the Western District polo teams pretty easy to beat,' he says. 'We knocked them off their horses with ease.'

Perhaps the matchless fertility of the Western District gave its inhabitants too much security. Oscar Wilde cynically said that ownership of property sowed the seeds of its own destruction: it gave one 'a position in society but it took away the means of maintaining it'. Hanging on to inherited property rarely has benefits in cold, hard cash.

Peter Learmonth has a unique perspective on this question. He was part of a founding pastoral family but spent his working life off the land, dealing with squatters – including some his own age – who treated him like a servant. He tells many stories about the snobbery and rudeness he encountered.

Like hawkers and tradesmen, Peter was expected to approach the homesteads by the back door, because the front door was reserved for family and friends. But even at the back door, he encountered trouble. One day he knocked on the back door of a homestead at noon. The owner, a man of some note, came out and asked him what he wanted. Peter says, 'I apologised for my timing, told him what I was about, and asked him for five minutes of his time. He replied, "We have lunch at 12" and slammed the door in my face. I sat in the car until one o'clock and then went again to the back door. He didn't invite me in for a cup of tea or a glass of water. I interviewed him for about ten minutes and then left. That is the first and only time I went near anybody at 12 o'clock. I always avoided the dreaded sacrosanct lunch hour.'

Another experience of Western District haughtiness came when he was asked to drop off some machinery parts for a man who had been a few years ahead of him at Geelong Grammar and was now operating the family property with his brother. Peter knocked and knocked on the back door, but nothing happened. 'I could hear them inside, but no one stirred,' he said, so he went to the front and rang a bell there.

'Out came this fellow. He looked me up and down and said, "What are you doing here?" I said, "I have brought the parts you ordered." He said, "Never ever come to the front door. In your position you come to the back door." I gave him the parcel, walked to my car and drove off with a little bit of speed, scattering gravel everywhere.'

But eventually Peter got his own back. 'I was sitting at my desk at Mortlake when my secretary came in and said, "There is a man to see you." We had a front door for clients and a side door, a goods entrance. I walked out and it was the same fellow. He was flogging drench for a pharmaceutical company. He had lost everything. I asked, "Which door did you come in?" He said, "The front door." I said, "Your type use the side door" and walked back into my office. It had taken 25 years, but it was sweet,' Peter said with a grin.

He believes there are two types of farmers in the Western District: the haves and have-nots. The have-nots haven't been born into families with 10,000 acres, but they have a good education, and they have had it drilled into them that they have to work.

'The have-nots are the people I admire,' Peter says. 'They're people who have worked hard, debt-free.'

Looking south-west from the spine between Coleraine and Casterton

The haves are more problematic in his view. 'The people who have it don't quite realise that it will run out unless they are prepared to put in and work. They have been born with a silver spoon in their mouth. And it *is* going to run out.' In many cases, their desire for the trappings of entitlement has squeezed the life out of them, leading to a terminal rupture of their connection with the land itself.

Bruce Whitson, who has spent his working life as a plumber based in Mortlake, remembers that the front drive was also out of bounds. You had to go in from the back or the side and wait until someone was ready to show you what needed to be done.

Bruce used to work on windmills out in the paddocks, and he talks of being driven for miles in the back of an open truck with dust or rain and cold for company, because the pecking order said there was no seat for him in the front. When he got there, his safety was the least of the squatter's considerations. He'd be stepping gingerly around a 10-foot head on a 6-inch board 25 feet above the ground with no safety railings. That was just how people did things in those days.

Kim McKellar, an equine vet in Ballarat, watched as the squatters' love of thoroughbred horses was moderated by economics. He saw rural landowners move out of speculative breeding as farming became strictly business.

'It was a huge social change,' he told me. 'All of a sudden the squatters had to go and work, and that was pretty hard for a lot of them to do. They were used to staying in the big house and occasionally strutting their stuff on the front lawn and going back inside again. Now they had to drive tractors and all that sort of stuff. That is when they said, "We can't afford to buy racehorses." They could still dress up and go to the carnival, but that was their one holiday for the year. The money wasn't there. They all used to pay their bills once a year. You never got anything until the wool cheque came in.'

The changing conditions in the district have placed a premium on skill and flexibility. One couple who were fortunate – or prescient – enough to avoid the worst fallout from the wool crisis were David and Kaye Blackburn of Eilyer, a property of almost 9000 acres south of Lake Bolac. Aware that problems were emerging when the wool price fell sharply in 1988, they had begun to diversify into cropping before the 1991 crisis struck. David told me, 'Traditionally, this place was all wool and some cattle. After wool collapsed in 1988, we went into cropping. Today we have at least 3500 acres under crops, while we still carry 6000 sheep and 300 cows.'

Kaye, a member of the Austin family, took over the property from her father Derek before he died. While other squatting families have retreated from the district, she and David have expanded their holdings. David said, 'We have bought places on our boundary, including two settlers' blocks that had aggregated into about 2000 acres.' The move was intended to help their two sons, both of whom wanted to go on the farm.

David and Kaye were glad their boys were interested. David said with a touch of pride, 'It will make eight generations occupying this land.'

The Blackburns' stand-and-deliver attitude stays with me as I drive away across the moonscape towards Lake Bolac. Their attitude to change and expansion reinforces some remarks Hugh Bromell made from his farmlet on the Bellarine Peninsula, a place he bought after selling his family property near Hamilton. He said, 'There are the aristocrats like the McArthurs and Winter Cookes who will never sell, the people like the Blackburns who have two sons included in the future, and there are those like me who had a son and a daughter who didn't want the place and had no other decision but to get out.'

Hugh's life as a pastoralist was once a fortunate one, with a social status impossible to achieve in town. That idea has gone now. Society has deleted the word 'romantic' from descriptions of life on the land, and off-farm careers in stockbroking, banking or the law have become the preferred options for farmers' eldest sons. Young women too, like Hugh's daughter, are more likely to choose life in the city after boarding school and university.

Travelling around the Western District today, though, I find a mood of steadfastness among those who have stayed, a stolid keenness to maintain the integrity of a dwindling minority. Some have turned to their daughters for continuity of family ownership, as Kaye Blackburn's father did a generation ago. But even this change cannot preclude the notion that the Western District has become a 'used to be' place. The people are leaving the vast landscape; it's even less likely you will see a human now than it was a decade ago, as services centralise and fewer people work the land. The dynastic people of the district believe its glorious past vanished with the wool industry. Filling the gap is both the problem and the challenge. A daring confrontation with the future awaits.

12
Blue Blood, Bluestone

I'm driving east on the Chatsworth Road, half an hour out of Hamilton, toward an enclave that was once the heart of Western District political power. Ahead are Blackwood and Nareeb Nareeb, two long-established properties whose labyrinthine homesteads were the meeting places for a regular salon of like-minded grandees, all of them related, occupying key sites of political and economic power from the 1950s to the 1990s. This group decided many crucial matters of the time, including the fate of their own people.

I doubt if Australia ever had another power mix quite like it. The salon included a prime minister, Malcolm Fraser; his brother-in-law, Hugh Beggs, who was active in woolgrower politics and would chair the Australian Wool Corporation; Fraser's sister-in-law, Victorian Liberal Party president Eda Ritchie; her husband, Robin Ritchie, chairman of Geelong Grammar; and Hugh Beggs's wife Frankie, whose father, Sir David Fairbairn, was a minister in successive Liberal governments from the Menzies years on.

I imagine the scene at the homestead on the Beggs's station, Nareeb Nareeb, famous for its affinity with the Merino. It's 1982, and this evening the machinations of Australia's biggest business seem as distant as the bleating of the sheep in the paddocks. Fraser and his wife Tamie (née Beggs), a daughter of the house, have arrived for a

The entrance to Nareeb Nareeb

late dinner. A large white Commonwealth car with flag and driver rests on the red gravel behind the homestead, a white brick villa built after a bushfire swept the old weatherboard house into smoke during the Second World War.

The prime minister and Tamie are on their way home to their property at Nareen, more than an hour's drive further west. Weary after a week in Canberra, Fraser often breaks his journey here. In minutes, drinks are served, and host Hugh Beggs draws his guests into the adjoining white dining room, where a polished mahogany table is surrounded by balloon-backed chairs. Hugh sits, gesturing to Malcolm with a bottle of red in his hand.

Hugh's conversation is always about his matter, wool, but if the others feel Malcolm has misfired on an issue during the parliamentary week, the wool story is interrupted and the Prime Minister is given 'a bit of stick'. Tonight, he is being pursued for using jargon, replacing a simple 'now' with 'at this point of time'. Hugh asks, 'Malcolm, at this point of time would you care for a glass of claret?' Laughter drowns out the reply, which is typically 'Yes'.

Hugh announces that the menu tonight is 'lamb killed on the place and probably as old as the wine!' There's more laughter. The dinner progresses amiably, sustained by a whisky, a glass or two of wine and the participants' unanimous support for the policies that assist their industry.

In jovial situations like this, power is unremarkable. There is no suggestion of collusion. The prime minister and his brother-in-law both answer to their own cabinets and boards, and virtually all their colleagues share their views.

Hugh Beggs has told me he seldom consulted Fraser directly on an issue, as he saw it as the wrong thing to do; the correct procedure was to approach the relevant minister. He did, however, agree that there was rarely a cross moment between the two men. They had the non-disruptive relationship of political friends who see the world through a similar prism.

Hugh remembered chauffeuring Fraser around at election time. 'I used to drive him around because I could stay relatively sober if I needed to, and I could buy rounds of drinks at the pubs on a Saturday afternoon. There were heaps of people there and I was able to buy them a round because for Malcolm to do that was against the law. I bought lots of beers.'

Their time together in 1982 was lubricated by a shared faith that the status quo would last forever. There was little overt talk of politics. Politics only becomes political when there are differences of opinion, but in this room there was no desire for dissent. Silent consensus ruled.

This was no Liberal star chamber but a gathering of moderate members of a broad church. Both Malcolm Fraser and later Eda

Ritchie would eventually ditch their party memberships when they perceived the Liberal Party as drifting to the right. For now, though, this meeting was a snapshot of an extraordinary moment when people from the Western District, identified as members of the squattocracy, held power in their hands, including power over their iconic industry.

Former MHR Stewart McArthur too recalls a time when Western District squatters exercised unrivalled influence in parliamentary politics. He believes modern rural power was at its peak during Henry Bolte's unprecedented term as premier of Victoria from 1955 to 1972. Bolte came from a rural background and owned land in the Western District at Skipton and Meredith. He was still in office when Malcolm Fraser became influential in the federal Liberal government. For a while, Stewart says, people presumed 'the country was run from Nareen and Meredith'.

Many other Western District graziers played important roles. Stewart mentions Victorian cabinet minister Tom Austin, a farming neighbour and mate of Bolte's, as well as John Silcock, an influential member of the Wool Corporation board, and Bill Weatherly, who was a senior figure in the Graziers' Association and a prominent opponent of the reserve price scheme. Malcolm Fraser, on the other hand, supported the scheme. Stewart says, 'He was under huge pressure from his grazier mates to do something – whatever that meant.' Fraser continued to back the scheme after he left politics, even mounting pressure through the media when the scheme was sinking.

If in 1982 the motif of Western District authority resides at this table, it won't last. A year later, in 1983, Fraser will lose power to Bob Hawke, and soon afterwards the floating of the Australian dollar will launch the wool market on a rollercoaster ride. Long after Fraser's defeat, Hugh will remain a prominent player in agri-politics, eventually finishing his career as the Labor-appointed chair of the Wool Corporation. In this role, he will become the public face of the wool industry during the crises that attend the collapse of the reserve price scheme in 1991.

With heavy debt and dwindling wool prices, the Western District's commercial dominance was dismembered. As Hugh's son Richard has put it, 'Twenty-five years ago you could drive from home east to Ballarat and probably see sheep with Nareeb blood in them most of the way. Now you hardly see a sheep'.

After Malcolm's tearful retreat to Nareen, the soirees at the Beggs and Ritchie homesteads continued until the mid-1990s, when the Frasers sold Nareen and moved to Melbourne. Their departure was a symptom of the eclipse of the squatters' power in the region. This was confirmed in August 2010, when Dan Tehan was elected as the Liberal MHR for Wannon, much to the horror of the Protestant pastoral establishment. Tehan, a member of a Catholic political family based in Mansfield, boasts a great-grandfather who grew potatoes on a plot of land at Port Fairy. Fifty years ago, as the establishment saw it, people like him wouldn't have bothered knocking at the Wannon electorate office door.

Stewart McArthur told me it was the first time in 30 years that he'd seen the Catholic position supported in the local Liberal party. 'It was sort of tap on the shoulder stuff. Tehan worked hard for it. There was a bit of unhappiness out of Wannon that we had to go to Mansfield to find a member.' For the Western District patriarchs who believed in their own right to power, Tehan's arrival raised the question 'Why am I still here?'

Hugh Beggs is like the basalt scoria strewn across his family property at Nareeb Nareeb, a rock in a hard place. A Western District loyalist not for moving, he's survived the vicissitudes of the wool industry over almost eighty years.

Hugh Beggs with melted silverware from the fire at Nareeb

'I was very young when trouble struck,' he tells me. When he was only five years old, Nareeb Nareeb was burnt out in a bushfire. 'It was during the war,' he says, 'and no one was here. It destroyed 100 miles of fencing, 12,000 sheep, the homestead. My grandmother got out with a parrot and a silver jug. With the law at the time, we had to pay excessive tax on the insurance payout, and then my grandfather died and we had to pay probate.'

He reckons the wool boom of the 1950s provided recovery money for his family after all the problems they'd been through. His father's spending was modest. 'The old man got himself a very nice shotgun and traded in the Plymouth for a second-hand Daimler, which was a big mistake. A lovely car, but not on our corrugated roads. It rained screws and other bits.'

Even his sisters' pet lambs were caught up in the boom. 'Dad said he would give them top price for their wool. Well, he had to pay them £20 each – it was a bit of money! Station hands were earning about £10 a week.'

Hugh has adapted to many changes in the wool industry. He says modestly, 'The most important decision we make is choosing our parents. I was very lucky. I had a father who ran the place well, conservatively. Loved his sheep, and was big enough to hand over responsibility to me at a quite early age, so I was able to do something useful as well.'

He moves from his armchair to throw a log on the living-room fire as he discusses the vastly different management systems that used to exist at the farm. 'In the past,' he says, 'your management was at a much higher level. My father had another place and used to come over one day a week, where he would discuss what was going on with an overseer. The place ran itself.'

But the system was under strain by the time Hugh took over. 'When I came here, there were ten men with an average length of service of 33 years. That was a problem, because we had no superannuation, so half of them were battling to do a day's work because they were so old. I remember one man resigned, to use his own word, when he was 92!'

Hugh, who had completed a rural science degree, was keen to explore new approaches to breeding sheep. The woolgrowers' standard practice had been to maintain the purity of their bloodlines and not introduce breeding stock from outside, but so many stock on Nareeb Nareeb had been killed in the fire that the flock was becoming inbred. To combat this, Hugh eventually persuaded his father to bring in new rams, and the results, he says, were 'pretty spectacular'. After that, his father basically handed over the management of breeding to him.

Like many established Western District squatters, Hugh's family lost land to soldier settlement after the war. 'My father tried to fight it but really couldn't. He had another property, and the commission was into absentee landlords. Here, there was only Dad's mother, so the edict was, "Give us half or we will take the lot." We were in the early wave in 1947. This place was valued at around £30 an acre, and I think we got £21 10s.'

Hugh says the results of soldier settlement were variable. At Nareeb Nareeb, the settlers got about 600 or 700 acres each, because the soil was quite light and the property was rabbit-infested. 'One day here we got 5500 rabbits off 180 acres. That is how thick they were.' The commission's rule of thumb was that a block should be able to carry 1000 sheep, which would earn the settler a living.

But the rule didn't always work to the settlers' advantage. 'On Blackwood, being a far richer property, the settlers got only 200 or 300 acres, which was really a sentence to peasanthood.' Ironically, those on Nareeb Nareeb did well out of what was assessed as inferior land. 'They got the money very cheap, they had the wool boom, and myxomatosis got rid of the rabbits. Those three things meant they did pretty well. Most of the settlers on our boundaries who had sons who wanted to carry on are still here. That is the way it should be.'

When I ask Hugh why he thinks the Western District families aren't represented on the main producer boards today, he says it's because younger farmers are under a lot of pressure. 'The whole industry has got a lot tighter. The young fellow on the land has little time to go to grower meetings and sit in cold country halls as I did.'

For Hugh, all those evenings in cold country halls earned him a crucial role in rural politics. While his name will always be linked with the reserve price scheme, he initially opposed it when Sir

William Gunn began travelling around the country promoting the notion to graziers.

Hugh recalls, 'When Bill Gunn was advocating a reserve price scheme for wool, I said to my father, "He's bloody crazy. You can't do that. First of all, you have to learn how to measure the stuff, give it an accurate description, then you could value it and then sell it." So my father said, "There is a graziers' meeting in Hamilton on Thursday night. Why don't you go in and tell them?" So I did, and that started a career in agri-politics.'

In 1963, Hugh joined the crusty Graziers Association of Victoria, where he earned the fury of Western District pastoralist elders when he supported amalgamation with the Victorian Farmer's Union, which represented small farmers. Then he was chosen to represent the Victorian Farmers and Graziers Association on the Australian Wool Council. This was his entree into the political machinations of Australia's biggest business.

Hugh became president of the Wool Council, and by now he had begun to embrace the reserve price scheme. He says, 'The things I said had to be done were done, and all of a sudden wool was being sold on length and micron so it could be commercially valued.' At first, it was seen as a temporary measure to set a minimum 'floor' price.

Hugh says, 'One of the major mistakes was when they changed the name from the floor price scheme to the reserve price scheme, because that changed the thinking.' The floor price was seen as a safety net below which it was unprofitable to grow wool, whereas the reserve price was promoted as the price graziers would like to get for their product.

For a time in the late 1980s, there was strong international demand for wool, which became more affordable when the value of the Australian dollar fell. Prices rose, allowing the Wool Corporation to dispose of the stockpile it had accumulated in previous years. Hugh recalls, 'There was a time under David Asimus when the stockpile got up to about two million bales, but they eventually traded their way out of it. And so the board was very gung-ho and said we could do it again.'

With demand strong, the corporation repeatedly jacked up the reserve price, raising it by 71 per cent in 1986 alone. Then, in June 1988, just as David Asimus was retiring as chair, the corporation decided to raise the reserve price to 870 cents a kilo. It was a controversial move, and Asimus installed Hugh Beggs as his successor just after the decision was taken.

Hugh says, 'I was not a part of the decision because I was not yet a member of the Wool Corporation, and that decision has been blamed as the cause of the disaster, which is quite justifiable, I think. I went to the meeting as an observer, and I remember David Asimus saying, "Can you live with that price?" and I said, "It would be difficult, but I'll do my best." Don't forget it was $5 a kilo under the market, and cool wool had just been developed, so it was felt wool had a completely new market for spring and summer clothes. Confidence was sky-high, although now with hindsight it should never have been done.'

Wool prices began to slide and the corporation and the government both floundered. Hugh says the main lesson he took away from what happened was that 'politics and commerce are mutually exclusive terms. The commerce part of me said, "Let's shut this thing down" and the politics of Mr Kerin said, "Hang on, we can't do this. We've been halfway around the world extracting promises from Russia and so on that they would be buying wool." This didn't eventuate, and I had to pull the pin.'

Predictably, there was a storm of criticism of both Hugh and the minister, with everyone involved seeking to blame someone else for the disaster. 'I was inclined to resign,' Hugh says, 'but Mr Kerin persuaded me not to, thinking it would be too disruptive for the whole industry. That was a mistake I made. That's history.'

It's ironic that many of these events, which became the bane of Hugh's public life, were not of his making. But in my discussions with him, there's no hint of self-pity. Rather, he can now view from a distance the irrationality of that moment and bring the wisdom of hindsight to bear on actions taken in a flood of panic. Hugh's life victory has been to survive on the paddocks of Nareeb Nareeb, tending his ewes and lambs with a woolman's hat on his head and an eager dog on the back of his ute. And at night, the music in his ear is the ruminant murmur from those starlit plains.

13

A Pillar Falls

The Western District – you are either born into it or you don't get into it.

                        Geraldine Doogue, ABC Radio National

Travelling east on the Hamilton Highway, as you approach the deadly intersection with the Penshurst–Dunkeld Road, you can just glimpse the iconic homestead at Blackwood on the right. Blackwood was sold to Chinese buyers in 2014 after five generations in the hands of the Ritchie family. The progenitor of the dynasty, James Ritchie, had walked sixty miles from Portland in 1842, eating boiled cockatoos and sleeping in logs, to claim his squatting run. His station was widely known as one of the best in the Western District, and the sale, when it came, was like a hammer blow. An unlikely pillar had fallen, and recriminations flared across the hinterland.

Before the sale, Blackwood had been run by Jason Ritchie, an engineer by training who owned the place with his brother Dan, a Sydney stockbroker. Jason did nothing to appease his critics when he told the local media he had 'lost his enthusiasm for farming' and decided to seek another path.

When Jason took over Blackwood, he decided to convert it from sheep and cattle to cropping, going against the advice of a chorus of locals. Among them was Peter Learmonth, who recalls, 'I told him that if he was to begin cropping it should be only in a small way. Instead, he began ripping all the fences out and even gutting a newish woolshed to accommodate large machinery. A lot of people saw no sense in it, especially on Blackwood, with its wonderful capacity to carry livestock.'

Others advised Jason he was investing too heavily in cropping plant, and that Blackwood's wet winters were unsuited to the growing of cash crops. Traditionalists probably saw him as endangering his heritage by turning his back on sheep farming.

Then, after a long visit to France, Jason enunciated his weariness with farming. Backed by his wife Kate, the daughter of former Reserve Bank governor Bernie Fraser, he made the bold move to sell. Blackwood was sold to the Zhejiang Rifa Holding Group, a textile company turned beef processor that is also involved in sheep production in north-west China.

The significance of Jason's decision was heightened by his parents' visibility. His late father, Robin, had been a high achiever both on and off the land, steering his old school, Geelong Grammar, through perilous seas as caretaker chief executive. His mother Eda also had a high profile as a former president of the Victorian Liberal Party with a wide range of accomplishments in education, charitable organisations and the arts.

The sale of Blackwood was a shift of tectonic proportions, confirming the arrival of a foreign corporation. The locals were further unsettled when the newly hired Australian manager was heard asking, 'How can I make money? What am I going do with the place?' He was told that if he wanted to keep the two manor houses on the property in good order, it would cost all he could earn.

I later discussed the sale of Blackwood with Eda Ritchie. A polished woman of determined conviction, she sat in the living room of her elegant Cape Cod-style home on Port Fairy's oceanfront. She seemed to be bearing up well. Tyrrell Evans had enunciated the Western District collective's view: 'Eda is being brave. The sale must have hurt.'

Eda, however, saw it quite differently. She told me, 'Robin and I seriously thought about selling Blackwood 20 years ago. Then our son Jason, who had been working with an engineering company, came home and said he would really like to have a go at running the place. He had a red-hot go at it and did some innovative things. When Robin was running it, he had slightly more sheep than cattle and just a fifth cropping, but Jason turned it into four-fifths cropping. He tried some interesting stuff, and I think he quite enjoyed that.'

Jason's wife Kate, however, wasn't interested in farming. Eda was very positive about Kate, whom she described as a 'goer', but she said, 'It is very hard to make a farm work these days unless it is a dual thing. There is no implicit criticism, but you have to want to be there.'

Jason and Kate went travelling and spent eight months in France, and that was when Jason came to his decision. Eda said, 'I think Jase came to the conclusion that he was finding it incredibly frustrating. You do everything that you think is right, and then the weather defeats you. I think he thought, "I don't want to live like that."'

At 43, Jason could still make a new direction for himself, but Eda understood that time was running out. 'I think he thought, "If I leave this for another ten years, it gets harder and harder and I can't leave it that long." Also, there are other family involved. I think we all decided it was the right decision. People I know say, "How could they sell it? It has been in the family forever." But nothing is forever, and given the circumstances if it continues it is totally miserable for everybody. We didn't want to do that. It was a huge decision and not easy to do it, but I am sure it was the right decision.

I asked if there had been anything said about selling to the Chinese.

Eda replied, 'Well, I don't know, people are too polite to raise it, but I can imagine it didn't go down too well in the district. But the Chinese can't take it away. You remember there was huge investment by the Japanese about forty years ago. They bought a lot of cotton farms, a massive amount of land. They weren't very good farmers, and it's all gone back to Australians.'

As I pass Blackwood now, cattle are grazing in preparation for export as safe beef. There is also a plan to breed first-cross Merino ewes and ship them to China to invigorate the grazing industry there. That is agri-business on the land where once the Ritchies strode, confident in their seasonal routine and rewarded for their generational craft. It now seems so long ago.

Not far north of Blackwood, the government of Qatar's agricultural arm and sovereign wealth fund, the Hassad Group, is preparing fat-tailed sheep for the tables of the Persian Gulf at Barton station in Moyston, a 20,000-acre property they bought in 2011. The year before, Qatar spent $25 million on the McKinnons' Kaladro station in Strathdownie, another historic 6500-acre spread, to act as a livestock finishing hub. That aim turned to dust, and Kaladro was sold on to South Australian land aggregator and stock dealer Tom Brinkworth, who has been building up a spread of properties, like the legendary Sidney Kidman, covering different weather zones to mitigate the risk of drought.

Sheep from Barton, meanwhile, are shipped directly to the Emirates, never to see an Australian saleyard. The process raises the question of how Australians and their government are rewarded for raising them. Obviously, foreign capital plays a very important role in agriculture, and it's said our lifestyle wouldn't exist without the boost to our balance of payments. But is it being done by non-taxpaying producers who operate outside our financial system, making use of our best breeding country for their own consumption? Local graziers are intrigued to see livestock being shipped with none of the fiscal scrutiny they must endure, although a company spokesman has said that they operate within the Australian tax law.

A different business plan can be seen in the push by international investors to broaden their portfolio risk by adding Australian

Eda Ritchie

agricultural properties to a wider mix. In a low-interest environment, the returns from agriculture look fair at around 5 per cent – plus, it is hoped, a capital gain. That was the reasoning behind the Laguna Bay Pastoral Company's decision to set the Western District alight by paying some $45 million for 17,000-acre Banongill station near Skipton in 2016. Laguna Bay is backed by numerous international institutions, including the Washington State Investment Board, which is a giant US pension fund. Its foray into the Western District marked the first step in a mooted program to spend $280 million acquiring Australian agricultural land for its Laguna Bay Agricultural Fund 1.

Laguna Bay's CEO and co-founder, Tim McGavin, has said that the company is aiming to build a diversified portfolio covering many sectors and regions. 'Interest in agriculture is strong. Everyone is chasing yield, and agricultural property is a good returning asset class in a low-yielding world.'

Investors are looking for 'real assets' that offer a higher return than they can get from term deposits and bonds, and Banongill is certainly real, with its flock of 30,000 sheep as large as any in the Western District. The sale also included 2400 Angus cattle and almost 4000 acres of cropping land. Owned by the Fairbairn family from 1897 until 1975, the property has a single-storey homestead that is 87 metres long and a garden designed by William Guilfoyle, who created Melbourne's Botanic Gardens. Famously, Major Fairbairn, an aviation enthusiast, used to fly his plane over the Banongill paddocks, instructing his staff by tipping his wings.

Yet the fortunes of Banongill exemplify the changing circumstances of the Western District. There is a clear trend toward more transient ownership. Banongill's owner of ten years, former AFL player Stewart Gull, told an interviewer in 2015, 'We are very proud owners.' Months later, he was gone. And the property that once had its own school, its own football and cricket teams, is now just a farm, with a hand-painted sign on the gate saying 'Ring Max on …'.

Questions of the changing ownership of land on the plains are with me as I pass familiar names, the Calverts' Hopkins Hill on my right and the Beggs's Nareeb Nareeb, both owned by the original families, giving a semblance of continuity. The roadside is broken by short gravel drives leading to soldier settlers' houses, once the refuge of returned soldiers. For a time during the wool boom, the soldier settlers' presence supported the local towns, and there was reason to hope that the Western District would develop a working society spread across all classes. But the hope was forlorn. Today these bleak weatherboards are cheap rentals or occasionally homes for surviving soldier-settler descendants who have been able to enlarge their farms by buying out their neighbours.

The settlement at the end of this road, Chatsworth, is the embodiment of failure, its once-thriving sports centre abandoned to the weeds of neglect. The people who lived here couldn't survive and moved on. It all seems a long way from the business ambitions of the Chinese at Blackwood and the fund managers at Banongill, which don't include a moment's care that they are investing in an increasingly empty land.

14
Succession

Leo Tolstoy, a member of Russia's rural aristocracy, once wrote, 'A ruling class is never terminated without a war.'

The great man was right about his own class but wrong about their Australian counterparts. The squatters of the Western District, who formed the core of the ruling class in the world's richest nation in the 1870s, have been displaced without a shot being fired. Ironically, in less than two centuries the Western District has twice seen its owners dispossessed: first the region's Aboriginal people, who were displaced after 1835, followed by their nemesis, the squatters, who are petering out today.

A 2015 volume, *Great Properties of Western Victoria* by Richard Allen and Kimbal Baker, demonstrates the magnitude of the squatting families' retreat. Of the 20 grand estates highlighted in the book, only four are in the hands of their founding families. Their manor houses and the surrounding land are now controlled by what the Scots used to call 'incomers' – city businessmen and professionals.

The shift in ownership is symptomatic of the dynastic clans' withdrawal from the 3.2 million acres of grassland that formed their home. To focus on their loss is not to equate it with the bloody dispossession of the region's Aboriginal people or to genuflect to the high and mighty, but to recognise the demise of a ruling class as a chapter of Australian history that is often overlooked.

When I asked Hugh Beggs why he thought so many Western District squatting families had disappeared, his reply was immediate: 'Succession.' Hugh said he could see the lack of succession planning when clients came to buy rams. 'The client will say, "I brought the boy along", and there is a 40-something man who has never seen a chequebook or had responsibility for anything. It's a tragedy.'

In dealing with his own property, Hugh set out to address the issue before a crisis could develop. 'I've spent my life trying keep this place together,' he told me. 'Richard, my son, and I own it.' At just under 7500 acres, Nareeb Nareeb is now smaller than it used to be. For a while, Hugh owned a couple of settler farms on the boundary, but when I spoke to him he'd sold one and was in the process of selling another.

'I wanted to liquefy the position so that if I fell off the perch, it didn't leave Richard with a massive debt and his brother and sister looking over his shoulder. Luckily, the family get along very well. I think I got the trifecta – I have a son who wants to take over, is pretty good at it, and we get on. He's running it now. I call myself the "Hey, Dad" man – if he wants a hand, he comes and asks me.'

Peter Allen, son of legendary Hereford stalwart Jim Allen, reckons Ronald McDonald's Angus burger killed off the breed in which his father had such unwavering faith.

Peter is talking with more than a few tears at the dispersal sale for the South Boorook Hereford stud near Mortlake. Building the stud had been Jim's life work, but Peter has decided to call it a day eight years after Jim's death.

When the Hereford was king, South Boorook's annual sales acquired rock-star status. It was the place to be seen in rural Australia, and the price of an insider's seat was the cost of a bull, which was

The last of South Boorook's stud females go under the hammer

sometimes north of $20,000. It could cost you even more to get in for a Scotch at the homestead later. That was the pole position, and Jim, the master salesman, knew it.

A ticketing system was introduced for the sales in 1974, and people used all their wiles to get there. On the property's airstrip, a bevy of aircraft confirmed its social cachet. At the peak, the sale attracted 2500 people, and 33 aircraft flew in for the event. According to Peter Allen, there was more aircraft movement at South Boorook for the 1974 sale than at Moorabbin airport in Melbourne that day.

Jim Allen was an entrepreneur, visionary and celebrity. At Melbourne Grammar in 1927, Peter says, he was almost sacked for running an SP book. 'But then they discovered he was taking bets from the masters and told him not to do it again.' His understanding of what customers were looking for helped him establish his Hereford stud, which he started in 1939. In the early 1950s, Jim imported eighteen female Herefords and several bulls from England. He once said that he preferred to buy bulls that looked over the gate rather than through it, because the taller they were, the better their shoulder and neck structure.

In the mid-1950s, when he was doing well at the annual shows in Sydney and Melbourne, he invited local people to look at his teams. Peter explains, 'He would parade them and comment on them. People came again to learn, and I think that was the beginning of the popularity of the sales. Knowledge was to be learnt.'

In 1956, Jim began holding annual sales on the property, a revolutionary move, and he was the first cattle breeder to include solid performance figures in his sales brochures.

'He had a lot of knowledge and was very happy to part with it,' Peter says. 'Everybody came to the sales for the judging and the points system. They came to learn from that.'

It's different these days because you can pick information up on the internet or in the department papers, but in those days there was no other source.

Jim was an identity wherever he went, particularly at the royal shows, where he cut a distinctive figure in bowtie and tailored tweeds. A super-salesman with a genteel touch, he made sure that South Boorook was lodged in the psyche of rural Australia as the nation's premier beef stud. Swish dinner parties at the homestead ran long into the night.

But Jim Allen could also be curt and wintry. Peter Learmonth, who for years was an agent for Jim's sales, remembered receiving a cool reception when he went to see Jim about a purchase. 'I had an order to buy 30 stud cows and three bulls from the Smorgon family, who were going to start their own stud.'

Peter had to drive about 30 minutes to see Jim, and he arrived just as Jim was leaving his office. Peter remembers, 'He swept past with the words "You make an appointment to see me," and that was it. So I went down to see Ralph McEachern, and he invited me in for a cup of tea. Of course, he got the order. I think it was a $30,000 deal. It was a lot of money then.'

On 28 February 2014, the South Boorook stud closed. The stud dispersal sale was organised by Peter and his sister Margaret. Peter told reporters that he was partly calling it a day because red tape around biosecurity was making it harder to run the stud. Underlying that problem, though, was the longer-term issue that demand for Hereford cattle had inexorably slipped.

Peter was very proud of his dad. 'We did a lot of work together. People commented what a good relationship there was between father and son. I looked up to my dad in every way you could. I just adored him. We would debate what we would do. Would we swing the gate on this side or that? And then we would agree and do it. A lot of father–son relationships end in tears. Ours didn't.'

In a Hamilton café, I have breakfast with six farming couples, four of whom have sons sharing the load. They're a disparate bunch with an average age above 70. Their conversation focuses on survival on the land, which they all see as a measure of success.

Ken Satchell farms at Condah, about 30 kilometres south-west of Hamilton, and his family has lived in the Western District for generations. There's not a trace of the squattocracy here. Ken is proud of the fact that he has built his farm up from a very small start. From an initial gift of 700 acres he received from his grandfather, the family now has 2500 acres and runs 8000 sheep.

They also have off-farm investments as insurance against farming downturns, but their main focus is on improving the productivity of the farming operation itself. When he talks about farming, Ken sometimes sounds like a graduate in business administration. He says an index of professionalism is to benchmark your operation against the top 25 per cent of farmers. 'That leading group today are very professional farmers,' he says. They use modern genetics and farm management methods to improve productivity and expand their operations.

On his own farm, Ken has wisely taken a holistic approach to family life and views women's wellbeing as a key part of the equation. 'It's important farming families have lifestyle for everybody,' he says. 'To attract women to farms, they need to participate in the success of the farm and have time to be part of the community. And the husbands need not to isolate themselves on the farm.'

In line with the need to provide a reasonably relaxed lifestyle, everyone on Ken's property sticks strictly to an eight-hour working day. 'It requires planning and efficiency,' he says. While other families have been plagued by conflicts and succession disputes, Ken has expanded his operation to provide a living for three families on the farm.

On the other hand, he reckons the bottom 50 per cent of farmers fall short on the efficiency front. 'They just don't drive productivity and have a low expectation of life.' Reluctant to spend money, they find they can't make money, so their prospects of survival are poor.

Succession disputes often trigger a final crisis. The situation is especially difficult when there are three or four children in the family. 'The eldest son quite often runs the operation, providing security for the others and paying school fees for the younger members of the family.' Then, when the parents die, the farm will be divided between the siblings, to the disadvantage of the farming son.

Ken outlines the effects. 'The one who has stayed at home ends up with an uneconomical piece of land. He is in his mid-fifties, and it's too late to change direction. He could end up out on the street. The other siblings have built a business, and midway through life they have the bonus of being left a third of a farm. I have seen it happen a lot.'

Over a lifetime in the district, Ken has seen many families succumb to disputes over probate, family squabbles and negativity about the future. He says, 'Unless the owners of a farm are positive about the future, they fail. And that is the story of the disappearing squattocracy.'

In the continuing story of the lost white tribe, the demise of the Russell family is an episode that shows two faces of the perils of succession. The progenitor of the family in the Western District was George Russell, a Scot whose squatting was as successful as his estate planning was not. George was born in 1812 in the village of Cluny, over the Firth of Forth from Edinburgh. (I took two days to find his birthplace, which Margaret Kiddle had rendered as 'Clunie' in *Men of Yesterday*, sending me across Perthshire on a very pleasant wild-goose chase.)

In Scotland, George Russell was one of 13 children in a tenant farming family. He was what became known in colonial Australia as an 'improver', a man who had overcome privation to attain prosperity in his mature years. A man of stern religious principles and some sensibility, he wrote about the squatting life and the 'loneliness of command' in a published autobiography.

After a childhood working on the farm, as was typical in the devastated Scotland of that time, George Russell migrated to Van Diemen's Land in 1831. Five years later, he followed John Batman to Victoria, where he managed the affairs of a Scotland-based pastoral syndicate known as the Clyde River Company. With some £8000 in his pocket to invest on the company's behalf, he took up land in various parts of Victoria and bought an estate for himself at Golf Hill on the Leigh River. By 1844 he'd become a partner in the company, and when it was dissolved in 1857–58, his share of the proceeds was £43,000. It was a substantial fortune and became the basis of a pastoral empire extending across the Western District.

When Russell died at his home on Golf Hill in 1888, he left seven daughters and a son. True to form, he made Golf Hill over to his son, Philip, while the daughters received shares in his other significant property, the hilltop Barunah Plains near Geelong. Neither property is now in family ownership. Both experienced succession problems, but they took a different form in each case.

On Golf Hill, Philip Russell struggled to maintain the property and found himself in debt after his father died. He died childless in 1898, having agreed to hand over management of Golf Hill to his youngest sister, Janet. Two years later, Janet married a former naval officer, John Biddicombe, and together they established what became one of Australia's foremost Hereford studs. Janet's husband died in 1929, but she maintained the stud's high quality, winning all the Hereford awards at the Sydney Royal Show in 1947.

The couple, however, had no children to take over the property, and in the 1950s Janet deliberately dispersed the stud. In October 1953, shortly before her death, she arranged for her remaining stud cattle to be sold by auction in the hope of improving the bloodlines of the Australian Hereford herd. The cattle realised record prices, and the proceeds of the sale were donated to charity. After her death, the Golf Hill homestead with its surrounding land was sold to John Barber, another Hereford breeder, and the rest of the property was taken for soldier settlement.

The story at Barunah Plains was different. At its peak, the property had the largest flock in Victoria, carrying 30,000 sheep. It was a huge station of 56,000 acres, unusually large for a property so close to a major town. The property was subdivided for soldier settlement in 1946, and Geordie Russell, who was managing it on behalf of the family estate, sold off the remaining blocks in the 1970s.

Over a corned-beef sandwich in the hayshed at South Boorook, I discussed the fate of Barunah Plains with retired stock and station agent Jim Hay. Jim said that as times got more difficult in the 1970s, the family decided to sell. 'It was sold in eight or nine major lots at an average of $70 to $75 per acre. Fred Herd bought Wingiel, and Clive McEachern bought a parcel.'

Sitting on a hay bale next to Jim was his mate Brian Wood, a lifetime stockman and auctioneer with Dalgety's, the firm that had been agents for the sales. Brian told me he'd known Barunah Plains since 1957. 'It was one of those lovely old Western District properties that was held in an estate in perpetuity. The family as they went on all had a share in it. It was one reason why a lot of those properties were eventually sold. It fragmented any profitability.'

He said that Strachans, a Hamilton-based firm of stock and station agents, had helped the family set up the estate, and the same structure was put in place for Mount Hesse, Ennerdale and other properties.

Brian was very critical of these arrangements. 'In the long run they were a disaster,' he said, 'because all the family members had a share in it and wanted their money. In the case of the Russell family at Barunah, there were 68 beneficiaries in about 1974, and more than half had never been on the place. All they were looking for was a return on their stake.'

In 1975, a block of 2200 acres on the western end of Barunah was put up for sale. Brian had a client in Hamilton, Leigh Medlin, who was looking for a block, and he went down to have a look at the land. 'It was a warmish spring day, and dear old Leigh was sweating up. We were bouncing around on the rocks in a utility, and the ground was covered in big white tussocks of inedible grass. Leigh Medlin decided not to buy it because of the tussock grass.'

But the next January, a bushfire started at Cressy, came down from the north and burnt every acre of the block, including all the tussock grass. Knowing that this would improve the pasture, Brian phoned

Leigh and said, 'We had better go and have another look at that land on Barunah.' Leigh went down and bought it for $80 an acre.

After the sale, Brian told me, he and Leigh sat down to have a cup of coffee with Geordie Russell, and Leigh asked him how many sheep you could run on that land. 'Geordie got up and found the stock book that had been on Barunah for 50 years. He said, "It would run 650 weaners if you're careful." On 2200 acres!'

Brian was flabbergasted. With modern stocking methods, the area would support more than ten times that number.

The biggest step was putting the homestead itself on the market. It was on 6000 acres and had numerous bluestone buildings left over from the days when the property had to provide all its own supplies. There was a bakery, a laundry, shearers' quarters, a huge woolshed, stables and a shed built specifically to accommodate the rams.

Graham Mills bought the block and restored the homestead, which became the basis for a hospitality business. Jim said, 'The shearers' quarters, which would hold 30 people, were a huge novelty. Visitors could play at being a squatter – they could go to the yards and handle fine-wool sheep, get the lanoline on their hands and feel the fleece on the skirting board. They would then go to the woolshed, where a huge table would be laid out for lunch.'

Mills had also built a golf course. The place catered for wedding receptions, balls, banquets and meetings. In 1998, the local council approved a proposal to build a country club resort on the site, but this never eventuated.

The property changed hands again in 2001 for $4 million. The buyer was internet entrepreneur Evan Thornley, who immediately sold 3000 acres to the neighbours. 'By that time, land was making between $1800 and $2000 an acre,' Jim said. The homestead block of 600 acres was on the market for several years, and eventually sold at the end of 2015.

Having risen from obscurity in Scotland to great wealth in Victoria, the Russells are no longer remembered in either place. The wealth George Russell accumulated in his lifetime was enough to keep his descendants in comfort for several generations, but the vagaries of descent and inheritance eventually saw the land dispersed. What is left is a vanished pastoral dynasty, paid-up members of the lost white tribe.

15

The Great Land Grab

The Western District squatters had enjoyed almost a century of economic and social dominance by the end of the Second World War, but then the compass began to shift. With a million people in the armed forces in a population of just over seven million, the federal and state governments were anxious to help soldiers return to civilian life. One way of doing this was to offer veterans land and capital to set themselves up as small farmers, but first the government had to overcome a problem: the soldier settlement schemes adopted after the First World War had failed spectacularly, and the authorities knew that they would have to devise a better approach.

When the First World War ended, the Soldier Settlement Commission in Victoria had been placed in charge of acquiring land for veterans with support from the federal government. Confident that the drier parts of the state would become more productive with intensive farming and keen to minimise the cost of the scheme, the commission had largely steered clear of the Western District, where prices were high, in favour of the Wimmera, the Mallee and parts of the Murray basin. Closer settlement policies also had to balance the needs of the land-hungry ex-soldiers with demands from sponsored British immigrants. Anxious to encourage new settlers for the sake of national security, the federal government had offered subsidised passage and land to practically anyone who spoke the language.

The Western District played little part in this stage of soldier settlement, and relations between landowners and soldier settlers there were generally benign. Lionel Weatherly of Woolongoon donated 880 acres for soldier settlement in December 1917 as an act of gratitude to the troops, then willingly sold another 16,000 acres for closer settlement at £7 an acre in 1923. It is a testament to the size of Woolongoon that he still had almost 13,000 acres left.

Other iconic stations where land was sold into the soldier settlement scheme included Mount Elephant, where Major Alan Currie sold his last 5600 acres on the south of the old property for £23 an acre in 1920 and used the proceeds to buy the spectacular Burrumbeet estate of Ercildoune with its sprawling stone buildings. Before leaving Mount Elephant, Currie donated his shares in the local butter factory to the soldier settlers as a token of goodwill.

But there were already signs of the problems that would plague the soldier settlers. The land on Mount Elephant, for example, was subdivided into 17 allotments, ranging in size from 77 to 163 acres, far too small to provide a living for a family. At first, the local press reported favourably on the Mount Elephant settlers' efforts, observing that many of them had built comfortable houses from the local stone, but as time went on, the reports became less hopeful. In 1931, an immigrant named John Jessop told a royal commission that he'd been allocated a block at Mount Elephant that was too stony to plough and impossible to crop. In a few short years, the block had three owners. The first settler committed suicide, the second escaped by walking to Queensland in search of work, and after Jessop too left, the block was abandoned.

Historian Ian Turner has sardonically described the soldier settlers as reaping the 'ashes of victory'. With the blessing of a grateful people, the veterans were banished to the parts of the country nobody wanted to own. One man said that being on his block in the Mallee was 'worse than the Somme', one of the most evil examples of trench warfare in France.

In 1929, after conducting a royal commission into what had gone wrong with soldier settlement, Justice Pike reported that the land supplied had been far less productive than the authorities had hoped. Furthermore, the high prices paid had saddled the settlers with heavy debts and annual interest bills running at 5 per cent or more. He estimated the national losses from the scheme at £23.5 million, with Victoria responsible for £7.7 million, about one-third of the total.

The story of these failures trickled down through the system. In the early 1940s, when the federal government started planning for postwar reconstruction, it appointed a Rural Reconstruction Commission to determine what was required to establish a more robust soldier settlement scheme. The commission's two most active members were C.R. Lambert, a banker with rural experience, and Samuel Wadham, Professor of Agriculture at the University of Melbourne. During 1943, the commissioners went around the country holding public meetings and listening to people's views. They travelled 33,350 miles and visited 232 country centres. By the time they began to produce written reports, they were ready to embrace a new, far more controversial game plan.

To avoid repeating the miserable failure of the previous scheme, the commissioners recommended that soldiers be offered bigger areas of better land closer to towns, with electricity and telephones and access to schools and doctors. But for this to be achieved, the soldier settlement authorities would have to take on the established landowners. This meant tackling the Western District pastoral families and either persuading or compelling them to give up some of their land. And there was no way the squatters were going to escape. Even before the war was over, the Victorian lands minister had announced that almost all the land being considered for soldier settlement was in the Western District.

The eminent historian Ernest Scott once described land settlement as 'the fundamental subject of Australian history'. In that light, it is strange that Australia's largest ever state-backed scheme of compulsory land acquisition has aroused so little commentary, at least from politicians. Since the mid-nineteenth century, progressive politicians in Australia, with one eye on the squatters, had adopted it as an article of faith that farming needed to be democratised and a yeoman class of small farmers established. After the Second World War, this egalitarian move to unlock the land under the watchful eye of the state appeared in the charitable guise of reward for effort and passed every fairness test of the time. And to object to the idea that war veterans should receive government support was a no-go zone for even the most zealous protector of land ownership.

Legislatively backed, the government grab for land was never billed as a socialised redistribution of wealth, but it was close to it. The impact is still being felt today. Older graziers find it a difficult topic and speak bitterly about the unfairness of the valuations used by the Soldier Settlement Commission. During the war, the price of land had been pegged at £5 an acre, and that was all that the commission would offer in the early postwar years. It was only after 1949 that the commission began paying close to market rates.

Landowners who took the valuations to court did so with trepidation. Many feared that if they objected, the commission would take the entire property. Their fears were justified, as the commission had power to acquire properties compulsorily if it couldn't reach agreement with the owners. By March 1946, it had already acquired 364,000 acres in this way, mostly in the Western District.

The commission mainly targeted farms where there was no active owner resident – second holdings where the owner only visited, properties owned by deceased estates, and even those whose owners were incapacitated. Keith Urquhart's father, who had had a stroke, lost half of Boonerah, near Mortlake, after a wasted legal objection in the late 1940s. Keith told me, 'We got £5 an acre, with a sheep to the acre in full wool.' When the wool boom arrived, the five settlers on

Boonerah paid for their land in twelve months, and some immediately sold out at a profit.

Similarly, the Lucocks' property at Ennerdale was reduced from 7000 acres to 4200 in 1949. The commission offered £6 an acre, and the family wanted £7. Chris Lucock recalls, 'At that time Ford Strachan, a Melbourne lawyer, was acting for us and he described the commission's reaction to a request for more money as a thinly veiled threat to take the whole place.'

But the family stuck to their guns, knowing that the land was about to become more valuable when the wartime price controls were lifted. 'They got their price,' Chris says, 'although the land was probably worth twice as much.'

On the other hand, once the soldier settlers had taken up their blocks, relations were good. 'My parents were never upset by the loss of some of their land,' Chris says. 'They were very good to the settlers. There were no trees on the land for the settlers, so they were allowed to cut firewood on our place and borrow any machinery my father had. Today there is a son on one of his parents' blocks and he has bought another settler out and has bought another piece of land.'

It's been estimated that across Australia, the failure rate among this second generation of soldier settlers was only 10 per cent, but Bim Affleck, who is writing a series of books on soldier settlement in the Western District, has told me that, of the 70 farms selected in the Caramut division in 1949, only seven are still in the hands of the first families on the block. When a soldier settler did fail, it was often another soldier settler who purchased their land, although the established pastoralists often took the opportunity to buy blocks back as well. The district now had a group of medium-sized landowners exploring more intensive farming techniques. The Soldier Settlement Commission claimed in 1953 that the soldier settlers were running three times as many stock as the same land had supported when it was being worked as part of larger grazing properties. Smaller holdings, the commission said, meant more topdressing and more sown pasture. The rise of dairying and cropping in the southern part of the district also owed a lot to soldier settlement. But it was a painful time for the pastoral families whose old way of life was suddenly taken away.

A near gale is blowing as we make our way across the gravel to the cottage Richard Jamieson shares with his wife Jane. Richard ushers us in from the rowdy day, unfussed by the wind. He is a man who has seen a squall or two. He moved down to this cottage in 2008 from the main homestead on Bolac Plains, where his son David now lives.

'We didn't get the boot,' Richard hastens to point out. His son's family lived in this cottage, but they now have two children and need more space. Richard is proud of the father/son house swap, which has avoided the sale and flight to the coast.

For Richard, farming survival has always been at the mercy of others, and the postwar soldier settler commission is a particularly sharp memory of unfairness.

The Jamiesons lost almost 11,000 acres to the commission, and the confiscation shadows all our discussions. It's a constant irritant to this gentle man, painful enough to make the subject taboo.

'This is the first time I've talked about the soldier settlement scheme,' he says. 'I was waiting for people to die. It should be documented – it happened, it is our history.'

He tells me of the devastating effect on his family. 'All of Connebar and half of Bolac Plains went. We were the last people to be dealt with under 1942 valuations.' The commission also pushed the family around. 'Dad had to come here, to Bolac Plains, under the threat of confiscation. If we didn't agree, they would take the lot.'

The family hired a QC in the hope of delaying the decision and getting a better price, but it didn't work. Richard says, 'In the court, our QC read from a foolscap page and sat down. We had no hope. In the end we settled for £6 10s an acre. A fortnight later, land was sold only three kilometres from our northern boundary for £28!'

The fact that his father had been in the army didn't help the family's case, and the local RSL club played a role in targeting land for acquisition. 'The work of the RSL clubs was critical. The clubs used to do surveys around the district and advise the commission which land was being farmed efficiently and where the productivity wasn't good enough. When Dad came back after being a prisoner of war in northern Italy, he joined the RSL, but he never went to a meeting, and before he died he refused the offer of an RSL burial.'

The effect on the Jamiesons was devastating. 'The commission had taken all of our family's reserves, the lot. We didn't have money in the bank. It was in land – that was our choice,' Richard says. 'They don't point the finger at you for having too much money in the bank but for having command of too much land. Quite an extraordinary thing, I think.'

The family's response was muted in public but despairing in private. This was a common reaction throughout the postwar Western District when graziers confronted the power of the Soldier Settlement Commission. The Jamiesons' angst was understandable, but in political terms the case against them was inarguable. Their privilege was there for all to see, their landholdings a vast advantage not given to others.

In any event, the Jamiesons still had the resources to pick up the pieces. They decided as a family to improve the efficiency of the property by investing in better sheep. 'The sheep we had were known as Western District possums,' Richard says. 'They were pretty short, low to the ground.' Richard put a lot of money into building up the size of the sheep. 'We used NSW Merriman blood, big-bodied sheep. We saw a big improvement in size, and that saved us.'

He says that most of the graziers in the district went for fine wool, while about a third were running South Australian breeds like the Collinsville sheep, which had coarser wool. The Jamiesons then bought Border Leicester rams, aiming to shift into selling lambs for meat, but it wasn't an easy business. 'We had trouble with lambing,' Richard says. 'It was hard work, and you had to run like hell or have a good dog to run down the ewes when they got into difficulty. It wasn't catastrophic, but we averaged around 85 per cent live lambs.' Others were getting 95 per cent and doing much better.

Richard believes that farmers in the Western District rely on periodic price booms. He remembers one wool clip in 1973 that sold at over 1500 cents a kilo to Russian clients who needed to get a ship out of port in a hurry. 'It was like winning Tatts,' he says. At the end of it, they had $250,000, which they nearly invested in the Pyramid Building Society before it crashed.

'If you don't get a boom every decade, you have had it,' Richard says. 'The history of the whole game is like that.'

16

Lost for Words

*'If those who rob,' says Kelly, 'are all condemned to die,
You had better hang the squatters; they've stolen more than I.'*

John Manifold, *The Death of Ned Kelly*

The story of the century that followed Major Mitchell is a tale of wealth creation in the Western District, of entrenched political power and social prestige, limited only by time. A sense of time's passage was at the heart of the seminal work about the region, Margaret Kiddle's historical treatise *Men of Yesterday*, which concerned itself with events and people in the Western District between 1834 and 1890. Kiddle did not hesitate to criticise the squatters' desire to exploit the land, and was especially scathing about the pious Scots who 'argued self-righteously that what they did was for the Glory of the Lord'. At the same time, she was acute in observing that they 'became rooted in the new world. In it they tried to recreate the old one they had lost but despite themselves they found and helped to build a new society.'

But a lot of water has flowed down the Wannon since then, and the biggest story of all, the squatters' demise, has broken since Kiddle's book was published in 1961. Yet the dramatic metamorphosis of the Western District over the last 60 years has been anything but an open book. The story of the rural oligarchy's exodus is buried away in remote crypts, scattered in family papers, or lurking in the stories of sixth-generation descendants saving face, their tales as elusive as gusts of wind across the pathless plains.

Historically, few writers have been attracted to the Western

District as a subject. In the nineteenth century, there were elegant, muscular words by Rolf Boldrewood and Adam Lindsay Gordon, both sometime residents. Boldrewood in particular celebrated the 'wondrous downs of the Wannon' and the 'celestial glory' of the light surrounding him there. In modern times, however, there has been no speaking of the past – no favourite storyteller comparable to the West Coast's Tim Winton, nor a poet to match Judith Wright, with her wonderment at New England's 'high lean country, full of old stories that still go walking in my sleep'. As a result, the stories that haunt this 'friendly wilderness' remain untold and its songs unsung.

One of the few writers born locally was John Manifold, a scion of one of the district's longest-established pastoral families. John grew up on Purrumbete, the dynasty's Camperdown homestead, but his rebellion began early. He wrote his poem quoting Ned Kelly – 'You had better hang the squatters, for they've stolen more than I' – as a fourteen-year-old student at Geelong Grammar. He then went to Cambridge, where he graduated with a degree in modern languages.

Like many of his peers at Cambridge, Manifold joined the Communist Party in the late 1930s. Fluent in French and German, he worked for British Intelligence during the war, then took a job at a German publishing house. He wrote what would become his best-known poem during the war, a tribute to his school friend John Learmonth, also a member of a prominent squatting family, who was killed by the Germans in Crete. At school, Manifold and Learmonth had shared their love of writing, but the war changed everything: 'Verse should have been his love and peace his trade, / But history turned him to a partisan.'

Manifold returned to live in Australia in 1949. He chose to live in Brisbane, turning his back on his genteel upbringing. He never recorded his thoughts on the Western District's highborn but spent much of his time writing, performing and collecting working-class songs. He was a founder of the Communist-aligned Realist Writers

Group in 1950 and compiled the *Penguin Australian Song Book*. By the time of his death in 1985, his poetry had been largely forgotten.

The most significant writer to record his childhood in the Western District was Alan Marshall, whose father had a modest store and worked as a horse-breaker in the village of Noorat. Marshall recorded his youthful memories of life there in *I Can Jump Puddles*, his rite-of-passage classic.

While he wrote about growing up in Noorat with the eye of a creative genius, *I Can Jump Puddles* wasn't presented as a specifically Western District story, but as the story of a boy's struggle with the effects of poliomyelitis, which left him with a withered leg, dependent on crutches to get around.

Young Alan was resourceful and wouldn't submit to the life of a cripple. With his friends, he explored his fecund surroundings, teaching himself to swim in Lake Keilambete and making his way through the bush around the volcanic crater that gives Noorat its uniqueness. He wrote:

> I began walking into the bush in the evenings so that I could smell the earth and the trees. I knelt among the moss and fern and pressed my face against the earth, breathing it into me ... I wanted to be like a dog, running with my nose to the earth so that there would be no fragrance missed, no miracle of stone or plant unobserved.

In Marshall's world, the squatters rarely made an appearance, except when a local squatter's widow employed one of his neighbours to chauffeur the district's first car. With his usual spare prose, Marshall described how the chauffeur was required to wear a uniform and open the car door for his mistress, standing at attention with his heels together.

Marshall and Manifold landed together on the left side of politics after the Second World War. Marshall flirted with the Communist

A sign outside Noorat, which unfortunately misspells Alan's name

Party after he left Noorat for Melbourne, but he never joined the party because he believed it would threaten his freedom as a writer. He became a strong advocate for literary freedom and was active in promoting the conservation of the environment around Eltham, the outer suburb of Melbourne where he settled. Unfortunately, neither Marshall nor Manifold wrote of the Western District as they saw it from opposite sides of the tracks.

Patrick White reckoned the landscape he knew made monsters of its inhabitants, but it's partly because of his literary efforts that we now walk around in an Australian context, interested in our own setting, fossicking for what is local. If the Western District was once a haven of wealth that could act as a source of patronage, it came to occupy a different role in a new chapter of its story.

An intriguing voice here is that of Gerald Murnane, the inspired imagist of the grasslands, who lived in the Western District for some years as a boy. Murnane's masterpiece is *The Plains*, an imaginative tale about the inhabitants of an unnamed grassland who have built a distinctive way of life around their own habitat and history. To tell their story, they have used their wealth to hire artists, writers and historians to record in detail every aspect of their lives. The narrative takes us into the grand houses of the plains dwellers, with their mazes of rooms, 'where the tastes and preferences of several generations were all evident under the one roof'. The narrator spends his afternoons in the library of a landowner's mansion, which is full of published books and bound manuscripts about the plains.

Murnane would not own up to anything so mundane as setting his novel in the Western District, but when reading it, I often felt it could only have been set in the disconsolate, shadowed recesses of a homestead I had once known, where thick curtains were perpetually closed against the brilliant light outside. When one of the landowners spoke of 'a drawing room where the curtains stayed closed from early spring to late autumn', I felt a jolt of recognition.

The novel even evokes an image of those that have fled the plains, 'the poor coast dwellers staring all day from their cheerless beaches at the worst of all deserts'. In *The Plains*, the grasslands are the heart of the country, while the coast is 'outer Australia'. Murnane knows a thing or two about the dynamics that formed the outlook of the Western District.

In non-fiction, however, the Western District today has almost disappeared. An example is Don Watson's prize-winning *The Bush: Travels in the Heart of Australia*, which only mentions the Western District on two of its 398 pages. When I visited Devon Park, my hostess, Susie Clarke, told me that Watson had also been a visitor there, but I searched his book in vain for any imprint of the Western District's welcoming warmth. Instead, I found a cold snap at its 'bunyip aristocracy'. Watson described attending an Anzac Day service 'in the west of Victoria's Western District, in the federal electorate of Wannon'. He noted how the differences of wealth in the district were indelibly marked by people's language and clothing:

> By their more rounded vowels and lack of rising inflection, their knitwear and sports coats, the bluer bloods of the remnant bunyip aristocracy stood out from the social middle,

and tracksuits and hoodies separated the lower rungs from all of them.

He also observed that in the surrounding countryside, the squatters' old mansions were set well back from the road, shielded by trees, while the soldier settlers' modest weatherboards were in plain view. Watson wasn't writing to please and his reputation as a wordsmith is secure, but the Western District's absence elsewhere in his book implicitly suggests that its contribution to past and present Australia can be safely ignored. The district doesn't even appear on the map at the front of his book.

Yet it is hard to ignore the distinctiveness of Victoria's western grasslands. The US writer Ron Rash, a proud regional voice at the southern end of the Appalachians, has written: 'Landscape is destiny. The environment you grow up in has to have some kind of effect on how you perceive the world.'

The Western District is not Rash's country, and historically, it has rarely produced a conscious outpouring by insiders in words or song. In art, its landscapes were brilliantly interpreted by painters of the nineteenth and early twentieth centuries such as Eugene von Guérard and Arthur Streeton, but it has largely been ignored as a source of inspiration by writers.

Ironically, Australian artists and writers have often found the creative swoon in places outside Australia. The Italian region of Tuscany, in particular, has been rhapsodised for its physical beauty and spiritual freedom. The art historian Janine Burke is one of many who have found in Tuscany an imaginative impulse unachievable in Australia. She has written:

> It would have been impossible for me to draw such an arc of inspiration without its curving hills and lambent light. The Tuscan landscape, so very human and humanised, and the golden light told me a true story.'

Similarly, Kate Grenville has said it was in Tuscany that she 'began to think about the issues of belonging and the power of place'. Ultimately, this led her to examine the deep history of her own family in Australia. And the late Shirley Hazzard, an expatriate Australian novelist publishing in the USA, found her voice in Tuscany because of its resilient humanism, which 'after so many centuries ... will not surrender easily'. Hazzard was clearly addressing the people of her adopted country, which she believed was beginning to see the death of humanism.

The seductive powers of Tuscany, however, do not lie in landscape as such, but in its antiquity and the long continuity of its culture, which gives its bucolic charm a primeval ambience. I sometimes wonder what would have happened if the Scots had done in the new world what the Italians did in the old when they left the pagan gods alone, creating a spirituality that softens the appearance of daily life and a reverence for nature that visitors can romance. Instead, the Calvinists narrowed the path and shook the life out of mythology, embracing a Protestant work ethic aimed at material gain, crowding many Western District believers into a blameless and stultifying conformity that left no space for revelation.

17
Northern Lights in the Western Sky

Love in action is a harsh and dreadful thing compared with love in dreams.

Fyodor Dostoevsky

Dostoevsky's emotive line enwraps two famous Western District love stories, poignantly describing their quite different endings mere kilometres apart on the open plains.

The joining of the scions of two rich Australian families with women who had found world fame thrust four lovers into the limelight of 'la belle époque' in the postwar Western District. Lindsay Nicholas of Terinallum married Europe's pianist Wunderkind, Hephzibah Menuhin, while down the road at Mooramong, grazier Scobie Mackinnon remade the old homestead in Hollywood style to honour his glamorous wife, silent movie actress and singer Claire Adams. And in between the grass estates of the two female stars and their pastoralist beaus lay the empty, often achingly lonely paddocks of Skipton, an unlikely and problematic background to their love, won and lost.

The headline 'ASPRO HEIR WOOS EUROPEAN MUSIC PRODIGY, 18, TO SHEEP STATION' fits a classic film script: sweeping vistas play host to a Beethoven soundtrack as the camera pans through the French windows of the grand homestead finding the pianist, wrought

Mooramong's swimming pool

and beautiful, her man in starched khaki, bewitched by the moment. In the role of Hephzibah Menuhin, perhaps a young Blanchett or Kidman. It is *Out of Africa* meets *Gone With The Wind*. The narrative is the very music of human drama; appropriately, it began backstage at the Royal Albert Hall in 1938, as Europe was about to go up in flames.

Lindsay and Nola Nicholas, siblings and heirs to the fortune of Nicholas Aspro, Australia's dominant pharmaceutical firm, are ushered into the green room by Bernard Heinze, later knighted as conductor of the Victorian Symphony Orchestra. The Nicholases are to meet the stars of the concert, violinist Yehudi Menuhin, 21, and his pianist sister Hephzibah, 17, already meteors in the world of music.

Something happened that night. Maybe it was the frisson of pre-war angst, but within a year brother and sister had married brother and sister. Hephzibah tried to make sense of it in her diary. She noted the 'freshness in the soul of these young Australians', while also admitting that she was making the unusual decision in order to stay close to Yehudi, with whom she shared 'a Siamese soul'.

It was a frenetic time, with the spectre of war, and the Menuhin careers already alight. They had recorded a highly successful album of Mozart's First Sonata when she was only 13. Four years later, Hephzibah had the world at her feet, including the offer of a debut recital at New York's Carnegie Hall, but she abandoned all career plans and headed for Australia with her husband Lindsay. On the new frontier of a Western District sheep station, she would be far from the conflagration in Europe, but also from intellectual stimulus and the familiarity of music salons.

Here amongst the dust and flies of summer and the withering wind noises through the strange stands of sugar gums, Hephzibah wrestled with what others saw as her privileged world as the wife of a rich grazier. It was never going to be easy for a strong-willed US-born idealist with a European outlook to adapt to the role of chatelaine of a large Western District property and live up to the social expectations that went with it.

There is no evidence that Hephzibah was inclined to play that conventional role, but neither did she turn her back on the rural district. In turn, she threw herself into organising the wartime efforts of the local Red Cross. She also launched her greatest Australian achievement, the mobile library service, which lives today, trundling the dusty roads of country Australia, bringing a library into the imagination of country kids.

Hephzibah and Lindsay saw out the war on Terinallum, occasionally visiting Melbourne for music and conversation. Hephzibah gave birth to two boys, Kron and Marston; she played the piano for guests in the homestead's living room, visited neighbours for afternoon tea, and at home sat down to scheduled meals prepared by a cook. It was a quiet house; there were no raucous drinking parties, no lascivious times. Most of the visitors to Terinallum were émigré Jews, plying their music and escaping the pogroms of Europe. They gave Hephzibah conversation from home and she gave them succour in an unlikely setting.

Hephzibah's biographer Jacqueline Kent describes her as 'warm hearted, humorous, astute, generous and occasionally ruthless'. She ran an ordered household in the unfamiliar terrain. We get a picture of a woman sharing a loving house with her husband and making the best of what there was to offer. Lindsay was reserved by nature, and there wasn't much going on. The nearest thing to hedonism was Hephzibah's habit of sunbaking on the cutout top of a golden cypress halfway down Terinallum's tree-lined drive.

'It was the one frivolous moment' remembers her son, Marston Nicholas, 70, now a retired veterinarian living in Melbourne. She was the focus of his life at Terinallum. 'My memories of my early childhood are all centred on her,' he says without venturing deeper.

'She never got out on the place very much, didn't go around the sheep with Dad. The lasting memory is of her cooking and her typically independent approach to it. She had a new-fangled pressure cooker. It was quite common to have the meal land up on the ceiling when it exploded.

'Because my dad was a disciplinarian, we always had to sit up for meals – no one allowed to talk, eat our Brussels sprouts, that sort of thing. Once, when he was away in New Zealand buying bulls, my mother announced that at dinner that night we would have no rules at all. Everything ended up everywhere, a complete mess, food on the walls. We all went berserk,' he says, laughing.

'There were times when Yehudi and Hephzibah were on the place at the one time. I remember the old man had a thoroughbred mare. She was a bastard of a horse. Yehudi walked up to her. He knew about violins but nothing about horses. He lifted her tail. My old man was petrified she was going to lash out and kill him.'

Marston remembers his mother as always alternative and exotic amongst the locals but still having an active public life in the district. He recalls an afternoon tea of sandwiches at the home of Keith and Flo Calvert at Terinallum South. A friend later suggested to Hephzibah that she should offer the Calverts a return serve at home. 'They won't be getting cucumber sandwiches!' Hephzibah exclaimed. 'I think she came up with a Thai concoction. I don't know how it went down, but that was Mum,' says Marston.

Hephzibah had abandoned her career for Terinallum and Lindsay, but Melbourne was only three hours away. Often she found herself in Lygon Street, Carlton talking to fellow Europeans in the first of the sidewalk cafes. She also performed in concerts during and after the war and was always a free spirit, enjoying her breaks in the city, gradually drifting away from the cloistered world of Lindsay and Terinallum.

In 1947 Hephzibah returned to Europe with Lindsay on a trip he thought would save the marriage. It did the opposite. In Melbourne, she had met a businessman, Paul Morawetz, who convinced her that while she was in Europe she should visit Theresienstadt, a German concentration camp and Jewish ghetto. This had a profound effect on the now 27-year-old, who began to question her own Jewish heritage and what she was doing to help. She realised that living at Terinallum not only isolated her but also stopped her philanthropy, which was fast becoming her life's mission. Mixed with this upheaval and self-doubt was her increasing emotional dependence on Morawetz's sophistication and the two embarked on an affair in Melbourne.

This was the beginning of the end. Hephzibah was tiring of Lindsay's emotional reticence and seemingly non-interest in ideas. After the Morawetz affair waned, she met another man in Sydney, Viennese sociologist Richard Hauser, who was to become her second husband. In 1954 she finally left Terinallum, Lindsay and her sons for a life with Hauser, initially in Sydney and later still in London, where the two ran a sort of halfway house for misfits. Hephzibah did not revive her musical career.

Marston says of his mother, 'She was a real rebel, would leave Germaine Greer for dead. She felt that nothing happened up there in the Western District, believed it was a dead place.' Her rejection of the district became more acute after her 1947 visit to the Jewish ghetto, which Marston describes as 'a life-changing experience'.

'Father was devastated. It took him a lot of time to get over it,' Marston says.

Hephzibah Menuhin's exit from Terinallum says little about the Western District. Neither partner was to blame. Terinallum was the backdrop to a sadly inevitable sequence of events. While the Western District was building to its most prosperous era, money meant very little to a man who already had enough or to a music prodigy and political activist for whom conscience was far more important than cash.

Was Hephzibah a romantic figure? Marston says no. 'A certain amount of hedonism goes with being romantic, and she certainly wasn't that. Life was about business, help people, get on with it. She wasn't a player. She was basically a non-drinker – didn't even drink coffee because it gave her palpitation.

'She was also totally non-practical, not the best trait for a farming life. The Menuhins were fantastic with music but when it came to real life stuff like backing a car, they were hopeless. Great ideas people, initiators, but when the time comes for action they are missing.

'Once in London I visited her and Richard Hauser. At that time the gypsies were being harassed and victimised, and mum organised for them to come over to their place and visit. I remember being surrounded by all these strangers and I looked around for Richard and Hephzibah and they were nowhere to be seen. That was typical.'

Terinallum was always too organised for Hephzibah. A farm run on mundane routine wasn't her at all. The place wasn't cosmopolitan enough, the quietness of the flat empty plains not a virtue. And what of her age? Surely she was too young, arriving as the lady of the house at 18, loaded with the impossible social expectation of the war years. For one so young, of such different culture and rebellious nature, it must have been doubly frustrating to deal with an introspective lover imbued by the responsibility and burden of inheritance. For most of la belle époque, Hephzibah Menuhin was indeed a northern light in the western sky. She lit up the savannah for 16 years, but in the end had no need for it or the people she left there. Love in action is a harsh and dreadful thing compared with love in dreams.

Down the road towards Skipton was another northern light, a very different mortal who hurtled through space at much greater speed and landed at Mooramong without a discordant note, in love with the plains and her plainsman. Claire Adams, a Canadian-born star of 40 Hollywood movies, was at a Mayfair cocktail party in 1937 when she met Donald 'Scobie' Mackinnon, an angular Clark Gable lookalike with an independent air, and decided he was the man for her. Claire had always been decisive and strong-willed. They married three weeks later, still in Mayfair. In the true style of a movie siren, Claire understated her age on the registry documents by ten years to match her 31-year-old husband.

'Scobie' Mackinnon was in London for a Cambridge rowing reunion and to witness the coronation of King George VI. He was the only son of the wealthy Melbourne lawyer L.K.S. Mackinnon, a Scot well known as chairman of the VRC, who had died in 1935. Scobie's whirlwind romance and marriage to Claire were reported in newspapers all around the world.

Scobie was a true son of la belle époque. For his twenty-first birthday, while still a Cambridge undergraduate, he had been given

 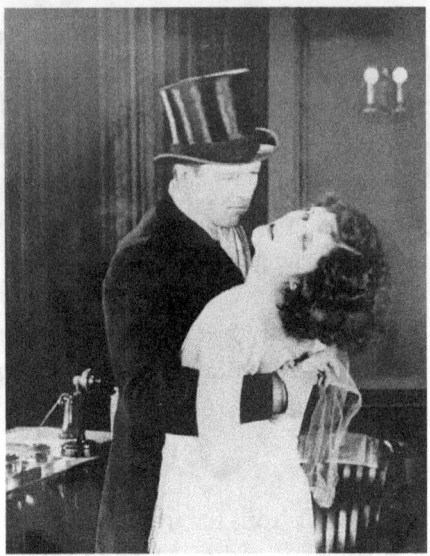

Dashing Scobie Mackinnon with his wife Claire;
right, Claire the actress

the title deed to the 7000-acre Mooramong. As a second birthday present, the keys to a Rolls-Royce had been delivered to him on campus! Ten years later, he was swept off his feet by Claire. After a year's honeymoon, some of it spent at the family's estate on the Isle of Skye, he returned to the Western District with his new trophy wife, scandalising the local establishment.

Quickly the locals softened, charmed by Claire, who was described prosaically as having film-star looks. She soon established herself on the shopping strip of Collins St as the toast of Melbourne's prestigious George's where she always ordered fashionable frocks in every colour and was never guilty of sending anything back. Claire had starred in melodramas and Westerns with Tom Mix and was a favourite of the studios. She had been married previously to a movie producer who had died, leaving her very rich.

The glamorous Claire, by Judy Cassab

The Mackinnons were childless, Claire being ten years older than Scobie. This was no hardship; the glamorous and popular pair celebrated the war years and later 'La Belle Époque' in the manner one would imagine, travelling between their estate and South Yarra villa in a chauffer-driven Silver Ghost Rolls-Royce, lighting up Government House parties and remodelling Mooramong homestead as an art deco folly, resplendent with a Hollywood-style cocktail bar, swimming pool, games room and bathroom.

The partying Scobie and Claire were said to have introduced cocktails to the Western District, an exotic competitor to beer or gin and tonics at first but taken up with enthusiasm in no time. Amazingly, there is no evidence of any meeting between the Mackinnons and Nicholases, although the two stellar couples were near neighbours. Russell Chirnside, who knew the Mooramong couple well, says he can never remember the quartet being together, although there were many soirees he wasn't invited to. He also said, not unkindly, that the Nicholas family 'had little in common with the Western District', while the Mackinnons were more adept at life on the land.

There were deeper heartfelt moments in Scobie and Claire's weekly visits to Melbourne. Claire would gather bones of beasts butchered on the property for distribution to the stockmen's dogs at the Newmarket sale yards. A passionate animal lover, she felt they were neglected by their owners, the stock and station companies, and would venture out to the yards at weekends, when the place was deserted except for the chained-up dogs. She also often served incognito in Melbourne's soup kitchens for the homeless.

Claire Adams and Hephzibah Menuhin were women of uncompromising stature and femininity, the Western District fortunate to have them. They shared not only a locale and international fame, but also had a nurturing need to put their caring natures into practice. These women were not of the idle rich, more idealist than decadent. They gave gravitas to 'la belle époque', the bejewelled Claire and the exotic Hephzibah standard bearers for the Gatsby era, northern lights in the western sky.

Claire and Hephzibah forsook their careers, Claire nearer the end when she came to Mooramong while Hephzibah's was truncated in the first flush. Both earned a reputation for humility. When she lived in the Los Angeles hills, Claire remained aloof from the Hollywood PR machines. She was indeed a star; one of her films, *The Big Parade*, was the second greatest box office success of the silent era and was credited with saving Warner Bros from bankruptcy, but she steadfastly eluded celebrity pap. Hephzibah's demons were closer to home, her devoted partnership with a beloved brother a difficulty that plagued her all her life.

Both Claire and Hephzibah were early feminists, driven by equality of the sexes and an elevated sense of social justice, active as fundraisers for the war effort with musical evenings in their homes and local halls. While forthright and independent of their wealthy husbands, they were kind to those around them. The exception was Hephzibah's abandonment of her boys at a tender age – Marston was nine when she left Terinallum. This was seen in the district as the ruthless act of a spoilt intellectual.

But the plains were empty for Hephzibah, while Claire, born to the expanses of Canada's prairies, was more at ease. She was also 24 years older without the desperation of time's ticking clock or the Jewish wartime angst for a lost generation. Besides, Hephzibah's love for Lindsay had run out while Claire's for Scobie was set in volcanic rock. That is the timeless truth of Dostoevsky; love in real time for Hephzibah was tough, but it lived longer in dreams for Claire, the actress attuned to keep the music playing.

Scobie, a reserved, sometimes desperately shy man, was popular in the Skipton district. He was also a Rolls-Royce enthusiast; it was said that he upset the Rolls executives when he had one cut down into a utility so he could carry dogs and sheep in the rear seat. The Beaufort agency for Rolls-Royce was censured for the wanton destruction, but not the owner.

Scobie would share the comforts of his luxury cars with local stock agent Bill Wood in regular tours of Mooramong. Bill remembers him as a kind man who was forgiving when put to the test. After a disastrous 1967 drought sale when 11,000 wethers from Mooramong averaged just $1 each, Bill was loath to ring his client with the bad news. 'I touched the phone 25 times before I picked it up and dialled his number. He listened and said finally, "You have done all you can do. I am very thankful."'

Scobie was said to know what was going on around the place, even if in later years he didn't actually roll up his sleeves. He had a manager and three stockmen to do that, while three housekeepers and a cook attended the homestead, and a permanent chauffeur watched over the limo. At one stage Mooramong had 25 staff.

Scobie, a heavy smoker, died of a heart attack in 1974, four years before Claire. He was 68. Claire was 84 when she died in 1978. She spent her widowhood between South Yarra and Mooramong, loving the property and the memory of Scobie until her last breath. They left rich legacies to animal welfare and the saving of natural habitats. In an especially touching legacy, the couple set up a trust at the local Skipton school, which still funds a trip away to a city in Australia for the children in sixth grade. Mooramong itself was left to the National Trust as testimony to the days of Western District hegemony, although you receive a sharp reminder of the fall a few kilometres away by Skipton, which is now a dispirited place of melancholic emptiness, not helped by a destructive flood. It remains a shiftless remnant of village life.

Arriving in the mid-1880s, L.K.S. Mackinnon was poles apart in economic and educational status from his countrymen, the desperate Skye émigrés fleeing homelessness sixty years before. His emergence as lawyer, businessman and racing administrator was both meteoric and lasting, while Scobie became a true son of the squattocracy, a gentleman squire whose father was clever enough to select Skipton's fertile soils and superior grazing for his son's farming life. Superphosphate and rabbit control saw young Scobie's flock grow from 5000 in 1937 to 28,000 in the late sixties. During the 1950s wool boom, Scobie was shearing over 25,000 sheep, financing a sometimes profligate Western District lifestyle.

It may seem problematic to place a 'belle époque' at a time of rationing and stifling social mores, but I would argue that this stern background only fuelled the blaze of hedonistic joy that boundless wealth brought to the Western District. And in that joy the Hollywood-inspired pool and cocktails at Mooramong and the salon of grateful émigrés gathered around a grand piano at Terinallum are surely the centrepieces of an extraordinary era.

    The Nicholases are long gone from Terinallum, which remains in private hands. At Mooramong the National Trust barely retains the homestead in an untouched state. A portrait of the handsome Scobie by Judy Cassab gives the games room a masculine glow, while over the fireplace in the cocktail bar is a luminous portrait of the patricianly beautiful Claire. A well-lived love from another time permeates the house and its generous bones.

18

Plain Speaking

> *The people of the Western District are all up themselves.*
> **Kate McEachern**

A broken-hearted Lindsay Nicholas sold Terinallum to cattleman Ralph McEachern in 1955 on very favourable terms, the compassionate millionaire believing in McEachern's down-to-earth ability to manage his beloved land. Nicholas had good reason to favour McEachern, a successful Hereford breeder who had sharpened his husbandry skills and his shrewd eye for pastoral property as a stock agent while still working his land.

Peter Learmonth remembered that famous sale with a glint in his eye. Lindsay Nicholas had engaged the firm Peter represented, Dennys Lascelles. 'We were much smaller than Elders and Dalgetys, who joined with us to sell Terinallum. It was an honour to be involved in such a prestige property.'

There were extraordinary scenes at the auction. Peter explained, 'Lindsay Nicholas wanted somebody who would look after the place and not just buy it and run it into the ground and sell it.' But on the day of the auction, the highest bid came from a man Lindsay didn't want to sell to.

Peter recalled, 'Bidding was closed and that was that, but Lindsay insisted "I'm not going to sell it to that man. I am going to sell it to Ralph McEachern." When told he couldn't do that, he said, "I will take the property off the market. Go back into the hall and tell

Terrinallum proved a headache when it went to auction

them the place is off the market." So there was a hell of a to-do.'

Lindsay had arranged for Ralph to stay on after everyone else had left. 'They went back to the homestead and Lindsay asked Ralph "Have you got enough money to buy the whole place?" Ralph said, "No, I can't." "Could you buy half?" "Yes, I could." Lindsay then said, "I will sell you half and the other 5000 acres I will lease to you for 10 years and then pay me." I believe Ralph paid it off in three or four years.'

Bill Wood, an agent with vast Western District experience, also remembered that transaction. He says, 'Ralph bought Terinallum after Lindsay Nicholas had spent a fortune on it. It was just starting to slip when Ralph bought it.' Ironically, Ralph hadn't been so keen on buying the country on the western side that he leased from Lindsay, but it turned out to be the best country on Terinallum.

Ralph's son Clive McEachern, whom I knew from our days at school together in Hamilton, inherited commercial wisdom from his father. When I caught up with him in 2015, he could still remember the heartache associated with the purchase of Terinallum. 'Obviously Lindsay was in distress from the sudden separation from his wife, Hephzibah Menuhin. Apart from anything else, she had left Lindsay with a telephone bill for £1775! Lindsay left the house more or less exactly as it had been with Hephzibah.'

Clive had fond memories of Lindsay Nicholas. 'Lindsay was a wonderful man. What he didn't do for the country! He almost built the Melbourne Show. He used to fly up to Terinallum for the shearing. He used to buy our sheep. He was a pianist as well.'

Since their days at Terinallum, Clive and his father had bought and sold several times. When I spoke to him, he and Kate, his second wife, had moved east to Wingiel, a large sheep and cattle-raising property outside Inverleigh that they bought from Geelong meat supremo Fred Herd. They had recently sold the Ardno business, a cattle stud his father Ralph had nurtured, beginning in the far west at Strathdownie in 1937 and building to a crescendo in the 1970s and 1980s, as Herefords reached their zenith.

Clive and Kate were now running a substantial operation with 15,000 sheep and 1000 cattle on 9000 acres, including some land leased for cropping. Clive had grown his inheritance with the help of Kate, who was originally from Melbourne but had since adopted the Western District as her home.

Not being bound to the district's sometimes Byzantine class system, Kate called it as she saw it. 'The people of the Western District are all up themselves,' she told me. 'They still think there is something special, but there is nothing to make them special. They think it's 1952, when they didn't have to work and still did very well. To survive now, you have to work and be smart with your decisions.'

I was in the kitchen of the McEacherns' homestead with Peter Learmonth, Kate and Clive. Kate's words are still on my tape recorder. Harsh as it is, her opinion is the voice of someone who lives on the land, invests in it and works on it.

The couple described themselves as Western District businesspeople. They were equally forthright about their own circumstances and the perennial problem of succession, particularly for Clive, who had four children from two marriages.

'Going through a divorce doesn't help,' he said, 'but thanks to Kate, we have bought more land. I have bought my two oldest sons out, so we only have us involved today.'

Kate told me their own children had remained on Wingiel as partners. 'Our son James has taken over. We also have a daughter Lucy on the place. We don't believe it all should go to the son.'

Clive and Kate also made sure that his older sons got something out of the property. They bought some land in the eldest son's name, and Kate later bought his interest out, while Clive bought his second son a property and he got the money from that when it was sold.

Kate added, 'For our two children we have bought extra land, to try and balance it a bit. This is big enough. It would be hard for James to borrow and buy this.'

Over a cup of tea, Clive was philosophical. 'We have done our succession plan. My accountant told me the other day there are more headaches in the Hamilton area with succession planning than any other district in Australia. The major problem is that land values have doubled in the last ten years, mainly through the inflated price paid by tax-driven tree developers. Farmers who tried to buy the rest of the family out during those times couldn't handle it.'

He remembered with horror the days when rural estates had to pay probate. He recalled, 'My mother's brother died of a heart attack on a plane from Melbourne to Sydney the night before probate was abolished in 1978. That caused enormous problems. They took half the value of the property. People took out huge life insurance policies to combat it.'

Clive was also relieved to be in the fortunate position of managing without debt. He'd learnt his lesson from a close shave in the 1980s.

He told me, 'Years ago, I bought a property at Alexandra on Lake Eildon with 1200 cows. I could afford to pay the interest and employ two men, nothing else. We put it up for auction just when the stock market crashed in 1987. One day there were helicopters with rich investors flying around looking at the place, the next day there was nothing.' Clive intended to sell so he could buy more land in the Western District. 'You could buy land west of Hamilton for half the price and you didn't have any debt.'

Bill Wood had been observing the McEacherns for many years and had great respect for their astuteness. He told me, 'Don't call them dealers; they are land improvers. I think Ralph McEachern was the most perceptive landholder that I have ever dealt with. I was in Mortlake when he was at Terinallum, and I remember saying to him, "Ralph, there is a bit of dirt on the market out at Darlington." "Which is it?" asked Ralph. "So and so block," I said. "Bill, thanks for ringing me, but I'm really not interested in country that hasn't any profile. I will buy a Carranballac or a Muralla or a Terinallum any time, because my skill is in redeveloping properties that have already got a reputation. You can't build a station name in a lifetime." It was a very interesting comment. He has been a very successful improver.'

The McEacherns' business model was never the norm in the Western District, where families stayed on the same property for generations or, as now, sold out and left. Not for the McEacherns, who have been singularly agents of change.

Clive was meticulous about everything on his property except his own health, which he largely ignored. In November 2016, five hundred members of the Western District's white tribe gathered to farewell Clive McKenzie McEachern in the cemetery of Inverleigh's resolutely Presbyterian Church. The service was led by a Scots-born minister who extolled 'The Land of the Brave' at the graveside and drew on images of Jesus as the Good Shepherd to illustrate Clive's own devotion to the breeding of sheep.

They buried Clive with one of his prize-winning fleeces, and then drove in a vast conga line to the McEachern homestead at Wingiel. I reflected that Wingiel's original owner, George Russell, a boy made good from the banks of Fyfe, would have appreciated the Scottishness of that mournful day.

At the homestead, under the spreading shade of elm trees, the tribe heard Clive's sister Helen Watson speak of their idyllic childhood on their parents' Ardno at Strathdownie, where 'life was free and easy and you made up your own rules'. In later life, Clive became a perfectionist. He had 'his heart and soul wrapped up in the belief that a well-run property with stock in great condition was the hallmark of his wellbeing,' Helen said 'For instance he insisted all the farm vehicles had to be washed on Fridays. That was part of running the property well.'

Helen closed her eulogy with a heartfelt wish that she and Clive would meet again in a place where 'we never have to worry about the shortness of the grass or the lack of rainfall'. There was a murmur of recognition, the universal angst of the stockowner understood.

That day at Inverleigh drilled down into the human core of the basalt plain, drawing together the fragments of the district's diaspora. All have an ancestral connection to the land, but many are now dispersed along the shores of the Southern Ocean.

Clive McEachern was not born into the squattocracy. His father began life as a small landowner and stock agent, but their combined success as progressive pastoralists gave them paid-up membership of this inland tribe, which these days routinely reconnects at births, deaths and marriages. And, unlike many of the multi-generation squatting descendants who attended that day, Clive was still on the land when he died.

19

A Voice of Reason

Tyrrell Evans is an outsider's insider. The son of a Melbourne-based meat company manager, he's lived in the Western District since he was taken by it as a young boy. He eventually bought a small block of land on Illira station from his former employer, John 'Jack' Bromell. He's had a peripatetic working life as a political fixer and sometime recruiter for the Liberal Party.

Evans has touched many lives, and his knowledge of the place is unsurpassed. He's worked with squatters, known them, understands their attachment to land and the rural life, and can also penetrate the underlying story of failure in its many guises.

Tyrrell Evans was 87 when we met in a Hamilton café in June 2015. He began his story at the beginning.

In his last years of school, he milked cows and did odd jobs for the Baileys on their Park Hill farm outside Hamilton. 'Then John Bromell asked me if I would like to jackaroo on Illira. I arrived in 1940 and left four years later. The war was on when I arrived and when I left.'

His next job was working as an overseer at Injemira, then a long-established sheep property near Grasmere outside Warrnambool. The station was owned by the Goode sisters, who were descended from the original owner. 'It was beautiful, heavy black soil, but when I was there it was susceptible to footrot.'

Tyrrell remembered the place as being seriously overstaffed. 'It was cold and wet, and there were fourteen men on the place. I spent a lot of time trying to find jobs for them. I remember about fourteen of us one day building a fence around the shearers' huts. It was absurd.'

The property was surrounded by dairy farms, and local footy games had to start at noon so the farmers could get home to milk the cows. 'When I left, the soldier settlement commission took over and made ten to twelve dairy farms out of it, leaving just the old homestead and about 100 acres. Later, Ian Watson took over and made a successful Hereford stud out of it.'

Tyrrell was there for six months, then helped a friend up in the Mallee for a while. He was working there when John Bromell wrote asking him to come back as overseer, and also offering him work as a share farmer.

'That suited me,' Tyrrell said. 'I used his tractor, and the oat crops were mine. Then John got word the soldier settlement commission was looking at Illira. There was about 10,000 acres in Illira at that time, and the fear was that they would lose it.'

They were all having dinner together one day when John's son Hugh said, 'Dad, if we're going to lose it, why not sell some land to Tyrrell?'

Tyrrell leapt at the idea. 'I bought 600 acres out of a 2000-acre paddock near Hamilton. I continued to work there and gradually built my farm up – built a house and sheds from nothing.'

Tyrrell got that initial parcel of land under the nose of the soldier settlement commission. The rule was that a transfer of land had to lie on the table for a month so the commission could review it, but by the time the commission came to Illira, it was too late to reverse Tyrrell's purchase. The commissioner pointed to the 2000-acre paddock, saying, 'That is the land we want,' but John Bromell retorted, 'You can't – that land belongs to Mr Evans.'

Tyrrell remembered the nerve-racking time that led up to that moment. 'I had been petrified, sitting there for a month awaiting a challenge to the sale. But they didn't notice the paperwork.' He felt justified, as his father had lost an arm in the First World War.

'Anyway, that is how I got it,' Tyrrell continued. 'And John Bromell gave me very good terms. I continued working for him and gradually paid him off. So I did get my farm. I was there 40 years. I eventually sold it and came to Hamilton to live.'

Tyrrell used super and potash to increase his land's carrying capacity, lifting it from half a sheep to five sheep per acre. Even so, it was hard to support four children on the income from 600 acres, so he took a job with the Victorian Farmers Federation. 'I was recruiting members for the VFF and the United Dairy Farmers,' he told me, 'so I spent a lot of time down south around the dairying districts.'

He was also involved in fundraising for Hamilton College. When he was on the board in the early 1970s, the college was 'just about down and out' until the Uniting Church came through with a couple of loans. Then Geoff Handbury and his wife Helen, who was Rupert Murdoch's sister, stepped in and helped to rebuild the school.

Tyrrell worked at the VFF for twenty years, with a break in the middle. After he retired for the second time, the Liberal Party persuaded him to do the same for them a couple of days a month.

'The Liberal Party had said to me, "You know everyone – you are perfect for this job." They paid me a bit and gave me travelling expenses.' He raised local party membership from 1000 to 1500, making Wannon the largest branch in the federal party.

The party and the local member, David Hawker, were suitably appreciative. 'I was given a nice little plaque, presented by Tony Abbott,' Tyrrell recalled, 'but I had had enough of this sort of job. People started seeing me coming and would cross the street. They'd say, "Here he comes. I wonder what he wants now?"'

When I asked what he remembered of the squattocracy, Tyrrell's first thought was of the squatters' Fridays, which were an institution in Hamilton. 'A regular Friday would be: come to Hamilton late in the morning, do a bit of shopping, have lunch at Harry Pentazzi's fish shop opposite the old Victoria Hotel, and then wander up to the Hamilton Club and play billiards, drink a lot of whisky and somehow get home. Most of them had managers on their properties that allowed them to play polo, go fishing and hunting.'

Tyrrell's boss John Bromell was an exception. 'He would do the Friday bit, but at other times would work beside me in the shed.'

Some of the young squatters were pretty wild. Tyrrell remembered Bill Moodie, 'a bachelor grazier with an eye for the girls, who would take ladies in his car and remove the inside door handle on the passenger side!'

Moodie also had a reputation for being stingy with his employees. Tyrrell was in the street one day when he saw a man going berserk, yelling 'I am going to kill that Moodie!' When Tyrrell asked Jack Ellis, Moodie's partner, what the fuss was about, he discovered that the man had worked as a shearer but had been underpaid by Moodie, who was in the habit of holding back part of his shearers' wages, saying 'They will only go to the pub and blow it all.' Moodie thought they'd all go to Queensland chasing work and forget about it, but this man wasn't going to let him off that lightly.

World War Two cast a shadow over many families, including the squatters, Tyrrell said. A lot of young men went to war, and quite a few of them were killed. 'There were also sad cases of alcoholism in some of the returned squatters.'

A lot of the older graziers on established properties had nothing to do with the excesses associated with the wool boom. 'I was on Illira at the time,' he recalled, 'and I remember materials were scarce. You couldn't get new cars easily. It was hard to spend your money.'

On the other hand, some soldier settlers got carried away. 'Suddenly they had this bonanza,' he told me. 'They had money they never dreamt they would have, and they went crazy.' A few sold out – 'Mick Hurrey on Mount Sturgeon got out and made a lot of money' – but most didn't, because they'd acquired the land on such favourable conditions: 'Two and a half per cent interest and didn't have to pay it off for fifty years!'

There was also a big lift to the squatters' incomes. Tyrrell told me some classic stories of excess, like that of the old fellow who bought a Rolls and asked the salesman to have a glass partition put along the back of the front seat to stop his dogs licking him on the neck.

Looking back on the squatters, Tyrrell told me, 'They were a class that is definitely gone. They pretty much socialised with themselves.' There were more of them around Mortlake than around Hamilton. 'The Kellys, Hoods, Weatherlys, Manns, Manifolds all lived that life down there.'

But some people around Hamilton made it clear that they considered themselves a cut above the rest. An example was Andy Gardiner. Tyrrell remembered sleeping out with Andy after a fox hunt. In the morning, Les, Andy's station hand, cooked a good breakfast, but Andy couldn't even thank him without pulling rank.

'Andy said, "You're a good man, Les, but I am a bloody sight better." That was pretty typical,' Tyrrell remarked. 'He was a great horseman and crack shot. I saw him one day shoot a fox from a horse at a gallop. That was the sort of people they were, and they let you know they were pretty good.'

But succession was a perennial problem. Some families sold up when the sons refused to take over. 'Then there were the sons who went onto the place because they thought they had to. Often that had a very sad conclusion, mostly ending in alcoholism and forced selling of the property.'

A more cheerful twist was when a successful son came back, bringing new money and new ideas. For example, Tyrrell told me, 'John Thomson had a very successful career as a money market operator and chose to come home. Now he is very successfully running Crawford River Wines at Condah.'

For the squatters who stuck with wool, however, things became increasingly bleak. 'I think financially it got more difficult,' Tyrrell told me. 'They just ran out of money.'

The sons who survived were those who built up bigger properties than their fathers, but others had their properties shrink, with land taken for soldier settlement and the remainder divided between family members.

Tyrrell cited the example of John Bromell's sons, Jock and Hugh. 'They finished up running 2500 acres each compared to their father running 10,000 acres,' he recalled. 'When I first went to Illira, there was a cowboy there who used to milk the cow and do odd jobs around the house, a Chinese gardener growing vegetables full-time, two station hands and me and John the boss.' A generation on, Jock finished up running his place alone. He eventually sold up and bought a house at Port Fairy, while his brother Hugh went to the Bellarine Peninsula.

The disappearance of the station workers had serious flow-on effects in the local towns. 'That is why it is hard to get a local footy team now,' Tyrrell said. 'There are no rabbiters, no station hands around. You are seeing that everywhere. The towns are dying. Look at Coleraine – it's dead. Even Hamilton has a lot of shops empty. I reckon it will end up with three big supermarkets, because the little shops just can't compete. And no Holden or Ford dealers. There were seven pubs in my early days. Now there are three!'

Hopes that growing plantation timber would fill the gap had proved illusory. 'The biggest change agriculturally in recent times is the blue gum invasion,' Tyrrell told me. 'Initially, it was like another wool boom.' It looked like easy money, and there were all sorts of tax benefits.

'The federal government can take a lot of blame,' Tyrrell said, reflecting on the problems that eventuated. The companies expanded rapidly and took up increasingly marginal land. At first, they'd only take well-watered land within 50 miles of Portland. 'But they soon ran out of country and started buying country around Branxholme and other areas that didn't fit the criteria.'

Timber production fell short, but the companies kept raising capital from investors until they eventually collapsed during the global financial crisis.

Tyrrell told me the effects had been disastrous. 'The blokes who leased their land have come a real gutser. The companies went broke, and these blokes still have the trees on their land, and no one wants to buy the trees. It's very sad. And if you do get rid of the trees, how do you demolish the roots? The mulcher/rotary hoe seems the most popular way, but the problem is the paddock hasn't had super for fifteen years, so you have to start again.'

Tyrrell agreed that the Western District had lost some of its economic and political clout in recent times. 'Politically, it certainly has changed. It's lost the power it once had. When you go back in time and realise the power they had, people like Niel Black – they ran the place.'

There was nothing like that now, but the district was reinventing itself. A long-time sheep-owner himself, Tyrrell saw the district's future as lying outside the wool industry. 'The dairy farmers are doing well – they have opened up big markets in China. Farmers are doing well out of fat lambs, not wool. You have revolutionary change.'

As he put it in a nutshell: 'We still have to eat, but we don't have to wear wool.'

20
A Manifold Misunderstanding

Sir Chester Manifold is ranked number eight in the Wikipedia list of Camperdown's twelve most notable citizens, sandwiched between Ross Thornton, a largely forgotten player for the extinct VFL team Fitzroy, and Adam Coote, an AFL boundary umpire. It's my firm belief that Sir Chester deserves an upgrade!

Yet I suspect the entry reflects community attitudes. If Sir Chester Manifold is now remembered, it is as the privileged son of the Western District squattocracy who became chairman of the Victoria Racing Club and established the TAB. It is a grievous insult to a man who is arguably the Western District's finest contributor to public life, certainly in terms of his monetary legacy.

Victoria's TAB was established at Sir Chester's initiative in 1961, and the other states followed. The TAB may not be everyone's idea of a noble bequest, but since its inception it has contributed about $45 billion to hospitals and education across the country. In New South Wales, the TAB paid almost $8 billion in state taxes over 50 years, and in Victoria, the TAB has paid $10 billion directly to government since its privatisation in 1994. The TAB also contributes much of the prize money that underpins horse racing, a $25 billion dollar industry that is an important employer and part of Australia's cultural fabric. Racing, like it or not, is part of the nation's DNA. Without the TAB, there would be no Melbourne Cup carnival and we'd lose small-town annual highlights such as the Dunkeld or Burrumbeet cups.

Before the TAB was established, there was no regulated funding stream to support horse racing. Starting-price (SP) bookies operated illegally in shops and pubs throughout the country, paying nothing for the privilege of taking the punters' money. Meanwhile, the licensed on-course bookmakers made a negligible contribution to the sport that sustained them. Sir Chester, or Chetty as he was known, had studied economics at Cambridge and recognised that racing faced a bleak future unless it had a guaranteed source of income.

In the 1950s, he became convinced that the best way to support racing would be to establish a decriminalised tote based on parimutuel betting, a system where bets are pooled and the winnings are distributed after tax and administrative costs, including racing's share, have been taken out. Governments and the public would benefit from taxing the turnover of gambling money, while punters could bypass the illegal SP bookies without having to pay for admission to a racecourse, which was too expensive for many.

The tote wasn't new technology – New Zealand had introduced it at Auckland's main racecourse almost twenty years earlier – but Melbourne, as Sir Chester discovered, was a particularly hard nut to crack. A conservative city on the surface, it had a virulent underbelly. Sly grog shops and SP betting syndicates flourished under punitive societal rules that prescribed six o'clock closing for hotels and prohibited off-course betting.

Racketeering Australian-style was indirectly encouraged by many of those who occupied the Victorian parliament and pulpit. When I was a young journalist, the Melbourne *Age*'s lead story on a Monday often came from the Sunday sermon at one of the city churches. The religion reporter was a major contributor to the newsroom, reinforcing the clerics' influence as moral guardians. To a man they opposed Sir Chester, piously turning a blind eye to the corrupting influence of the ubiquitous SP bookies, who were criminally intent on defending their stranglehold over Australian gambling.

Sir Chester was certain that bringing the totalisator to Australia would defuse the influence of the wowsers and attack the crime fostered by illegal bookmaking. Unfortunately, a huge section of Melbourne's body politic didn't share this vision. He'd upset the Protestant puritans while endangering the livelihood of the predominantly Catholic SP bookmakers. Getting them both off side was quite a double!

But if the Calvinists, Catholics and crime figures of Melbourne thought they could beat Chetty Manifold, they were wrong. He'd never run away from a fight. During the First World War, he'd financed his own passage to England to serve on the Western front, where he was quite seriously wounded at Ypres at the age of 20, and he wasn't cowed by the opposition now. He cut them off at the pass by financing the first TAB branch himself in service of his beloved racing industry.

In the spring of 2014, I spoke to his 84-year-old daughter, Mary Schlight. We discussed his private trials and tribulations over prawn twisters and pies in a charming café on Camperdown's elegant main thoroughfare, the suitably named Manifold Street.

She emphasised that her father wasn't a gambler, but he was distressed to see all the money invested in racing disappear into the bookmakers' pockets. The illegal SP bookmakers were a particular threat. She spoke about the family consequences of her father's dream.

She told me, 'We had a flat in Tivoli Place, South Yarra, and often the phone would go late at night with a threatening voice saying they knew where we lived and that he should be frightened for the safety of his wife and daughters. My father was never upset by these calls. He would just hang up without a word. I always remember him as calm, saying they were just fools trying to change his mind with violence and that needn't frighten any of us.'

When Sir Chester was away, however, her mother had to deal with the calls, and that was a different matter. 'She would become very upset. Easily the worst incident was when a man tried to blackmail my mother by accusing her of being a hit-run driver, saying she had run over a man on the way to the races at Moonee Valley and hadn't stopped. He said she had both her daughters with her in the car and named the date.'

Sir Chester followed this up with the accuser, and both Mary's parents met him at their solicitor's office, where they proved the claim baseless. 'Mum hadn't gone to the races on that date because our horse Misting had been scratched,' Mary said, 'and I was in England at the time. He was arrested, but my parents didn't want to press charges and police let him off with a severe warning.'

While Mrs Schlight's story seems less shocking today than it would have been to a young girl then, it's clear the Manifold family didn't emerge unscathed from Sir Chester's campaign.

After we spoke, I drove to the top of nearby Mount Leura and looked out over Camperdown, which is part of the Western District's south-eastern green hinterland. It's volcanic country close to the Southern Ocean, with opulent basalt soils that will grow anything the heart desires. It's what old farmers call 'soft country', lusher than most of the land further north and west, suited to intensive dairying, cropping and vegetable growing.

When you approach Camperdown from the west, the golden plains give way to rolling emerald-green country punctuated by hills that are the cones of extinct volcanoes. Between Camperdown and Colac lie the stony rises, whose rugged terrain, almost impassable to horses, halted the squatters' westward march for some years in the 1830s. It's said the Manifold brothers, Sir Chester's antecedents, were almost ready to turn back in 1838 when they spied a freshwater lake at Purrumbete. The prospect of plentiful water induced them to stay, and Purrumbete became the family's base.

Today, Camperdown's main street is dominated by a 100-foot clock tower, Australia's finest of its kind, bequeathed by a grateful Manifold pioneer. At Purrumbete itself, the original station of 100,000 acres was broken into four to accommodate four sons, and the parts have since been sold off.

The head station with its historic homestead has repeatedly changed hands. In the 1980s and 1990s, stockbroker Rene Rivkin and property investor David Marriner both owned it at various times. It's said that Rivkin sold it because he couldn't construct an airstrip for his private jet.

The land attached to the homestead is now just over 400 acres, far too little for a working farm. The same applies to the impressive Talindert, Sir Chester's family home, which was built on a subdivision of the original estate. Both historic buildings now stand virtually on their own, cut off from the landed wealth that financed their construction so many years ago.

I don't know who told my mother about Talindert Road, but she seemed to find it easily as we swung off the Princes Highway just east of Camperdown. A minute or two later, the car with all four kids aboard stopped, giving us time to admire a deep green glade opening to a fine house on a rise above horses grazing. There was mystery here for a ten-year-old. Windbreaks lined the paddocks, forming a borderline that delightfully narrowed the view. This idyllic scene became a regular for our family, interrupting the long haul from Melbourne to Hamilton for a snack break in a fine, evocative location at the centre of Western District privilege.

The Italianate mansion at Talindert ran with my imagination for 60 years until 2015, when I drove that shadowy drive with Mary Schlight as my guide. She showed me a living but empty homestead

The elegant Talindert

of elegant dimensions, a timeless classic with high windows and timber-lined hallways, vast entrances and a ballroom, the bandstand ready for the next waltz or Pride of Erin. Now living in a small stone cottage at nearby Danedite, Mary was unhappily conscious that her family home was rarely used by her siblings, who lived interstate, but there were no plans to change when I was there. It seemed the home of Sir Chester Manifold was to continue as it was, lovingly cared for but abandoned, representative of a time long gone.

Here, I could feel a golden age living and breathing – the tennis parties organised by the Manifold girls, the lawns strewn with people and cocktails, a band at night, and the warm sounds of horses settling in the towering stables, intimately close to the house. That was the stuff of Chetty's loves: living the outdoor life, breeding good stock, raising beautiful horses and enjoying a couple of whiskies at sunset.

The stables at Talindert   Mary Schlight

Other times, he'd arrive home from town after visiting a family he knew were in need. He had a true sense of duty and an overriding concern for those around him. He had a grumpy mien as he got older, but that was skin deep. Even in today's Camperdown, decades after his death, there are those who remember his kindness.

Fortunately, he didn't live to see the Kennett government privatise the Victorian TAB, a move that still hurts the racing administrators who were helpless to stop it at the time. Kennett would have found Sir Chester an implacable enemy, but politics was not in the old warhorse's blood. He briefly joined the Victorian State Parliament as an MP and rose to Minister without Portfolio in Argyle's coalition government, but abandoned this folly with the verdict: 'The insincerity of politics was hard to take.' An apt epitaph for the great man.

21

The Last Squatter

> *A hundred thousand sheep and upwards require a professional man cook and a butler to look after them; forty thousand sheep cannot be shorn without a piano; twenty thousand is the lowest number that renders napkins at dinner imperative. Ten thousand require absolute plenty, plenty in meat, tea in plenty, brandy and water, colonial dishes in plenty, but do not expect champagne, sherry or made dishes.*
>
> **Anthony Trollope**

Trevor Clarke of Devon Park personified the landed gentry, and he knew it. He wore a tie every day of his working life and enjoyed the services of a butler; he lived on his property outside Dunkeld with the perfect symmetry of a gentleman to the manor born. Decades after his death, he is still known as 'the last squatter'. He was proud of his ancestry while accepting that his affluence was a lucky accident of birth.

Yet Clarke was nothing like his forebears. The respect he commanded was something the founding squatters aspired to but never really attained, often because of their own brutal behaviour. Trevor shared the initials of his most famous ancestor, W.J.T. 'Big' Clarke, but he was far more civilised than the nineteenth-century sheep owner who founded the family fortune.

On his death in 1874, 'Big' Clarke was said to be Australia's wealthiest man. He left an estate of 215,000 acres of freehold land and funds of £2.5 million, which today would be worth many billions of dollars – just how many billion varies depending which measure you use. Clarke had been a drover in Somerset and a butcher before taking up property in Van Diemen's Land and then extending his interests to the mainland. He belonged to a group of 'newly rich squatters ... regarded as socially inferior peasantry' by genteel Melbourne society. After he died, one local newspaper remarked that his only motivation in life was 'to make as much money as he could'; his name was a synonym 'for roughness, wealth and meanness'. A reporter at another paper claimed he had worn out his shoes vainly tramping the streets of Melbourne in search of someone to speak in Clarke's favour.

The first-generation squatters were wild men, driven by survival and the pursuit of money, and not caring about much else. Although many of them, including Clarke, built large, impressive houses, there was nothing sophisticated about them. But things had changed by the time Trevor Clarke was born in 1903. He grew up as part of a fourth generation that could finally enjoy the spoils of the fortunes their forebears had assembled.

Trevor Clarke bought Devon Park in 1928 from Marcus Oldham, who donated some of the proceeds to found an agricultural college outside Geelong for the sons of Protestant gentlemen. Clarke went on to bestride Devon Park as owner for 55 years until his death in 1983. He was true to his class and time, but not always to everyone's taste. Some read him as an indomitable snob, a latter-day member of the class derided as the 'bunyip aristocracy', famous for their meanness and habits of command.

But meanness was never Clarke's style. His daughter-in-law, Susie Clarke, saw him daily at close quarters after she married his only son, Jim, and moved to Devon Park in 1968. Susie liked her father-in-law enormously. 'He loved women,' she told me. 'He was good to them. He was incredibly good-looking, wore wonderful clothes.'

At the same time, she said, Trevor was quite shy. He was six feet four inches tall and was uncomfortable about his height. She remembers him as 'a kind man who never let a drover go past the

Devon Park, and its Juliet balcony

front gate without offering him some meat for his dogs, a shower or any other comfort he was missing on the road'.

Her memory is supported by a story I heard from local farmer Michael O'Shannessy over a drink in the makeshift bar of a Dunkeld café. Michael told me of an incident when he was a kid helping contractors cart hay on Devon Park. It was very hot, he said, and all five of them were 'buggered'. Then Trevor Clarke rode up and told them to call at the homestead when they finished the day's work. Michael recalled, 'We arrived at the house to be greeted by ten chilled bottles of Melbourne Bitter and five glasses!'

Trevor's gesture was memorable because it was out of the ordinary. 'On another place,' Michael remembered, 'we were told that if we wanted a drink, there was bore water at the woolshed, and that was good enough for hay carters.' Those were the days of a pastoralist paternalism that is now largely gone.

Even so, Trevor Clarke had not lost the habit of command. Many felt the sting of his stick and heard his barked orders. Peter Learmonth recalls an incident when he was assistant steward to Trevor at a Mortlake show, judging the best thoroughbred. Learmonth was momentarily distracted from the job at hand by a girl rider going through her paces in the next ring, until he received a thwack on the back from Trevor's ubiquitous stick and the order, 'Concentrate, young man!' Trevor didn't apologise, but he later remarked to Peter, 'She was rather attractive, wasn't she?'

Chas Armytage remembered Clarke as 'an imposing figure, often misunderstood as pompous'. Chas told me the story of local jockey Butch Power, who had a series of run-ins with Trevor Clarke. There was a big falling-out when Power was rabbiting with some mates on Devon Park. 'They'd cleaned out a warren that included a lot of young ones. When they'd finished digging out the rabbits, they shook a bag full of the young ones back into the burrows to assure there would be a constant supply.' But Trevor had silently ridden up behind them and seen them. Incensed, he ordered them to re-dig the warren and retrieve all the baby rabbits.

Power was also a jockey, and after a successful race meeting, he'd often launch a spectacular pub crawl, which might go for four or five days. Clarke disapproved and would threaten to drop him as a jockey if he got into trouble again. But Power came to respect Clarke and rode a lot of winners for him.

One day in the 1970s, Trevor Clarke attempted to impose his authority on the Dunkeld postmistress, Olive Stimson, by leap-frogging a queue of six people patiently waiting to be served. He breasted the counter with his impressive stature and announced, 'Clarke, Devon Park.'

'Yes, Mr Clarke, I know,' the postmistress replied. 'Now, if you go back to the end of the queue, you will find that you will be served when it is your turn.' Trevor did as he was told, and Ms Stimson continued on her orderly way.

Hugh Beggs, who knew Trevor Clarke well, described him as 'an extraordinary fellow', adored by all his family. 'He could be very abrupt but had a great sense of humour,' Hugh said.

Trevor's sense of humour helped to obviate family conflicts. Hugh Beggs recalled, 'I remember going over to Devon Park – I was conned into helping prepare for his daughter Georgina's wedding. I got over there at 7.30 in the morning and sat around the back door with these fellows. Trevor emerged, saying "Hello, how are you?" and then, stretching to his full height, said, "Now today, a day before the wedding, could have difficulties. It shouldn't so – we will hope for the best. But I will say this: if Mrs Clarke says she would like the wood heap on the roof, then just put it on the roof. If she then decides it doesn't look nice up there, then just get it down. If we do that sort of thing, the day will pass uneventfully."'

Susie Clarke also remembered Trevor Clarke as 'one of the most gorgeous men I have ever had anything to do with. I loved him.'

He was very sociable and accommodating, while his wife Sandra was more reserved. Living with them at Devon Park, Susie came to realise 'it was Mrs Clarke who stirred the pot, and it was Trevor who was the gentle soul. He was the kindest man.'

But many also remember his gruffness. Dinner guests who tried to help the staff by stacking empty plates would be stopped in their tracks when Trevor said imperiously, 'We don't stack at Devon Park!' It was a relic of those halcyon days when there were servants to tend to the boring bits of every meal.

James Kimpton, who was an occasional visitor from Melbourne, sometimes stayed with the Clarkes at Devon Park. He remembered, 'They had a large staff and wore black tie for dinner. Dinner was at a particular time, and you were expected to be on your best behaviour. One evening after a mate and I had tried to earn a dollar for the local hospital by drinking one-cent beers at a local race meeting, it would be fair to say I was fairly sloppy over dinner.

'So I was bundled out,' he said, evidently unperturbed by having breached Devon Park protocol.

'The Clarkes were the last to have a full staff,' Susie Clarke recalls. An English married couple lived on Devon Park for many years. Charles, the husband, was Trevor Clarke's valet/butler, and his wife Paula was the cook.

Charles had been a gunner during the Second World War and was shot down over France. 'He worshipped Mr Clarke,' Susie says. 'He was the bravest and nicest man. He could do anything. He could wash, iron and mend and get up on the roof and mend it.'

Paula was a wonderful cook, and glamorous as well. 'Used to go to the races and look more elegant than anyone else.'

Sandra Clarke was a member of the extended Baillieu clan. Born in 1907, she was a tall, imposing figure, always beautifully dressed, and with a lifelong love of horses. As a child growing up in Toorak, she and her friends would ride from her home in Linlithgow Avenue to shop in Toorak village, and periodically she'd load her horse on a special train to Cranbourne to hunt with the hounds.

At Devon Park, Susie says, 'Everything had to be utterly perfect.' Sandra's role was to be beautiful, and to make her house beautiful as well. 'She always had exquisite flowers in the house.' She did a lot of gardening and was constantly on a diet.

Georgina Weir, who worked with her mother supplying Western District wives with fashions from Paris, told me, 'People like Sandra Clarke stick in my mind because she was so fabulous. The most elegant, fabulous woman. She could put a hat on and just touch it and it would look right.'

But Sandra could also be down to earth, especially where horses were involved. 'When the chips were down, she got in the truck and drove it with the kids and their ponies in the back. Very capable and practical.'

Sandra outlived her husband by almost 30 years, dying at Devon Park in 2010 at the age of 103. She managed the stairs at the two-storey Bluestone Hut until the last week of her life. She outlived two of her four children – Carmen, her eldest daughter, and Jim, both of whom died of cancer.

Sandra's death left Jim's widow Susie as the last family member on the place. When I drove out to meet her, I missed the cunningly disguised bluestone front gate and sailed past, then realised my error some distance down the road.

I called her on my mobile and found her in the midst of her morning ritual of cleaning up dog poo in the dining room. She had a new puppy, and house training was a problem. I knew then that things would be pretty relaxed at Devon Park.

I arrived to find Susie in the garden, shifting sprinklers. We met and walked toward the homestead, a bluestone pile that has grown under three building regimes over the years. Large, flat stones emerged from the skin of the well-worn driveway, and there was no mistaking the volcanic base of the place.

Over lunch, Susie proved to be a dispassionate and witty observer. She was philosophical about having shared Devon Park with her in-laws. 'I have lived 50 yards from my mother-in-law for 46 years,' she told me.

Melbourne born, Susie was fascinated by the Western District of the 1970s and 1980s, with its class stereotypes, divisions and tribal ways. 'I was aware of the strata of society when I arrived. I was accepted because my grandparents were friends of Mrs Mann. They played bridge together. The pecking order was the Clarkes, the Manns and the Ritchies, the Kellys and Manifolds, followed by the Beggs. It depended on who your relations were.'

Susie felt there had been a generational shift since then. 'My parents-in-law were old in their sixties,' she said, 'not like today. My friends didn't get old like their parents did.'

The Clarkes, for example, did the same thing every year. 'Their social year was set in stone – the Sydney Show, the winter races in Brisbane, the spring cup season in Melbourne. It was terribly regimented.'

They always stayed in hotels, and there was no small talk. 'They travelled overseas very little considering their wealth,' Susie said, 'and when they did, they did the same thing. They stayed with her family in England.'

Susie said the wives and mothers played a crucial economic role in the district. 'It's the only way capital has been injected into the land in the last 80 years.'

Some money also came in through BHP. Two Western District families, the Kellys and the Weatherlys, were among the original twelve shareholders in BHP back in the 1880s. Susie told me Bill Weatherly still had the original scrip when he died.

Susie cited Garry Carnegie's book *Pastoral Accounting in Australia*, a compilation of many of the Western District properties' accounts, as giving solid evidence of how important off-farm money was to the stations. 'The properties were never very profitable,' she said. 'It was a very tenuous existence, and the real money came from the protein that was sold on the gold fields, or from off farm.'

When I asked her how she saw the future of Devon Park, she replied, 'I think its future is probably limited. My daughter Sarah owns the place. She has married a very successful solicitor, who isn't a farmer but will probably put enough money in to keep it going. She adores this place and is a very competent stockwoman. But they're not going to live here, and it needs to be lived in. Sarah said the other day, "I realise if you weren't here and we didn't come to a place that was ticking over, it would be a very different story." The cost of staff is prohibitive when the margins are so low.'

Susie had three men working on the property. 'We still breed horses and do all our work on them,' she told me. 'A lot of our country is stony, and our cattle are so quiet. We actually have to ride motorbikes through the weaners so they will be acclimatised when they go to their new places.'

Most of the plains were open, park-like country when the first settlers came. Susie was struck by how familiar the landscape was when she attended an exhibition of von Guérard's paintings. 'Returning home along the Hamilton Highway, where he had painted so many pictures, I realised nothing had changed. If you drive up through this country, you will get exactly the same views as Thomas Clark painted.'

Susie saw the Scottish settlers as being oppressed, but oppressing in their turn. 'They came out from Scotland and Ireland and did to the Aborigines exactly what had been done to them. Who am I to pass judgement on their behaviour? They had been cleared off their land as tenant farmers by the aristocrat owners.'

She was obviously fond of Jim, with whom she shared a lot of laughs, but she told me she could never understand why he chose her as his wife. 'Jim could pull birds off the tree,' she said. 'I don't know why he married me, except he said I could lift hay bales and when the chips were down I did as I was told. At parties he used to dump me at the door and run off with the best-looking woman in the room.'

When Susie looks to the future, she can envisage a life outside Devon Park. 'I have told my children I could live anywhere in the world. My son is totally independent, and I have said to Sarah, "You have to do what you have to do." I have had a wonderful life here. You have to make the decision when it's right for you. I live as if it's going to go on forever, but it won't.'

On my second visit to Devon Park, I found the place empty. I poked my head in doors and windows only to discover that Susie was off the farm picking up machinery, having spent a long, hot day mustering steers in 38-degree heat. She'd left me a message the previous day to say she couldn't meet up, but it hadn't been delivered.

I spent a few moments of repose in the garden of the iconic house, replete with its romantic Juliet balconies, which probably hadn't seen flowers delivered with passion for some time. Even out here, in this privileged sanctuary, there was no time or patience for Jane Austen stories. Such is the reality of today's bucolic life.

I walked around the green lawns and flower beds, wondering about the future of Devon Park. I thought about Susie's son Tim, the only son of Jim, who was in turn the only son of Trevor. It seems so obvious a line of inheritance. But what is routine about handing down sacred family land?

Tim was running Minjah, a grazing property south-west of Caramut. In 2004, he and Jim sold Mount Schank, a cattle station outside Mount Gambier that had been in the family since 1860, and a year later, Tim bought Minjah from 'Bim' Affleck, whose family had owned the 3,500 acre property for more than a century. Minjah, famously painted by von Guérard, was a showpiece 30-room bluestone homestead dating back to 1870.

After acquiring the property, Tim and his wife Jenny spent a lot of time and money updating the home and adding 3,000 acres to the farm. Just replacing the homestead roof involved importing 28 tonnes of Welsh slate. Tim also upgraded the yards and water systems, improving stock management infrastructure in the interests of keeping running costs low.

He outlined his global business plan to Richard Allen, author of *Great Properties of Western Victoria*. Tim's scheme involved exporting processed meat as well as live cattle and sheep in a joint venture with a Chinese partner. The most valuable stud sheep would be exported to China by chartered plane as part of a triangular trade: having offloaded the sheep in western China, the plane would take on computers for export to the USA, where it would then load for the final leg, bringing white goods and clothing to Australia. It was a very ambitious plan, but when I phoned Tim from the garden at Devon Park to ask about its progress, he made it clear that he didn't wish to discuss it with me.

I left the matter and wandered Devon Park's environs, watching water birds settle for the night on the dam beside the house. As I walked, I thought about the Western District and its vanished ways. The old white tribe of squatters had largely vacated this land, but some echoes of the past remained. Jane Austen, with her keen eye for the foibles of the landed gentry, would be right at home looking out on this estate from one of the bay windows of Devon Park.

22

The Pistol under the Pillow

We make up our own past.

Doris Lessing

One lesson of adulthood is that the child in us never dies, living on as memory. Yet our recall torments us as adults because it's incomplete. It may be the purest memory, but that doesn't mean it's true.

My memory of Waratah, near Cavendish, traverses more than sixty years. I first went there around 1955 to visit my school friend Charles Reid, and found a world very different from my own. Charles's parents, Don and Elizabeth, were revelling in the largesse of the wool boom. Don drove a black Bentley, and his beautiful wife visited Hamilton every fortnight to have her hair blonded.

Like most Western District graziers in the 1950s, the Reids seemed to be living the good life. Waratah gleamed as a showplace and nursery for thoroughbred horses. Its racing credits included four Melbourne Cup winners – Gatum Gatum, Rainbird and Rain Lover (twice). The post-and-rail fences were painted a glamorously different red and white, the stables sparkled, the gardens were immaculately groomed, and there were staff everywhere.

Although she never really spoke to me – maybe didn't even notice me – I remember the young Mrs Reid as being particularly glamorous in a Grace Kelly kind of way, with an air of unconventional mystery. My most treasured memory of her is that Charles and I once stole

Waratah

into her bedroom to test a rumour we'd heard, that she slept with a pistol under her pillow. We were both agog when we discovered the tale was right.

But was this memory just a myth that had grown in me? If it was, a phone call seemed the best way to explode it, so I picked up the phone and called Waratah.

When the phone was answered, I heard the voice of Andrew, Charles's younger brother, for the first time in six decades. Andrew, now 64, was perhaps three or four when I last saw him. I'd already rung Charles, who moved away years ago, but he hadn't answered. I was worried he might be avoiding me. And I was worried about speaking to Andrew. Would he be sympathetic to a stranger? Would he understand my need to know if his story matched my own recollection?

The introduction was awkward. 'But I don't know you,' said the distant voice.

I explained quickly. He recognised my father's name and remembered him at Hamilton College. I talked about Charles and

Elizabeth Reid (left) at the races in Melbourne

Waratah. He softened slightly, but I soon realised that Andrew was very much part of the story.

He told me he'd been living on Waratah since he left Geelong Grammar in 1970. He worked the place with two station hands, who had each been there for more than forty years. They ran 14,000 sheep, operating with complete synchronicity. If one of the three was away, Andrew said, 'the place just continues as if everyone is here.'

Andrew was a bachelor and, in his own words, 'nearly a hermit'. He had a housekeeper three days a week but cooked at night and washed and ironed his own clothes. He often spent his evenings reading about war over a glass of beer. Napoleon and Rommel were his favourite generals. Occasionally, he visited Melbourne or Adelaide, where he stayed in expensive hotels, but he never looked up other family members, though they were numerous in both cities. He didn't have a mobile phone or a computer.

The Reids were not part of the classic Western District tribe, though the family did have a pastoral connection. Andrew's grandfather, Malcolm Reid, who bought the 6000-acre property in 1938, was, according to the Reid family, a self-made man from Adelaide who started his working life at the age of fourteen, hammering roofs with his father. He went on to establish a large furniture store and was active in the timber business. One of his brothers, Sid, married Sir Sidney Kidman's second daughter, Elma.

Andrew remembered his grandfather as a frugal man, mindful of expenses on Waratah, which he controlled until his death. Malcolm used to take long walks and enjoy a Dewars whisky at night. He rode a horse until he was 75.

'He would come to Waratah every three months from Adelaide and stay a week. He would go through the books and was careful to let Mum and Dad know that he owned most of the place, especially if they were overspending. And Mum and Dad liked to spend.'

Andrew told me his mother liked fast cars. He remembered his parents tossing up whether or not to buy a Ferrari in 1960. 'It was then £8000, and that was a lot of money.'

But in those salad days, the Reids were minor players in the Western District squatters' hectic social round. Andrew said his parents rarely held parties. They were introverted, if not antisocial.

'The last significant party here would have been in 1960, when we had a polo party with probably 100 guests,' he said.

I remembered his father, Don, as being always dressed in a shirt and tie, clothes that hadn't seen any toil, but Andrew told me my recall had let me down. He said his father physically worked the place and only wore a tie once a year, when he went to the wool sales in Adelaide.

Don was a patriarchal father, a returned serviceman who had fought in the Middle East. He liked a beer at the local pub, played polo and was 'always well horsed because he could afford it,' according to John Gubbins, a member of the Hamilton Club who played polo against him.

Don Reid was not withdrawn, but had few close friends locally and was said to have had 'a difficult war'. He did most of his socialising back in Adelaide with old school mates from St Peters College.

One particularly hot day in January, my mother dropped me off at Waratah so that Mr Reid could take me by car to the family holiday home at Adelaide's Henley Beach. Before I jumped aboard the huge, stifling Bentley, he advised me sternly, 'Now listen, young fellow, we are not stopping until we get to Adelaide, so you'd better have a drink of water.'

I was staring at a seven-hour journey that had all the allure of a walk across burning sand. When we reached Murray Bridge four hours later, he took pity on me; he stopped and bought me a milk shake, which I consumed voraciously in one of those deep leather booths that graced milk bars of that era. He must have noticed my flushed face, because I hadn't said a word.

Now I edged toward the question of Andrew's mother. Andrew didn't remember her as beautiful, but he agreed that many people in the district did. 'She was eccentric,' he said. 'Probably a male in female clothes – she loved guns and knives and flew Gypsy Moths before the Second World War.'

Elizabeth Reid was the daughter of an academic. Her father won a scholarship to a German university, and she lived with her grandmother until she was nine years old, when she joined her parents in Germany. She spent two years at school there in the tumultuous late 1920s. By the time she left school, her experiences had forged a character that would later label her a Western District misfit.

For Elizabeth, like many women who move from the city to the country, the Western District meant drab loneliness and dislocation. It was an uncomfortable life for this beautiful, vivacious girl.

'My mother probably should never have come to Waratah,' said Andrew, reflecting. 'In 1940, she had a great life in Adelaide. She got a lot of publicity as a woman pilot and lived life to the fullest. Here, it was very primitive.'

There was no electricity, and the phone was a party line. She missed her life in Adelaide and had nothing in common with the locals.

Andrew said, 'She made herself unpopular by telling the locals to get rid of their milking cows. She told them with good wool prices they could afford to buy a pint of milk!'

Over the years at Waratah, Mrs Reid retreated into herself, relying increasingly on alcohol but always keen to maintain her looks. She would never venture from her bedroom suite without full makeup.

I asked him about the pistol, and to my relief he confirmed the story. 'Yes, she owned a .25 automatic pistol, and it could well have been under her pillow. The police eventually took it off her because they reckoned it could be too easily concealed.'

As Andrew told the story, 'On one stormy night with thunder and lightning, Mum was alone. She heard a noise in the house, grabbed her pistol and made it out into the hallway. There was a man silhouetted against the nightlight.' She brandished the pistol at him from four feet away, but when the man saw the pistol he shouted out to her. 'He was one of the workers on Waratah, who had come over to see if she was all right,' Andrew said.

Mrs Reid outlived her husband by many years. After she died

in 2003 at the age of 84, Waratah was left in the hands of four shareholders: Andrew, Charles and their estranged sister Kristin had a half share between them, while the other half was owned by their father's brother, Peter Reid.

All the shareholders were getting 'quite good dividends', Andrew said, but the family's ownership of Waratah was thrown into doubt after their uncle Peter died in August 2015 at the age of almost 101.

Peter Reid was a character, in the tradition of this not straightforward family. He lived in Sydney most of his life, married at 65 and had no children. A great favourite of Sir Frank Packer, he had been a director of Consolidated Press Holdings and worked out of its Sydney offices, but things changed when Frank's son Kerry took over and demanded payment of rent. Wounded at the rejection, Peter Reid severed his ties with the Packers.

At his death, he left a sizeable fortune. As well as his share in Waratah, there were great rafts of bank shares and myriad other properties, including a waterfront abode in Point Piper. The estate was said to be worth between $50 and $100 million, and 22 objectors disputed the will. There were bitter allegations that the will had been changed in later years, when Peter Reid was suffering from dementia. When I spoke to Andrew, the outcome of the case was very much in doubt.

Among those contesting the will was Peter Reid's niece by marriage, Peta Roberts. A sensational Sydney Supreme Court hearing in June 2016 was told that Peter Reid had made a pass at his much younger niece during his wife's funeral in 1998, and an intimate relationship had begun soon after. Over the next 17 years, Peta had travelled to Point Piper from her hobby farm in Tasmania at least twice a week. She had received over a million dollars in payments for her children's school fees and the upkeep of her farm.

Then, from the detritus of this unedifying squabbling, there eventually came a breakthrough. A Supreme Court judge upheld Reid's wish that his brother's three children should inherit his half share of Waratah and have full ownership of the property.

When I heard this, I made another phone call to Waratah. This time, the call was answered by Charles, my old school friend, who hadn't returned my earlier calls. We arranged for me to visit Waratah, where he was overseeing a building program to restore a semblance of gentility to the homestead and outbuildings.

From Balmoral to Waratah, the paddocks were blond after the hot winds of March. Paspalum waved as high as the car windows, reminding me that I was on the pampas and this was their grass. Ahead lay the Grampians, the azure signature of Western District elegance. Was this the view that turned Malcolm Reid's head when he bought Waratah in 1938?

From the road, Waratah's homestead and outbuildings were a shadow of their former glory. Assorted horses were grazing a stock route behind a rude electric wire, and the sheds were full of secondhand trucks and floats. At face value, the property seemed to have fallen on hard times.

Charles emerged from the tired homestead, which was now mired in dead grass. When we were boys, this was a manicured lawn. Stories of the house's failures spilt from him, along with his plans for restoring the outbuildings, which were in various states of disrepair.

Andrew had obviously let the homestead and its environs go. He had no interest in keeping up appearances, but he was now giving his older brother free rein with the repairs. There had already been a setback when part of the roof collapsed the day before I arrived.

Andrew had gone away for a few days, and he had told Charles that he wanted to retire.

Charles, a successful Canberra businessman, had long ago declared his preference for commerce over the uncertain path of farming, but in the moment of his inheritance he had to deal with the certainty of ownership. He viewed keeping the land as a matter of pride. 'I am third-generation,' he told me across a dining-room table laden with sandwiches and tea. 'My grandfather was self-made, and I am very conscious of not stuffing up. If someone gives you land and you lose it, that's stupid.'

'Do you have any plans to sell?' I asked, knowing that Andrew and Kristin were childless and Charles's own children, a boy and a girl, were not interested.

'No, the plan is to keep it – install a manager to run it.'

But his wife Jenny broke in, 'Nothing is guaranteed.'

Charles was full of praise for Andrew's farming ability, saying he had done a first-class pastoral and financial job.

When we went for a tour around the paddocks, I realised the appearance of decay was deceptive. The wandering horses and the clutter of equipment that made Waratah look derelict from the road belonged to a tenant in one of the cottages. Although the homestead was forlorn, the rest of the estate was in pristine order. The fences were immaculate, and each paddock had its own mystery and beauty. Around each dam, a wood lot had been fenced in, allowing acacias, she-oaks and red gums to flourish and providing superb sanctuaries for waterbirds. The trees had also reversed dry-land salinity and provided shelter for newly shorn sheep during cold snaps.

The man responsible for this initiative was Peter Watt, a Reid employee for 45 years. On his way to one of the reserves, he saw us and stopped his ute for a chat. He told me the trees had made a huge difference to stock mortality.

'One night before we had them, we lost 600 young ewes in a cold snap,' he recalled. 'It was cruel, a terrible time.' Their losses now were far smaller. On a freezing October night after shearing, they lost just 30 lambs from a mob of 3000.

I was surprised at Peter's long hair, unusual for a man of the land. He talked easily of how well the Reids had treated him, contrasting them with the meaner squatters in the district. For example, he said, the Reids always paid fortnightly, where other squatters paid their men monthly, so they got almost thirteen months' work for twelve months' pay.

We drove on across the paddocks. Charles told me he was proud of their bountiful condition but concerned about how to manage ownership from afar. Like so many in the Western District, he faced the question of whether to hold the land or sell when there was no family member interested in hands-on management. But whatever the Reids decide, Waratah's dreaming paddocks will continue to grow the miraculous grass that spawned three Melbourne Cup winners.

23
Last Man Standing

If there is one man who epitomises the Western District, it must be Stewart McArthur, a man of startling eyebrows with a face as rugged as a Highland crag. He is of a past age, an establishment conservative, vitally interested in today. We meet in Camperdown, his home town. The cafés are noisy, so we talk in a car parked on the charmingly expansive main thoroughfare, Manifold Street. In American terms, it's a 'McArthur on Manifold'.

Stewart starts at the beginning, cutting a long story short. 'My family came from the Isle of Islay, off the west coast of Scotland, in 1839, and are still on the same piece of ground near Camperdown. I was born in 1937, rode a horse to school, and then at nine went to Geelong College as a boarder. Later I went to Jesus College, Cambridge, for three years. Then I came home and ran the farm on behalf of the family for 25 years.'

Stewart became chairman of Marcus Oldham College, the distinguished agricultural education institution, and sat on the boards of the Pivot Fertilisers and woolbroker Dennys Lascelles before launching his political career in the 1980s. He became president of the Victorian Liberal Party in 1982, and two years later was elected as the federal member for Corangamite. His seat, which extends from the fertile farmland around Camperdown to the western suburbs of Geelong, became increasingly marginal as the population mix changed. Stewart held the seat for more than twenty years, but was defeated at the 2007 election.

Stewart, a Western District partisan and standard-bearer for his locality, believes the land around Lake Bolac and perhaps Streatham is the best cropping land in the world. One of the Western District's great advantages is, of course, its fertile volcanic soils. The red-gum country to the north-west is of lower quality, and most other parts of Australia are sandy because their soils were formed under the ocean.

The advantages don't end there, Stewart says. 'Western Victoria has an advantage with reliable, good rainfall of 25 to 30 inches and a moderate climate, except for a winter that is pretty cold. As Major Mitchell said in 1834, when he described Western Victoria as Australia Felix, there was an abundance of grass and herbage that he had never seen before.' Yet many people in the Western District take its unique qualities for granted.

The families who came to the district in the 1840s and 1850s had a pretty hard time at first. The first McArthur was a Scottish crofter and would have had a bit of money, Stewart thinks, but most of them didn't come with much. 'The Manifolds had some money to start with. Others just managed to survive.' In the diary that the original McArthur kept during the depression of the 1840s, 'the diet was damper and mutton one day, mutton and damper the next.'

But with wool prices strong and the flock growing, established families in the Western District had a head start. The gold rushes helped, opening up new markets for those who could produce meat as well as wool. 'The Manifolds walked their cattle to the goldfields and made a killing.'

Real prosperity came with the rapid growth of the wool industry from the early 1860s, at a time of high wool prices. 'Obviously the big families had a substantial lift in their incomes between 1865 and 1890, when the big houses were built and the big holdings consolidated and the families enjoyed an enhanced standard of living. If you look at the material structures that emerged from that time, there was a lot of money around.'

He says there aren't many of the old squatting families still on their original land. 'The cutting up of the big estates through soldier settlement and high living has taken its toll.' He cites the example of the Cumming family, who had 100,000 acres around Darlington and Mortlake, but now don't own an acre in the district. 'They are one example of a family who thought the good times would roll on.' Other families lost their land as a result of personal misfortune, soldier settlement and the imposition of probate.

'Probate was a major threat because it took half the farm. The probate was 50 per cent of land value to be paid within a year – 30 per cent to the state government and 20 per cent to the federal government. It was always an iniquitous tax.'

The other big threat was soldier settlement. Public opinion favoured soldier settlement, he points out. 'It was driven by an attitude that the diggers had done a good job in both world wars, and soldier settlement commissions were active after both.' Soldier settlement after the First World War was rarely successful, because the blocks were too small. 'There were many disasters after 1918 in both Victoria and New South Wales.'

During the Second World War, there was a lot of discussion about how to handle breaking up the big holdings. 'There was a social attitude that families who controlled a lot of land – the Manifolds come to mind – could afford to lose half their country. The government said, "We will take three of your farms away, leaving you with three." They did that after the war basing their buying price on 1942 valuations.'

This was a real inequity in Stewart's view. It helped the soldier settlers, because it made it easy for them to pay off their land, but it meant that the existing landowners received far less in compensation than they should have.

Stewart says, 'The Victorian Commission after the Second World War did it better than anyone else. It was very well organised. It happened a conservative minister, Sir Rutherford Guthrie, was in charge in 1948, when it really started and became a topic in the Melbourne Club. Some of his mates never talked to him again.'

It was a difficult time. There was a belief that they could make economic units by dividing the big runs, Stewart says, and squatting families whose properties had been singled out found themselves defending the way they ran their farms.

'The RSL was very active, with sub-branches saying, "So-and-so doesn't work very hard and has no sons, so get stuck into him." The RSL clubs sent a subterranean message to the commission.'

The soldiers had such kudos that it was impossible to stand against the scheme. Stewart says, 'The diggers were heroes. They had survived the war – they were untouchable – and the RSL was hugely influential. Their smoke nights went from 8 p.m. to 3 a.m., and they had lots of influence in the parliament.'

Stewart believes people were also reluctant to oppose the commission because they were afraid of its power. 'Inherent in their threat was "We will leave you with your house and take the bloody lot."'

At first, the soldier settlers did quite well. They got cheap loans, some good soil and the benefit of the wool boom. But then the size of the blocks was cut, so that those who came in after 1951 only got 500 acres or less, depending on where they were.

The old properties now had soldier-settler families trying to make a go of it on their borders. Boortkoi suddenly had 20 new neighbours and Meningoort, the McArthur family property, had ten.

Stewart reflects on the scheme's overall impact. 'The soldier-settler scheme changed the whole social fabric of the district, sometimes for good, sometimes not so good. Some of the settlers were under such strain they just battled, where others made a major contribution.'

It wasn't the only change that affected the Western District in the postwar years. There was a major shift in the pattern of marriages between squatting families. For generations, Stewart says, 'sons and daughters of graziers tended to marry each other. Generally the girls had attended a single-sex private school in Melbourne or Geelong and came home to become a nurse or secretary locally. We're now seeing a change in the social structure as the daughters of the landowners are being encouraged to go to university and get a qualification. So the level of intellectual discussion has moved up a notch or two. The potential wives of graziers now want to live in Melbourne and go to the theatre or have a conversation with their contemporaries who have a tertiary education.'

These newly educated women don't necessarily want to move back to the farm. The problem has been compounded by the demise of the country schools. 'The nice local schoolteacher no longer emerges in the community. So suddenly the real problem is the lack of women.'

He is sure the problem is serious. For example, if a man has a job running a farm outside somewhere like Camperdown, what does his wife do?

Then, if women go back to the big homesteads, how do they fill in their time? 'Are they going to get on the internet?' he asks. Women used to play cards, go to the club and interact with their peers, and have three or four children, who were generally cared for by somebody else. 'Now, economic pressures have pushed the women to look after the children themselves and often have part-time jobs, so this has created a lot of new pressures that were never there before.'

Schooling has changed markedly as well. 'These children now go to private schools at fourteen, where previously it was about nine. Older families even sent their children to school at the age of six, which is unheard of today. Fifty years ago, it was almost taken for the norm that sons and daughters went away to school about ten as boarders and stayed away for the full term and came home for holidays a couple of weeks and then went back to school.'

Meningoort as seen by Eugene von Guérard in 1861

Clearly, the current lifestyle is far more demanding than the squatters' old way of life, and it extends to the man of the household as well. 'The husband of the day is out working with probably a large overdraft, worrying about the drought, stock prices and interest rates. Meanwhile, the wife is busy looking after three young children, driving them to school, often long distances. A lot of these wives spend a lot of their lives in a motor car.'

Stewart believes this is one reason that the political voice of the Western District squatters has become much less influential. 'I think they have been busy surviving day to day. Most of these big properties were run on an extended management basis. Usually there was a manager and a number of station hands, but most of the current owners are busy doing the job.

'That wasn't the case in the previous generations. They had time on their hands and time for political debate. In my youth, the Graziers Association used to have their meetings at two o'clock in the afternoon. It took a long time, but we of the younger generation said, "We will have the meetings at seven o'clock because we are working at two." It was quite a social change.'

McArthur of Meningoort has seen quite a bit of that.

24
A Mann and his Daughter

Richard Mann, I'd been told, had an encyclopaedic knowledge of the Western District and knew where the bodies were buried. In the fire-lit living room of his farmhouse at Branxholme near Hamilton, I tested that claim out.

When I asked about the wool boom's effects on the district, Richard was ambivalent. 'It actually brought all sorts of problems,' he said. 'Of course, people coming into money … it's like winning Tattslotto. People generally don't know how to handle it. My family were pretty thrifty – my father shared it with his kids. But others just had no idea.'

He cited the case of the Falkiners, a famous family of Merino breeders in the Riverina. 'They were reputed to light the fire with a ten-quid note. You can imagine the amount of money they were making – it was colossal! But it came and went very quickly.' The Falkiners now are out of the industry.

Taking a long view, he says the wool boom was an exceptional time. 'Over the years I have been involved, the tide comes in and goes out, but it has never come in as far as it did then.'

Richard was young during the boom, and he didn't take part in the general carousing. 'My parents had dances. It was a fairly artificial sort of life. I loathed it. My mother and father were always entertaining, having people to dinner. Of course, they were their age, not mine. I don't think I enjoyed the social life. I didn't want to be a part of it, because I knew one day it would come to an end, and it did.'

Richard had an older sister and brother, and most of the dances were held for their benefit, either in Melbourne or out on the property. 'My mother was a very hospitable woman,' he said.

His partner Julie agreed. Julie first came to the Western District after she married William Agar at The Gums, near Penshurst, although it was Richard's mother who went out of her way to make Julie feel welcome. 'My mother-in-law, Rosemary, although local, did nothing to entertain people or introduce us. She was so shy. But Richard's mother, who had no idea of who I was, had Will and me for dinner. Richard's mother was very generous. It was early television times, and entertaining was far more important then.'

Julie said that sort of entertaining had largely disappeared now.

Richard rated this as being one of the biggest changes of the last fifty years. 'The social life is almost dead, if not completely gone.' On the rare occasions when there were big events, he said, they were hosted by stock agents, not by property owners. 'We did go to a masked ball recently based on the Charleston era. The girls had to dress up – that was as good a party as I have ever been to. It was breath-taking. But that party was given by a successful local agent, and he had a lot of his best clients there. He would have written it off.'

I asked Richard how soldier settlement had affected the district after the Second World War. He said there were positives as well as negatives. 'Generally, if governments do something, they mess it up, but in this case there was a lot of land that wasn't being utilised. The graziers didn't have to do anything with it, so they didn't.'

But the scheme upset a lot of people. 'The government came along and told you, "You don't need that 10,000 acres. We are going to take it from you." And they did.' The Minister for Lands at the time, Sir Rutherford Guthrie, said he was offered bribes on the steps of the

Melbourne Club by pastoralists hoping to escape having land taken under the scheme.

Richard remembered, 'We lost some land off Brie Brie. It was difficult for the landowners, because they saw their land being taken for a lot less than it was worth.'

The effects on the soldier settlers were mixed. 'Some went up and others went down – all over the place,' Richard said. 'It was a volatile time. Down at Caramut, they gave the soldiers 1000 acres and they cashed in on the wool boom. Then the government thought in future they could make a living out of 300 acres, which of course was absurd. When the prices fell away, the settlers on those smaller blocks went broke.'

Sometimes soldier settlers rubbed the established landowners up the wrong way. Richard said, 'I remember an old soldier-settler bloke over at Woodhouse saying something to my father about graziers complaining, and my father replied, "I've been to the war too, you know."'

On the other hand, his parents weren't prejudiced against the new arrivals. He remembered the words of Nan Wawn, the wife of a soldier settler near Penshurst. 'She said to me, "Your mother and father were wonderful because they didn't resent us. We felt difficult coming into the district as soldier settlers." But Bardie Wawn had flown in the Battle of Britain – he had gone away and fought for his country. They became great friends.'

In recent times, Richard watched many long-term squatting families leave the industry, while others had their wealth seriously depleted. 'The Russells, Fairbairns and Austins are gone,' he said. 'The Kellys of Barwidgee once owned a fourteenth of BHP.'

When I asked Richard why he thought that pastoral ruling class had disappeared, he replied, 'There was a complete lack of reality in some of the older families about money.' He cited the case of one of the Cummings, who came back from his annual six-month trip to

England only to be confronted by his bank manager, who told him his assets were $100,000 and his borrowings $120,000. When the bank manager asked what he was going to do about it, Cumming replied, 'What are you talking about? We have all this land!'

'The Cumming family eventually lost it all,' Richard said. 'Another wonderful story is the Chirnside lady confronted by her bank manager over her overdraft of $3000. "Don't worry," said the old girl. "I'll just write you out a cheque!"'

One approach adopted by several established families was to buy properties in Queensland but continue to live in Victoria. 'I remember driving out from Winton in Queensland once with my uncle, and he said the property we were passing once shore 100,000 sheep. It was a Chirnside place.'

They made money up there, but in the long run it wasn't enough. Like so many other people on the land, Richard identifies succession as the crucial issue. 'The problem with the land is it's such a poor yielder. It just doesn't make enough money to pay daughters out. You can't keep going on and splitting the family farm up. Unless there is an influx of money from somewhere, like a wealthy wife or something, it is bound to go backwards.

'The Ritchies of Blackwood are a classic example – 160 years of ownership, and now it's gone. When I was a child, we were absolutely in awe of the Ritchies – the wealth, the social position. They are as good as non-existent now. People say "What a pity." Well, does it matter? Things change – they change while we are talking.'

Education for the children of Western District pastoral families has changed as well. Richard went to boarding school at Glamorgan in Toorak when he was eight. 'My brother Ted went when he was even younger – he was six. Another friend went when he was five. But it was considered perfectly normal. We didn't know anything else. My mother wouldn't send us to the local state school – we were little princes, far too precious to go to the local school. At Glamorgan, we were allowed two afternoons off a term, so we didn't see much of our parents. I don't think it mattered. Of course, you wouldn't do it in this day and age – wouldn't even think about it.'

When I asked what parents did today, Julie told me that many country families were sending their children to Hamilton College. 'A lot of people keep their children at home and send them off in the bus. I know children who travel daily up to Hamilton College from as far away as Port Fairy. It makes a long day.'

Hamilton is much closer than Melbourne or Geelong, she said, so students in the junior years can attend as day students, but this changes in senior school. 'As the children get older and busier at senior school, they either board at Hamilton or go away to Melbourne or Geelong if the parents can afford it. It is very expensive – around $57,000 a year to board at Geelong Grammar – but every generation seems to find the wherewithal. I don't know how long that can go on.'

Richard also doubts that it's a viable option. 'With the way wool and cattle prices are, there would be very few people who could afford $57,000 after tax. I was in my mid-forties when my last child left school, and since then the fees have blown out of all proportion.'

Richard has been fortunate in establishing a succession, though he hadn't been planning for it to turn out the way it did.

Julie told me, 'On this property, it is Richard's daughter who is taking over. Richard was lying on the ground seeing stars after coming a buster off his motor bike when his daughter said, "Dad, how would you like me to take a bigger responsibility on the place?" and Richard replied, "Great idea!" Now you are not just thinking about your sons, the daughters are assuming much bigger roles.'

Richard said, 'Yes, I never ever thought I would be handing over the reins of my outfit to a daughter. But I have, and she has done a fantastic job. She's 25 and doing it on her own.' He added with brutal frankness, 'And doing things I don't want to do.'

The remark typefies Richard Mann's slightly cynical view of the idiosyncratic business he's in. He also observes wryly that his family 'haven't been around that long. We're not like the McArthurs – we've only been around 100 years.' By Western District standards, they're newcomers. And when he describes the industry's boom/bust cycle in terms of the tide going in and out, his mature appreciation of long-run economic change comes together with a deep bucolic dread of being caught high and dry.

25
Two Weeks' Work in One

Like Stewart McArthur, Chas Armytage is a son of the establishment, but that is where the similarity ends. Chas is a workaday farmer on a property near Dunkeld once owned by his wife's family, the Barr Smiths. On the day when I visit, Chas sweeps out of the paddocks to greet me.

He tells me the property used to be part of Mount William, which was a key part of the old Chirnside estate. Chas is now working approximately 3000 acres at the southern end of the property. His wife's grandfather, Robert Barr Smith, bought Mount William from the Chirnsides in 1920.

Descended from the founder of Elders, the largest pastoral company in Adelaide, Barr Smith was keen to escape the city after he was 'shot up in the First World War'.

'He was the first of the Barr Smiths to leave Adelaide,' Chas says. When he bought Mount William, it consisted of 20,000 acres, much of it uncleared. Fire was a constant problem, and he had barely acquired the property when most of the homestead was destroyed in a bushfire. His Russian wife, Eda, oversaw its replacement with an unusual arched structure, which survives today.

Over the following years, the Barr Smiths cleared much of the property and planted it with English grasses and clover. They eventually retired to the Mornington Peninsula and left the property to their son, Robert Mitchell Barr Smith, who became a noted breeder of Charolais cattle.

In 1985, he split the property up between his four daughters. Chas says, 'The daughters married an Armytage, a Baillieu, a Handyside and an Abbott.'

'So they all married well?' I ask.

'Their mother would probably say they all married down,' Chas says, laughing.

I ask him what happened to the Armytage family place, the nearby Mount Sturgeon. He explains that after his father retired, Allan Myers bought the homestead block, but this came at the end of a much longer process of dispossession.

At the end of the Second World War, Mount Sturgeon was owned by his great-aunts, who were living in the family mansion at Como in South Yarra. This made Mount Sturgeon a 'prime candidate' for subdivision, Chas says. 'The first big properties the commission took were where the owners were not living on it. The old aunts lost two properties to the settlement commission, Mount Sturgeon and Fulham at Balmoral.'

Mount Sturgeon was divided into 32 soldier settler blocks, and Chas's father, Peter, received 1500 acres on the eastern edge in recognition of his service in the air force during the war. Peter had been shot down over Germany and spent the last part of the war in a prison camp.

On his return, he married his long-time girlfriend, Diana Officer, and the couple moved to the property at Mount Sturgeon, where they raised four children. Peter called his block 'Caviar' – the best of the sturgeon.

As well as losing rural land to soldier settlement, the Armytages saw their holdings in Melbourne greatly reduced. 'I suppose losing Como, 58 acres in the centre of Melbourne, didn't help,' Chas says.

In 1958, the family gave Como to the National Trust. Chas was eight years old when they handed the keys over to Sir Dallas Brooks, the governor of Victoria.

When I ask what his father said about the loss, Chas replies, 'At the end of his life he wasn't that bitter, because the pie in the end has to be divided in a family, and inevitably they get smaller pieces. Como could never have been kept by the family. After all, the National Trust has trouble looking after it!'

Peter Armytage later became chairman of the Victoria Racing Club and chaired the Liberal Party's Wannon electorate committee while Malcolm Fraser was prime minister of Australia. The Armytage family also still had substantial private resources. In 1970, Peter added the old homestead block to his holding after its previous owner died. They also had a good property at Hughenden in Queensland, and Peter Armytage was involved with that. 'He had his own plane and used to fly up there,' Chas recalls. It was good sheep and cattle country, and a lot of family members had stakes in it. It was eventually sold in the late 1970s.

Chas believes it was inevitable that the big landed estates in the Western District would eventually be broken up. 'What do you do with all the returned servicemen?' he asks. 'You had to do it.'

The results of soldier settlement were mixed, with positives as well as negatives. 'I think half of them on Mount Sturgeon probably failed and the other half did pretty well,' Chas says. 'Some of the families are still around. They got some good land at Mount Sturgeon. It was one of the first places subdivided, and they were lucky.'

Chas says some members of the old landowning families took a pretty frivolous approach. 'If you look at my father and his generation, they loved a party. What the war did to them … they weren't living for yesterday or tomorrow. Every day was party day. Also, wool was a pound a pound. They were buying motor cars.' That postwar rush of wealth 'buggered half of them,' Chas reckons.

He is also sceptical about the argument that cropping offers salvation for the Western District landowners. He believes the dividing line is about the Glenelg Highway, which separates the cropping country from the rest. 'Fellows down south have a go in the last eight years, and I don't think it's been successful. It's too wet.' The prospects are better to the north, around Ballarat, Lake Bolac and Dunkeld. 'But all the more successful farms have a mixed enterprise approach. Even with the demise of the wool industry over the last ten years, fat lambs and mutton have been very good.'

Chas runs Charolais cattle. 'My late father-in-law was a foundation Charolais breeder in 1969, so we run purebred Charolais and cross them with Angus to breed commercial steers. It is a very good cross. But this is primarily sheep country, so we have a Merino-based flock and we have put South African dual meat/wool sheep and crossed those into the Merinos.'

Following in his father's footsteps, Chas has been heavily involved in horse-racing administration. He is on the local Hamilton racing committee and the Country Racing Board. 'I try and go to as many country race meetings as I can,' he says. 'I reckon if you started up a farm and had no outside interest, life would be very boring. I suppose being brought up with racing, it's a bit like a religion.'

He says that depression is quite common among farmers. 'It can be lonely, going out there on your own, knowing there is two weeks work but you need to do it in one.'

The other big negative is when farmers have difficulty sourcing capital to keep the property going. 'Every time you drive past a rundown farm, you can see it,' Chas says. 'There is just not enough capital to keep the thing going. The only time you get a real quid out of a property is when you sell it.'

Like many others in the district, Chas was shocked by the suicide of David Baulch, who was a year above him at Geelong Grammar. 'His suicide hit us all,' Chas says. The worst of it was that David kept his depression to himself. 'Nobody, probably even his closer friends, knew that he had a problem. Obviously the state of his farm and finances weighed heavily on him. It's just a tragic thing where people don't come out and confide in their close friends and hand the problem on to them to deal with. We have seen it all happen before.' He believes that farmers who have their backs to the wall need to face their bankers and say, 'Well, this is how it is. It is very serious, and you have to come to the party too.'

So how does Chas see the future? 'I have a son, 30, and he is on the place. And I'm bloody lucky! If you look around and see these old farmers who haven't got any kids involved, there is no future. They should get out. They just let the places run down.'

26

The Practical Stockman

Keith Urquhart sits on a horse as if put there by God, an instinctive stockman with a deep inquisitiveness about the animals he nurtures. At 86, he still works the land on a former soldier settler block he bought some years ago, ironically carved from his family's original property, Boonerah, about 20 kilometres west of Mortlake. Keith's daughter Helen and son-in-law Nick now run Boonerah. Today he is sitting in a big armchair, looking at me with the quizzical eyes of a man wondering what is going to happen next.

I ask him how he thinks things have changed around here. His first thought is of the tax-driven timber schemes that drove up the price of grazing country from the mid-1990s. 'It is shocking,' he says. There was further pressure on land prices from New Zealand dairy farmers, who were buying land at inflated prices in the southern parts of the district.

'They thought land was cheap here compared to what they could sell their own land for. They came here with a nice old roll of money and could buy bigger farms for the same money.' They were paying $6000 an acre, but fifteen years later they'd be fighting to get $3000, Keith says.

Prices for grazing land also fell as the timber schemes came undone. 'A lot of land around here would make $1700 today, where in the blue-gum purchasing days it was $2500.'

His cousins, the Armstrongs, were also his neighbours at Hexham Park, but they're now gone. Keith doesn't seem surprised. 'David was never really keen on the land,' he says. 'Uncle Walter, David's grandfather, he would sit in the yard and study the sheep's faces for hours. Walter would say at four or five o'clock, "Let's call it a day." It didn't matter what they saw on the way home – Walter would say, "I've called it a day."'

Keith says things are different now. 'Today, you have to make everything work. Those who don't just don't survive. It's very sad. We don't have to go very far from here to see farms that have disappeared from the family in three generations, where none of the families were really interested in the land.'

Keith's succession plan is in place. His daughter and her husband have taken over Boonerah. 'Helen and Nick have two sons who are keen on the land and work pretty hard. Nick's father had a farm at Ballan. Lachlan, my grandson, does a lot of work on computers at night, and he's great on figures.'

When Keith was running Boonerah in the 1950s and 1960s, he says he spent a lot of his time producing bulls for sale, but sheep are now the main business. His grandson Lachlan has done a lot of the work to build a stud of Coopworth sheep, a New Zealand breed that has a high birth rate. 'He seems to sell a fair few rams. He fell in love with them when he was at ag. college in Christchurch. A lot of the young fellows about here went there.'

Keith nominates the emergence of cropping as another big change in the district. 'A lot of people went into that in a big way, and a lot of them found that not very profitable in this area. Too many wet years. They have stopped that now. They just put in crops in a few better-drained paddocks.'

Keith himself has experimented with many sheep breeds. 'When I was at Boonerah, I had Corriedales,' he says. 'I could see they weren't doing us much good, so I tried a South Australian breed, Collinsville.

They were very good sheep, but I found when they were three years old, the wool was disappointing. So then I went off on my own bat to the Litchfields' Hazeldean stud near Cooma and bought 24- and 25-micron rams out of there and they did me a lot of good. They cut a lot of wool.'

At those dimensions, the wool would be strong and thick in the fibre. Keith says that Nick, his son-in-law, has bought sheep from there with much finer wool.

Keith has nothing to do with Boonerah now. 'I run this place. I started over here with 1200 acres and have cut it back to 350 acres. I run 900 first-cross ewes and I buy a few cows this time of the year and sell the calves, just to eat the grass.' His daughter and son-in-law have enough knowledge to run Boonerah, he reckons, and they don't need him to help.

People tell him he should retire, but he says he'd turn cranky, and he has a long-time helper on the property. 'I've got an old bloke who has been with me for sixty years. He's just a bit younger than me. He can do things I can't do, and I can do things he can't do. He's hopeless with stock, but very good at repairing things – welding, carpentry, all the things I can't do – so we fit in very well together. He lives in Mortlake now, used to live on Boonerah.'

Keith is taking advantage of the smaller scale of his block. 'I join my ewes for six weeks, then I pull the rams out. After 35 days I scan them, then I put the rams back with those not pregnant. And by doing things like that, which you can on a small place, I get good results. From 900 ewes on the place, only eight were empty. They are first-cross ewes, and every lamb gets sold.'

He says he doesn't get a chance to work as hard as he used to. 'Well, I can't work as hard as I used to. We still get things done. I have my grandson help me sometimes.

Keith still has a quarterhorse he bought as a yearling, and he rides once or twice a week, though it's more difficult to get on a horse these days. 'I broke my hip a few years ago, so I have to more or less climb on. I can't swing my leg over like I used to. I enjoy it and it does me a lot of good. I wish I could ride more.'

Keith became famous for his horsemanship. He was a great polo player and pioneered the stock-horse movement. He often appeared at shows. I remember seeing his stock horse pick up his hat from the ground and give it to him.

He also broke in a huge number of horses. 'I broke in 100 horses when I left school. Some of them never saw me in the daylight – we used to start early.' When he was in his twenties, he had a boy of about 14 living at Boonerah, and they broke in horses together. 'We broke in 103 horses in a year,' Keith says.

Keith says he hated school. He ran away from Geelong Grammar at one stage, but he didn't get far. 'I only had two and sixpence. That got me a second-class ticket as far as Colac. I met my cousin Helen McCullough on the train between Colac and Terang. She asked me what I was doing. I said I had cleared out from school and didn't have a ticket to get me home. She said, "You will be arrested!" She got off at Camperdown and got me a ticket, then she drove me home. I was sent back next day, of course.'

Keith left school when he was 17 and was supposed to go to Queensland jackarooing, but then his father had a serious stroke while fighting a fire at nearby Woolongoon station. 'He never did any work again,' Keith says.

Old Mr Urquhart was the first person in the district to have a TV set, and David Armstrong and I would sometimes cross the river and walk up the hill to the homestead to watch the last quarter of the football in the splendid drawing room. The set was reverently placed in the centre of the room in its own mahogany display cabinet. The old man never spoke or showed any emotion, no matter the state of the game. Now, when I see footage from the fifties, players in boxer shorts and short back and sides, I find it hard to believe I watched it live and not in some ancient newsreel.

After the Second World War, Boonerah lost 3000 acres to soldier settlement at a very low price. His father was already sick, and Keith doesn't believe they were receiving good advice from their lawyers. Even so, he is quite positive about the scheme. 'It gave a lot of people a chance,' he says. Many of the new settlers didn't stay, but those who were still there a few years later paid for their land and the sheep in the first year of the wool boom.

It was fortunate for Keith that Boonerah had a good manager, Mac McLean, and Keith initially worked under him.

Keith remembers Mac with a mixture of admiration and apprehension. 'Working under him was probably the best thing I have ever done. He was tough, tough as anything. He hated public school. "You college boys, you never learnt anything," he would say. We had a couple of young fellows that worked for us, and we used to think he was an old bastard.

'He would need to get in a mob of sheep and send me way out here. By the time I got back, it was dark. Mac shouted to me, "Next time when you take so long, could you write to me?" He was very sarcastic, and he made me do everything on the place.'

Killing sheep to supply the workers on the property was one of the less appealing jobs. 'He used to send me down to kill three sheep at 5.30 in the afternoon. I would have to get the mob in, and there was no yard at the killing pen, so I would have to hold the sheep with my dog.' Keith would kill the sheep, skin and gut them, and then put them up on his shoulder to take them to the house or to the huts.

'I was always sent to do that when everyone else was going home,' he remembered. Mac later told him that he chose the time on purpose. Mac said, 'I achieved what I wanted to, because I knew you would want to get home. If I had sent you there at three o'clock, you would have taken two hours, but at five-thirty you went like buggery and got good at it.'

Keith reckons about the worst jobs Mac ever gave him was to clean out the septic tank at Boonerah. 'I don't think it had ever been cleaned out before. When it was done, he said to me, "What was it like down there?" I said, "It's so big down there you could have a ball." He almost laughed.'

Reflecting on the four or five years he spent working for Mac, Keith says, 'He made you do things right and quickly. It was very good for me to learn from him and then to manage after he was gone. When I was 22 he said he was leaving, and the trustees said, "What are we going to do without you?" "Well," he said, "if Keith can't manage it now he never will."'

I ask him what Mac taught him about horses. 'Oh, a lot,' Keith replies. 'He was a good horseman. There were fifty horses running around here after the war, and they had never had a hand on them. He said to me. "We have to break them in. Do you want to have a go at it?"'

Keith said he did, but he didn't know much about it.

At that, Mac said seriously, 'I will give you one word of advice. Stay like that, because once you think you know it, no bugger will ever help you and you won't learn anything.' It was the best advice Keith was ever given.

When Mac died, Keith tells me, 'I went to his wife and said "I owe more to him than to anyone else. He kicked my backside and taught me how to work."'

27

'The Equal of Anyone'

I think farming is far too important to treat simply as a business and food too important to treat as a commodity.

James Rebanks

James Rebanks is a Lake District shepherd, a member of a family that has farmed the same area for more than six hundred years. In 2015, he published *The Shepherd's Life*, a book that diarised the ancient routines of shepherding through the seasons and set out the deep-rooted practices of sheep farming, which he describes as 'another form of culture, just like Picasso or punk'.

The book became an unlikely bestseller, and Rebanks now spends his nights tweeting to 70,000 followers, who are entranced to read a modern tale from an ancient landscape, written by a man with an authentic connection of the kind so many have lost. It is a story of permanence, of fulfilment in a working life. Rebanks has proved the words of Beatrix Potter, who left 4000 acres of Lake District farmland to the national estate: 'Shepherds are the equal of anyone.'

Rebanks is the antithesis of the Western District squatters, in that the people he's writing about aren't trying desperately to leave a place but are trying just as hard to stay. Even so, his inherited life experience is not so dissimilar as to be dismissed by Western District folk. Like them, he faces the strictures of an arduous workload, sometimes in a hostile environment, for modest financial returns. His commercial world is dominated by a rural cost/price squeeze, and only dedication has seen his family survive.

Rebanks celebrates an uncomplicated way of being, his own immersion in the Lake District a touchstone for his critique of modern existence. The modern way of life, he says, is emptied of meaning, 'rubbish for so many people ... It bores them so much they can't wait to get smashed out of their heads each weekend.'

Survivors who are still at the helm of Western District dynasties could read Rebanks and relish their life anew. Many of his sheep-farming neighbours have family links to Western District settlers. And to the north the remaining Scottish crofters – small farmers, sometimes owners and sometimes tenants – are still working the country today, some thousand years after taking up land there, though it is far less fertile and its climate far more cruel than the Western District.

On Scotland's border country and the Hebridean isles, there are still many crofters doing daily chores that the Vikings would recognise. Fiercely protective of that way of life, Rebanks celebrates the values of the shepherd and his ilk, who he says always act decently, don't give up, and 'hold on to who we are'. His litany of virtues was still in my mind when I went to Scotland to see where the squatting families had come from and speak to the relatives and neighbours who were still there.

As my plane floated out of white-grey clouds into clear air, below me was the Isle of May, the flat basalt gatekeeper to Edinburgh, where for centuries it has been a landmark of welcome and forlorn farewell. This is Scotland rock, symbolic of a country mixed with Australia in blood and history, but so foreign in the grey light of this summer afternoon.

Yet the island rock was familiar. I had seen it in the lava flow near Penshurst and the Stony Rises, a lichen skin softening its basalt hardness. Two-thirds of the pioneer settlers in the Western District were Scots from the lowlands and the borders. For them, seeing the basalt on their runs for the first time must have been like greeting an old friend.

The Lake District and Scotland itself seemed to be in a rural revival when I went there in 2015 – the summer pastures mown, the fences strained, all in neat order. EU subsidies and regulated commodity prices had taken the gamble out of farming. In the country north and west of Edinburgh, helped also by oil revenue from the North Sea, Range Rovers crowded the market towns, where sophisticated boutiques and top-end homeware shops mushroomed in the high streets, and gourmet meals have replaced the traditional doughy sandwiches in the cafés. Nowhere is the revitalisation as graphic as on the once-benighted Isle of Skye, where the crofters' stone houses shimmer in freshly painted whiteness and the locals glory in their stunning homeland by staying at home. Skye's population had been falling since the mid-nineteenth century, when the chieftains turned from patriarchs to pariahs, burning tenants' houses and driving them into poorhouses or onto ships, leading many to emigrate to Canada and Australia.

By the 1960s, the population had fallen to just over 6000, and it stayed at that level for twenty years. Today the populace is roughly twice as large, stark evidence that there are jobs for Skye's children and a future for their offspring in this mountainous island of magnetic fascination. A subject for classic British writers such as Dr Johnson and Walter Scott, its landscape painted by Turner, Skye's violent past and its splendid ruggedness have created in its people an almost epic sense of survival.

At Glendale, a British gunboat was despatched in 1883 to suppress a rebellion by tenant farmers demanding land ownership and fairness in their blighted lives. It was the last time Britain deployed force against the Scots, and in the village I find the facts of modern-day Skye. At the quaint store and post office, I meet Stuart Bell, the proprietor, whose English accent and economics degree from the University of London give a hint of the vast changes that have occurred in the island highlands since that handful of Scottish martyrs changed

Westminster's mind and eventually transformed tenants into owners.

In a way, Bell is completing the job of the Crofters Act of 1886, which gave the small farmers security of tenure and gradually allowed them to buy the tenanted land. The Scottish Nationalists are now spruiking the tenants' rights to buy their land even if the landowners don't want to sell. Despite all the reforms since 1886, the SNP point out, 432 people still own half of Scotland's private land, and fewer than half are actually Scots. At Glendale, helped by a handful of English incomers, Stuart Bell and a group of crofters have become a vital part of local estate management, buying up the trust that controls 18,000 acres of the grazing Highlands, which was traditionally owned by Oxbridge-educated Scots, who now prefer life in London.

A saviour from an unlikely place, Stuart talked modern economics and farm techniques, using satellite photographs to track fertile soil that could be sown down. It was surreal to see a smart-as-a-whip Englishman at isolated Glendale, amid the very Scots who attracted the last British gunboat, but from the stream of visitors interrupting our discussion I could see he was accepted not only as local but as a leader of the new order, where crofters could live without fear or favour on their own land.

That evening, in the refined bar of an isolated private hotel, I met a couple from Devon, a social worker and a horse-loving businesswoman. They had decided that day to move to a farm on the moors of Skye. Slightly shell-shocked that once-wild Devon had become urbanised, they were fleeing England. It made me think that emigration from Skye had come full circle. This island of people-exporters had become the importer.

I'd come here to follow up the Mackinnons of Mooramong, who came to Victoria from Skye. They wouldn't have been bothered by this modern-day boom. The progenitor of the family, L.K.S. Mackinnon, prospered after he came to Melbourne in 1884, eventually part-owning the *Argus* newspaper and chairing the Victoria Racing Club. The family would return to Skye on holiday, which meant a reunion with their former neighbour's son, Dr John Maclennan.

When I spoke with Dr Maclennan, a retired veterinarian and practising crofter, he suggested the rivalry between Skye's farming families was a reason for their conspicuous consumption. In a Scots brogue as dense as his birth island's tweed, he charmingly explained that the 'young ones' on the island were 'highly geared'. Raised on the Isle of Harris in a house without running water and lit by paraffin lamps, Dr Maclennan had experienced an austerity that taught him to live within his means. These days, the crofter farm he ran with his son was making a small profit. Awarded an MBE for his services to the crofters of Skye, Dr Maclennan was confident of their survival and insisted on having his photograph taken with me in front of his summer grazing mountain, known as the 'Hill of the Old Lady'. Legend says that a Viking princess who died on Skye wanted to be buried atop the mountain so that the winds of Norway would blow over her. Dr Maclennan told me a local shepherd claimed to have seen the grave, though not the princess!

Dr Maclennan spoke of the Mackinnons, and I told him something of Scobie's role in the Western District's belle époque. In the darkening afternoon light, I noticed a tear in the old Scotsman's eye. He may have been feeling sad about his friend's inability to have children, or simply moved at remembering Scobie's visits over the years.

Next day, I discovered that the Lake District in August was no place to 'wander lonely as a cloud'. Wordsworth's adored lakes were in danger of being swamped by people led here by his wondrous words. There was a visitor by every rock as I surfed the incoming tourist stream. Waves of people with backpacks sought solace in the fast-filling space, fogging the dreaming air with frustration.

In brief moments of aloneness, the winding traffic yielded glimpses

Jean Wilson, imperious astride a quad bike

of shaded glens and sheer green cliffs of summer grass, where tightrope-walking sheep had been grazing for a thousand years. I was among their shepherds' families at Matterdale, a gently sloping patchwork of crofter houses and paddocks at the end of a perilous mountaintop journey.

This was where James Rebanks was living, but I'd already decided not to disturb him. Instead, I turned up a road that said 'Town Centre'. It was narrow, one car wide, with just enough room for a lady approaching me on a quad bike, her border collie camped on the carry-all behind her. I edged into the undergrowth spilling onto the unused road and we both stopped, my car her annoying roadblock.

I couldn't believe my luck. The lady looking uneasily at this stranger with his head out the car window was Jean Wilson, heroine of *The Shepherd's Life* and breeder of its author's favourite Herdwick sheep. Slowly she relaxed and her arms slid down from their defensive crossed position to dangle by her side. She was in her working clothes and spoke in a shepherd's matter-of-fact way about her line of sheep, about the vital importance of teamwork among the shepherds and the ever-present dangers they faced in the lethally fickle weather up on the fens.

I was charmed by her easy manner as the story of her life as a sheep breeder unfolded. Jean was fiercely proud of her instincts for breeding sheep that would be equally admired by the butchers, her fellow shepherds and the judges of the show ring. She was proud too of her economic successes, which had increased the value of her crofter home and the farm she shared with her husband. Practical, a realist, she did not need to talk of the theoretical and showed a healthy scepticism of James's newfound fame. There is a quiet reserve in those who have found their way. In her face was the soundless joy of doing what she loved, of a life fulfilled.

I left Matterdale, again braving the endless traffic snarls between the towns, fuelled by the human search for comfort in movement and diversion. What did all these tourists think was around the corner? And was this mass invasion a vote for antiquity or simply a quest for rural beauty?

As I crawled between the villages, I felt a pang of nostalgia for a different landscape, one where I could view rural beauty in peace. I remembered travelling the Henty Highway between Hamilton and Horsham in the luscious spring of 2016. It was God's road into heaven, classic Western District pastoral country – succulent green pasture with regal red gums and newly shorn sheep white against the cobalt blue of the Grampians, now lit by the midday sun, exposing the sandstone face of the eastern range. We were at the centre of an Arthur Streeton painting, at the core of Australia Felix.

But 'we' was not entirely accurate. I was alone on this road on a Sunday morning. There were no road sidings, no viewing platforms, no need to stop or even to pause. I may have passed one car. Despite its overwhelming beauty, the Western District is no tourist destination. The Henty Highway was on mute, waiting for someone to sing its praises.

28

Diary of a Farmer

Last night I thought I dreamed – but when I woke
The screaming was only a possum skiing down
The iron roof on little moonlit claws.

Les Murray

Last night, no self-respecting possum would have risked skiing the roof as the wind ripped at this settlers' house near Woorndoo, in the middle of the old Salt Creek weaner paddock. Warm in bed, I thought of the shepherds who once tended their flocks here. It would have been a miserable place to live in a tiny hut on a barren, windy night like this.

My host, David Barry, has bought two of the thirteen soldier-settler blocks subdivided off Salt Creek station in the 1950s. David came here in 1969 from the harsh part of the Wimmera, seeking the things only good land and rain could bring. His wife, Pauline, was born around the corner at her dad's soldier-settler block on Ennerdale. Since they came here, the Barrys have thrived.

David is a down-to-earth farmer with the poetry of the soil in his heart. He talks wistfully about the geology of his country, the soil and seasons. He tells me the neighbouring volcanic country always sprouts grass quicker than his lighter Grampians loam, because the rain splashes off the stones, softly spreading the drops.

'You can see the grass is always fresher earlier in the basalt country. The sheep will walk over the lighter loamy soils and seek out the new shoots in the stony rises,' he says.

David has experimented with native grasses, joining in a

A sheepfold near Lake Bolac, dating from the 1840s

community project to develop kangaroo grass along a stock route on a stretch of the Lake Bolac–Woorndoo Road. He knows that it's impossible to return to native pastures because of their uneconomic carrying capacity, but he does it out of interest in the past.

He tells me that the lakes and swamps in the region all have lunettes, which are banks of soil or sand blown out of the bed when it is dry. The lunettes often look like dunes, but they don't move around, and some of them are very large. He says the lunette at Bolac Plains is forty feet high.

'These lunettes show that climate variation has been with us a long time. They are the result of extreme weather changes. The soil needs to be wet so that grass doesn't grow, and then it has to be hot to dry it out so that it can blow when the winds get up.'

David is dedicated to his farm, which he runs with his son, Chris, who lives on another block 15 kilometres closer to Lake Bolac. He has sketched a diary of his working year. It seems extensive, but he tells me it would fill another 20 pages if he detailed every day.

He has 3000 Merinos and 2000 first-cross ewes producing prime lambs; he also has 300 acres of land under crop, with 120 acres of wheat, 100 acres of barley and 80 acres of Monola, a variety of canola that has been specially bred for making oil.

This is his routine.

January

Usually feeding sheep twice weekly

10	Cull older first-cross ewes
15	Buy 200 first-cross ewe lambs
	Send 500 prime lambs to [cousin's property at] Warracknabeal to fatten on bean stubble
	Few days off
20	Put rams out with first-cross ewes and take rams out of 5-year-old ewes

February

Still feeding twice a week

2	Join maiden first-cross ewes, sell culled first-cross ewes
20	Start crutching Merinos

March

4	Finish crutching Merinos
	Drench Merino weaners
6	Cull one-year-old Merinos and go through two-year-olds
15	Have grain cleaned and dressed ready for sowing
20	Sell 400 lambs off fodder crops
25	Begin shearing first-cross ewes, take rams out. Put rams out with Merino ewes
30	Spread super 120 kg/ha on pasture paddocks
31	Finish shearing first-cross ewes

April

Still feeding sheep, prepare machinery for cropping

10	Sell lambs from Warracknabeal
12	Deliver Manola out of silo for seed
20	Burn stubble ready for cropping
25	Start sowing pasture seed 40 ha, oversow lucerne with oats 30 ha
26	Give 5-year-old Merino ewes 2mls Eweguard ready for lambing

May

Feeding slows down

6	Spray paddocks prior to cropping
10	Start lambing five-year-old Merino ewes
	Start sowing Manola, followed by barley and wheat
	Get super + zinc + nitrogen from Lake Bolac as required for cropping
11	Start spraying paddocks after seeding with pre-emergence sprays for weeds
25	Finish cropping, take Merino rams out of ewes
28	Have contractor do replacement fencing

June

Finish feeding sheep

10	Give first-cross ewes 3 mls Eweguard prior to lambing
	Drench Merino wethers prior to winter
20	Start lambing first-cross ewes with prime lambs
25	Mark Merino lambs off 5-year-old Merinos
28	Have one week's holiday in South Australia

July

Lambing first-cross ewes

15	Clean up Merino ewes for shearing

20	Wean Merino lambs off 5-year-old ewes
22	Spread urea on crops
28	Start shearing Merino ewes

August

2	Finish shearing
5	Start marking first-cross lambs
14	Finish marking
19	Start lambing Merino ewes
20	Clean up Merino weaners ready for spring
25	Sell wheat to dairy farmers
28	Shear Merino weaners
30	Spread urea on crops

September

1	Finish shearing weaners
8	Go to Canberra for one week to visit daughter
14	Put hay booster onto hay paddocks
16	Sell 5-year-old ewes, sell cull ewes
28	Start marking Merino lambs

October

8	Sell wool
12	Sell young wethers
18	Start cutting, pressing and carting hay

November

1	Drench Merino sheep and first-cross ewes and lambs
10	Wean Merino lambs, drench and jet for flies
14	Drench all Merino and first-cross ewes, jet for flies
20	Clean up first-cross lambs, crutch first-cross ewes
28	Windrow Monola

December

1	Sell first-cross suckers – 80 per cent, retain the rest
2	Start harvest, Monola
20	Wean and shear remaining first-cross lambs
25	Xmas with family
28	Finish harvesting

Phew!

It's the morning of 15 June when David shows me his diary, so I look up today's date. According to the calendar, the ewes are about to start lambing. Is he going around to check them today?

'I've already been,' he says. 'They started a fortnight early this year.'

I'm reminded of James Rebanks, who wrote that on any given day in the Lake District he could say exactly what his neighbour was working at without looking. It's the same in David's life, where the same thing happens every year. It's how things are done around Woorndoo.

Farmer's like David Barry restore the faith because like Rebanks their soul is the land and life a caring for the animals who grow from it. And always it is attended by the spirit of kindness.

At the Adelaide funeral of tribal member Geoff Baulch, originally 'Rose Park', Hawkesdale and more latterly the Coorong, SA where he bred Hereford cattle, there was mention of that kindness. Geoff, it was said by his daughter Emma, would gently walk his cattle, mainly cows and calves, to the yards for routine treatment where they would be kept strictly in yards of friendship groups to avoid any disharmony when returned to their own designated paddocks.

29

A Gentleman Politician

Rain was falling as I drove east from Edenhope, which now boasted a sign: 'Things to do in the West Wimmera'. West Wimmera! I had friends at school from Edenhope who saw themselves as very much inhabitants of the Western District. Besides a few miles west of here was the home of David Hawker, the former MHR for Wannon, which is quintessentially Western District. It would have been a quick political death if Malcolm Fraser's successor had said he was from the West Wimmera.

This was not the only blow. The road wound down into the damp and lifeless town of Harrow, where sheer slopes plunged to the Glenelg River, to discover that the local branch of my bank only opened on Friday mornings. Surely, now safely in Harrow, I thought, I'm out of the West Wimmera and into the Western District! But no, like the bank customers, I had to wait.

When I asked for guidance from the postmistress, who is the only upright soul visible, she said, 'I haven't a clue if we are in the Western District or not. No one ever mentions it.' She did, however, admit that she'd only been in Harrow for three years. After some instant research, she cried out with a hint of victory in her voice, 'Harrow is indeed a West Wimmera town!'

I was in the federal electorate of Wannon, which became famous as the parliamentary seat of Malcolm Fraser, Prime Minister from 1975 to 1983. It was the epicentre of the Western District, covering its two most populous towns, Hamilton and Warrnambool. Fraser was elected to parliament at the tender age of 25 in 1955, when the Liberal Party's new boy could watch the district revel in its newfound wealth.

Despite his patrician air, his estate at Nareen not far from Harrow and his marriage to Tamie, a member of the fine-wool Beggs family, Fraser was not a true son of the Western District. The hauteur side of the squattocracy regarded him as a Johnny-come-lately. I have never forgotten David Armstrong's mother, Joan, scathingly saying, 'His father is a blow-in from up north – the Riverina, I think.'

Fraser's father, John, had bought Nareen in 1946, but this was too recent for the old families' taste. Joan's view was mirrored elsewhere in the electorate. Still, Malcolm, a Melbourne Grammar old boy and Oxford graduate, won Liberal Party pre-selection for Wannon with help from the Hamilton Club and the western branch of the Melbourne Club. As a result, between 1955 and 2010 the federal seat of Wannon consistently returned an establishment son of the soil, if not a direct member of the squattocracy.

Previously, Wannon had been a swinging seat, represented at various times by all shades of politics, including long years under the ALP, until the Labor vote was seriously weakened by the sectarian split of the 1950s. With the formation of the Democratic Labour Party, the Catholic church intervened actively to discourage its parishioners from voting for the ALP. The Labor years had been galling for the squattocracy, which had become used to getting its own way in politics, but after the split, the Liberals were back in control.

As Prime Minister, Fraser won three federal elections and gave the Western District what they believed to be their right, political leadership and social pre-eminence in all the right places. He left parliament after his defeat by Bob Hawke and was replaced at a by-election in 1983 by David Hawker, a university-educated grazier with a property at Apsley. Hawker's Newlands was about 15 kilometres from the border to South Australia, the state of his birth, where he was viewed as having a top-shelf rural pedigree.

Hawker went on to spend 27 years as MHR for Wannon, He was assiduous in his care for the electorate and eventually became Speaker of the House, yet he always seemed to operate in the shadow of Fraser, who was the last prime minister with a bespoke accent, a knowledge of the names of prominent Western District families, and a property with a large holding of sheep and cattle. I remember Fraser as being very much a man of his time. I once played in a charity cricket match on a dusty ground at Warrnambool and was the operating bowler when, much to my surprise, he appeared as the incoming batsman dressed in a waistcoat and tie!

After searching the map for the property where David Hawker lives, I find him close to Apsley. It's in the Western District, but by the barest of margins. The same thing could be said for his elevation to parliament in 1983, when he surprisingly won Liberal Party pre-selection from the local favoured son, Ian Smith, a former minister in the Victorian Hamer government, who had quit his state seat of Warrnambool on the assumption that he would be on his way to greater things in the federal sphere.

Hawker tells me his victory was helped by the fact that Smith's support base in the south was fragmented. Eighteen budding politicians contested the pre-selection, and many of them came from the south. In the end, Hawker clearly won the exhaustive vote and the hapless Smith ran third. Hawker gained support from both north and south, perhaps even including Malcolm Fraser, by then an aloof figure who rarely bothered with local electorate matters.

Hawker remains a rarity amongst politicians, a man easy in his own skin who treads the earth gently. His unassuming modesty may have cost him a cabinet seat. One thing is certain: reputation is effortlessly shredded, and it's easier to find a good word about Hawker than Fraser in the Western District today.

One key achievement of Hawker's political career, he says, is that he played a part in converting Tony Abbott to climate-change scepticism. I'd previously heard him mention this during a countryman's lunch at the Melbourne Club in 2014, on my one and only visit to the conservative fortress in Collins Street. At the time, I was sure that, if reported, Hawker's story would have made headlines the next day, but I resisted my newspaperman's urge to report it, conscious of the gentleman's rule that prohibits reporting speeches delivered in private, even if they're of public interest. Now, in the privacy of his extended kitchen, the story unravels.

It all happened when Abbott had to travel from Adelaide to Beaufort, west of Ballarat, where he was due to address a Liberal Party meeting. He flew to Mount Gambier, took a charter flight to Ballarat and then travelled to Beaufort by car, and Hawker travelled with him.

'We got on to the business of climate change and the carbon tax,' Hawker tells me. 'I was quoting Ian Plimer's book *Heaven and Earth*. Plimer is a very interesting bloke – professor of geology at Adelaide University and someone who says we should talk to old farmers about climate, because they know the trends and how it changes. He spent a lot of time out in the bush looking at rocks and studied a lot of long-term changes to the geology, and from that he can identify the changes, which he says have been going on for 500 million years. The more Plimer talked about this, the more he was criticised, forcing him to put it all in a book.'

Hawker is obviously a strong supporter of Plimer's views. He outlines some of his arguments about long-term climate change, then continues, 'Plimer talks about the fact that we are the first generation to fear warmer times, which history tells us are the most productive.'

Hawker has an engineering degree from the University of Melbourne. 'I am not for one minute arguing we haven't got climate change,' he tells me. 'Of course we have, but we should be putting our efforts into living with it, adapting to it. If we were serious about it, we could be like the French and engage nuclear power. However, Australia has a hang-up about it.'

He tells me that nuclear power nearly came to the Western District in the 1970s, when there were a lot of strikes at the Latrobe Valley power stations. The State Electricity Commission had worked out that a new power line from Yallourn to Portland would not only connect with the South Australian grid but would also run near a site outside Portland that was the most geologically stable place in Victoria. So if you put a nuclear power station there, you could send the power to Melbourne and replace the troublesome plants in the Latrobe Valley.

Hawker says he discussed all these points with Abbott. 'People', he said, 'mistakenly think they can actually do something about carbon dioxide levels, given that Australia's emissions are only 1.4 per cent of the world's output and the three biggest culprits are doing nothing about it.'

Abbott listened but didn't make much comment. Then later some of the farmers at the Beaufort meeting raised the issue with him. Hawker says, 'When I introduced him to the audience to speak, I also announced the editor of the local newspaper was in the room, so Abbott knew he was there. And you could hardly pretend it was a private meeting with 500 people in the hall. Abbott was specifically asked about climate change. Whether or not my chewing his ear had impressed him, but he said the now famous line – "Of course, the science behind all this is crap." I could see the editor get excited, and that was the headline in the *Pyrenees Advocate*.'

Then the local state Labor member sent it through to the federal Labor MP, so Abbott immediately started getting parliamentary questions about it. 'He said in interviews that day had changed his mind on the subject. He spoke to Nick Minchin about it, and not long afterwards the challenge came to Turnbull.'

'So you could say the history of Australia was changed traversing the Western District?'

'Yes,' says Hawker. 'You could say that.'

30
Life on Loan

We're now well into the second decade of the twenty-first century, and the squattocracy's failure can't only be blamed on unfair family expectations or the generations who succumbed to hubris or the personal tragedies of loneliness, alcoholism and suicide. The Western District has been disfigured by them all in equal measure.

Suicide is by definition the death of one, but it's also the murder of many. It hangs like a spectre over the Western District. It may not be more widespread here than in other rural areas, but speculation is sparked by every 'accidental' death – the house fires, the trees hit head-on, the shotguns that go off when the owner is climbing through a fence. There is always a suspicion that they may not be what they seem, and there are private discussions that never reach the Coroner's ears.

This wasn't the case with the death of David Baulch in September 2013, when he was just shy of 60. I'd just begun my first round of interviews when the district was unnerved to learn of David's suicide. He was a member of a multi-generational grazing family and president of the Port Fairy Golf Club, a role that placed him at the centre of the Western District elite. An effervescent man, each year he would host one of the Warrnambool Racing Carnival's best parties, yet subsequent medical evidence revealed that he had been hospitalised with depression shortly before his death. Whether or not he should have been released from hospital will forever haunt the memory of David Baulch.

It's hard to explain the disenchantment of people living in a kind of paradise, let alone when it leads to suicide. Why does the Western District echo with such sadness?

Peter Learmonth once told me of a Mortlake man, Ralph Laidlaw, who seemed rather inhibited and shy, but nothing more than that. Peter said, 'He was a man you really couldn't talk to save the bare necessities like "Good morning" or "Nice to see you." He came into our sales and bought steers he then fattened on his country outside Mortlake.'

Then one day Ralph came in to his wife and told her he had just drunk a cup of lavacide, a poison used for fumigating rabbits, and would be dead in an hour. The doctors vainly tried to rescue him, and he went through hell. It would appear he had suffered tremendous depression in a very private way.

Suicide is never a pointless or random act. To the suicidal, it is an answer, a way out. But in the Western District suicide has a historical and generational context. I don't think it's drawing too long a bow to link suicides with the Scots' desire to live within the restraints of the Bible and the constant strain of striving to be among the chosen people. Even from this distance in time, I suspect many of the district's desperately sad people didn't arrive at their final desolate conclusion without their austere heritage playing its part.

Frugality and unyielding hardness were part of the Western District survival kit, forged in the DNA of graziers.

The last words Arthur Gubbins of Coolana uttered before dying peacefully in his sleep on 6 August 1990 were to tell his son-in-law, Andrew Manifold, 'Look after that money young man – it's only on loan.'

Arthur Gubbins's grandson Simon committed suicide in March 2003. He was 43. More than a decade-and-a-half later, Simon Gubbins's suicide is still discussed in the Western District, because he had so many reasons *not* to take his own life. He was what they used to call a 'pin-up boy', a successful man from a privileged background who had built on his inherited wealth. Being seen to enrich your birthright counts in the Western District. Simon had done that, and he knew it.

But it wasn't enough when the weight of expectation began to outweigh achievement. With privilege came remorseless responsibility.

In the Western District, as in other places, society can be punishingly judgemental. Material success is prized, but failure in relationships is often met with savage gossip. Simon Gubbins received little reward for his scintillating farming performance to counterbalance the sense of failure he felt over his fractured family. Simon saw his disappointment with himself mirrored in others, and a sense of defeat came to permeate his life.

Simon, the eldest son of John and Jenny Gubbins, was managing his mother's family property near Hamilton, the 4300-acre Murroa. He enjoyed a high profile in agri-politics and research, and had overseen enormous improvement in pasture quality, doubled stock numbers and cash flow in his 20 years there.

He had also separated from his wife and children, but was in a relatively new but reportedly happy relationship.

The *Age* ran a major story on the suicide five months later, in August 2003. Simon's car had been found in a gully and his body a short distance away. His family had decided from the outset that there would be no pretence about the manner of their son's death. His father John sent an email to friends the next day, telling them that Simon had shot himself.

'That's what happened, so there was no point saying otherwise,' John told me.

At his funeral, Simon was described as one of Australia's most innovative sheep and beef producers. Busloads of farmers, students, academics and overseas visitors had made the long trip to Murroa to benefit from his advice. Simon had been a district councillor for the Victorian Farmers Federation, president of the Grassland Society of Victoria, a director of the Australian Beef Association, chairman of Rural Industries Skill Training, an adviser to Melbourne University's agriculture faculty, and captain of the local Buckley Swamp fire brigade.

While every individual suicide conjures a victim's own demons, Simon Gubbins was struggling to strike a balance in his relationship with his former wife. The two shared custody of the children, but increasingly he began to believe he was failing his boys, according to those who observed him closely. He saw himself as inadequate, even an obstacle to their development and happiness. 'I think he felt very alone with this problem,' his mother Jenny told me.

A wry, stoic woman whose family has farmed in the Western District for more than a century, Jenny Gubbins rejects any suggestion that her eldest son's death was triggered by depression. 'It shouldn't have happened, simple as that,' she says bluntly. Paradoxically, everyone who knew Simon Gubbins commented that they had never seen him so happy, in large part because of his new relationship with an old friend, Fiona Mercer.

Family friend and former State Liberal Party MP Ian Smith, who spoke at the memorial service, said that Simon had confided in him about his sense of failure. He had set high standards for himself, Smith said. 'To Simon, just doing your best in the circumstances you faced was not good enough – he had to make things right, and in his mind, he couldn't. To Simon, the honourable solution was not to fail, but to remove himself as the obstacle.'

Jenny and John Gubbins have walked each step of their son's last day in their minds a thousand times since his body was found in that gully. It had been a family day – gardening, playing with the kids, making plans for the coming week. But early in the evening, he drove the boys back to their mother's home in Hamilton, and something apparently snapped during that 25-kilometre journey. 'Fiona told us that when he walked in the door, he was ashen-faced,' Jenny said quietly. 'He had a shower, sat down to eat, then suddenly pushed back his chair and said "I'm going to get rid of the problem." He then grabbed a gun and left.'

I visited John and Jenny on their property, Coolana, in February 2014. Like many ageing graziers, John had moved from the homestead into a smaller house on Coolana South, allowing his son Mark to take over. He was preparing finally to move off farm to retirement in Port Fairy. His father had followed the same path, except that Arthur had chosen Barwon Heads.

The heartbreak of Simon's death was now eleven years old, but it hadn't been forgotten. Jenny mused, 'The *Age* feature upset a few of those funny people in Hamilton who said we should never have co-operated with a newspaper. But [the journalists] came to the table and had lunch with us and talked sensitively. It was on the front page and did get people talking about suicide. But none of our friends mentioned it to us. They wouldn't say a word. I would mention Simon and there would be silence. Even people we knew well.'

Jenny emphasised the importance of Simon's relationship with his children. 'The last day I talked to him, the day before, he sort of said, "The district has gone against me."' One of his friends had said that he couldn't be Simon's friend because he was friends with his ex-wife.

John, who had emailed the facts of Simon's death so honestly, seemed less inclined to talk about it. He closed the subject by raising something else over a cup of tea and some lunch. It was sad and telling at the same time. But perhaps the saddest thing of all was John's eulogy at Simon's farewell. While it was brave, his speech was virtually a dry rendition of Murroa's history, sad for what it didn't say about his feelings for his much-loved son.

31
The Incomers

As the squattocracy leaves, the void is filled by others. In a socioeconomic twist, the sons of soldier settlers have acquired thousands of acres in the Western District over the second half of the twentieth century. Colin McKenna and Stirling Draffen are two of those rewriting land ownership in the district.

Colin McKenna is the Western District's resident tycoon. At Woolsthorpe outside Warrnambool, he drives an around-the-clock dairying empire based on the Union station, an iconic property that dates back to 1843. Nearby he has dramatically increased the productivity of land the Askews grazed somnolently for a century. His commercial meat operation, Midfield Meats, holds a total 10,000 acres. It employs 1500 people in the district at its Warrnambool abattoir, which caters for export markets and has a turnover of $800 million annually.

McKenna enjoys travelling in his helicopter and private jet. He explicitly contrasts his attitude with that of Stirling Draffen, who is famously closefisted and drives an ancient Mercedes. McKenna says, 'Unlike Stirling, I like the toys, the trappings of money.'

An acquaintance had described McKenna as 'an angry little Irishman' before I met him by accident in the lounge of Melbourne's RACV Club during the Cup carnival of 2016. McKenna had followed the traditions of the wealthy Western District squatters, becoming an extensive racehorse owner. When we met, he was celebrating having won the Caulfield Cup with Jameka. McKenna, his wife and friends were sipping beers in big leather armchairs at the fashionable city club, and he waved me over to join them.

It immediately became obvious that there was no comparison between McKenna and the squatters or their predilections. Indeed, it was dangerous territory. A self-possessed man in the manner of a magnate who found the building of a mega-business within his reach, McKenna told me he was staggered by their mismanagement, and he marvelled at the speedy downfall of the people he knew as an untouchable ruling class. He was scornful of most of them, especially those he describes as 'shiny arses', and he reeled off stories about being treated with disdain by haughty squatters as a young stock agent.

He was warming to the tirade, pushing himself half out of the chair with both arms, giving dramatic emphasis to the injustices a working-class Catholic endured in the Western District of the 1960s. He especially remembered an incident when he and some friends were rabbiting on a squatter's property. The owner had ridden up to the group and went 'right over the top of one of my mates. He rode over him, such was his contempt for us.'

His resistance to this discrimination only made him stronger and more determined. He inherited a strong work ethic from his parents, who took up a soldier settler's dairy block on Injemira, near Warrnambool, in 1955. In those days of scarce accommodation, the whole family, including three children, had been living in a single-car garage, anxiously awaiting the commission's decision.

McKenna's rise and rise from there was based on hard work and skill, with an eye to new opportunities. His three sons were now in the business with him. 'I couldn't do it without them,' he said. At that, he bade us all goodnight.

Stirling Draffen grew up on Merrang at Hexham, a traditional Western District estate owned by the Hood family, who lived there as landed gentry for 150 years. Stirling was the son of a returned soldier who had been granted 690 acres of Merrang in 1948 after a war in which he was one of the famed Rats of Tobruk and was repatriated from New Guinea with malaria.

Since Stirling's childhood, things have changed dramatically for both the Draffens and the Hoods. Today, Stirling owns most of Merrang except for the house block, and the Hoods have retired to Barwon Heads. Like many of the long-standing Western District properties, Merrang had a grand bluestone homestead surrounded by extensive gardens, but Stirling didn't buy it.

'I could have bought the homestead,' he told me when I met him in Warrnambool, 'but I have two sons, and their wives would have argued over who lived in the grand home. It is easier not to tempt fate.' He was also practical about the potential problems. 'It would cost a fortune in upkeep,' he said. 'Probably cold and hard to heat.' At the end of 2012, the Hood family's connection to Merrang came to an end when the homestead was sold to a neighbour.

Stirling Draffen is a Western District legend. He owns a little over 12,000 acres of land, running 50,000 sheep and 2500 cattle on a variety of terrain. He has two sons and seven hired hands on the payroll of his agricultural powerhouse.

Draffen has turned recent history on its head. Where others have retreated, he has advanced, where they have downsized he has acquired, and instead of courting failure, he has found success.

When I asked him whether he considered himself to be the contemporary equivalent of the old squatters, he replied, 'To a certain extent. We are second-generation, where the squatters who are still here are fifth or sixth. My father was allocated 690 acres on the Hexham–Woolsthorpe Road, on a property owned by the Hood family for 150 years.'

Stirling remembered Robert Hood, who owned the farm when they took up the land. He told me, 'Robert Hood only died a few years ago. A nice fellow, a good man. Robert was shire president for a long time and did other community work. That is where he got his self-esteem. As a farmer, he didn't do a lot of physical work himself, but he was a very innovative fellow, had a lot of ideas on the farm. But the next generation were the ones who sold out.'

The problem, in Stirling's view, was that the property was left to the extended family, and this took all the incentive away. 'There was no desire to build it up, make the property bigger', because the profits would just go to his siblings or cousins. 'Why should the poor fellow running the place work his guts out?' Stirling asked.

Stirling's father saw what was happening, and it convinced him that children who came back to work the farm should be able to do so unencumbered. He applied this philosophy in dealing with his own children.

Stirling explained, 'I have four sisters and a brother. My brother came back and worked after I had been there twenty years, but he was thirteen years younger than me, and we had different attitudes. He was of a different generation. He didn't want to borrow and go into debt, so he went to my father and asked for his inheritance. He now has a farm and is debt free. At the time I thought it was a bit rough, but over time I have come to see it as a good thing.'

Stirling's four sisters were also given what he described as 'a fairly nominal amount' of $50,000 each.

Stirling himself had four children, including two boys who were now working with him. He said, 'They are probably smarter than me but don't have quite the ambition I have – but not far from it.'

One of his sons went to university and did mathematics. Around the farm, he was good at fixing tractors, while the other son was a good stockman. 'The stock are my priority,' Stirling said. 'We have 31,000 sheep plus 21,000 lambs and 2500 head of cattle.'

I noticed that Stirling's story unfolded in a series of short sentences, without artifice. He struck me as a man happy in his own skin.

He spoke of how much his family had sacrificed to establish their strong financial base, particularly his wife. 'She works very hard. In the early days, she would be in the woolshed skirting the wool and the baby would be in the basinet under the table. She would come at 10 o'clock in the morning and stay all day.'

He added, 'I inherited my dad's ambition – I went to wool school. You get focused on it. Rearing stock is a big challenge. We have purchased property and endeavour to pay for it as soon as we can. The last ten years, we have bought property without worrying the bank – we have had the money. It's not easy to get into that situation.'

I commented that his present holdings were a long way from the 690 acres originally allocated to his father.

Stirling told me that his father had started the process of building up the family holdings. Of that first block, he said, 'Fortunately it was good land. My father went onto the land in 1948 and in 1956 got a couple of hundred more acres. Then he sold that and bought another 900 acres. I came home in 1969 and we had 1500 acres and slowly since then increased the size.'

The secret to their expansion, he said, was that they did most of the work themselves. 'We pride ourselves on being pretty efficient in what we do. We fix windmills and fences. Do all the plumbing work, which is expensive; we do the rouseabouting in the shed, fix buildings and a lot of the mechanical work.'

I asked him what he did with the houses on properties he'd bought.

He replied, 'A couple of the men working for us live in them, but largely they are a problem. Renting them is a problem – the problem is drugs. People let you down and they lie, borrow money from you and never pay it back.'

Stirling was ambivalent about the remaining Western District squatters. He recalled, 'We had a wool classer called Jack Stephens who went around all the big sheds in the past. He said he was treated appallingly by the big squatters – told to go around the back and basically keep out of sight.'

His family had little to do with the squatters socially. 'We don't socialise with them. We are not in that social group. In a business sense we do get respect, but only because of our size. They don't socialise with us because I haven't been to a private school. I went to Mortlake High and did as much as I needed to get into wool school at Geelong.'

Stirling saw formal education as having both advantages and disadvantages. 'Sometimes people who have been educated think "I can't do that because I haven't been taught", where people who aren't educated just use their brains.'

When I remarked on his frugal way of life, Stirling said, 'It's just part of me. I don't like wasting money. You get into the habit of saving a dollar. I drive a nice motorcar, but it didn't cost much. I live in a basic house. My wife deserves more than I have provided for her, but houses are a liability, cost you money. My sons live better than I do.'

He said his priority wasn't to chase agricultural fads and fashion. 'We didn't go into farming to be millionaires. If you are looking to make dollars, you will keep chopping and changing. Change from one breed to another, always looking for the more profitable enterprise. We stayed with the one thing, and the wheel turns. We try and leave the place better than when we found it. If we grow a crop, it's to feed animals; that's our main priority. The squatters sometimes have other priorities. The Manifolds recently were complaining about the diesel bill to heat their swimming pool!'

Stirling was sure that the old families who had survived were in much the same boat as him. 'It's just their living standards are much higher. It costs them more to educate their kids, holidays and so on. My kids went to high school, but the next generation will go to private schools. I don't think they need it, but it does put them in that social setting, which does open doors. Whether that is a good thing, I don't know. You get contacts, mates, a circle of friends. But unfortunately for a lot of those doors, there isn't much money left behind them.'

32

The New Medici

The Renaissance of the fifteenth century may seem a long time ago, but it seems closer than you think when you look at the life and times of Allan Myers. There are many similarities between Myers and the Medici family, and I am sure the Western District patriot is aware of the parallels. Like the Medicis, who hailed from Tuscany, Myers is from a noted farming area, the Southern Grampians. He is a wealthy man involved in the wool industry, as were the Medicis, but like them he was not born into the elite. A sixth-generation Dunkeld native, he is the son of a local butcher; the source of his wealth is his whip-smart intelligence, not any aristocratic lineage. Like the Medicis, he is of the Roman Catholic faith, and he is a pre-eminent philanthropist with a strong interest in the arts. He is also adept at the backroom politics for which the Medicis became famous.

Myers' philanthropy is significant. Among his major donations, he is reported to have given the University of Melbourne $10 million and the National Gallery of Victoria $9 million. His current position as Chairman of the National Gallery of Australia, while one of the most sought-after honorary jobs in the nation, invariably comes at a cost to its holder and in January 2017 he was installed as Chancellor of Melbourne University. Active as a barrister, commercial company director and volunteer committee member, including as titular head of the influential Grattan Institute, he has escaped publicity by his insistence on privacy.

In Dunkeld, his residence is surrounded by a vast sandstone-walled garden designed around a series of pavilions, bringing Tuscany to the Grampians. Gardeners till the soil and tend vegetables for both his personal table and his nearby Royal Mail Hotel, a refuge he has fashioned for Australia's gourmands. I imagine his lifestyle as resembling that of the cultured Florentines, with fine French wines taken in an art-bedecked library amid erudite conversations.

By nature a robust democrat, Myers is a disaffected ALP supporter. His allegiance to the party was sorely tested by the factional and religious split of the mid-1950s, and he and his father John are now more Liberal than Labor. John Myers was active in the Liberal Party as treasurer of the Wannon branch when Malcolm Fraser was the local member, and Allan engineered Dan Tehan's pre-selection for the seat of Wannon, arm-twisting him into a Liberal seat ironically made safe for half a century by the sectarian split in the Labor vote.

As a pastoralist, Allan Myers owns 25,000 acres of Western District grazing country, a holding larger than that of the entire Manifold family, who came to the district in 1836. His well-judged philanthropy has made Dunkeld a destination for both tourists and epicureans. The main focus of his philanthropy in the town has been to make Dunkeld more liveable. Among other things, he had power lines put underground and established the innovative Royal Mail Hotel, coaxing it from a country pub into a 40-room residential retreat with panoramic views of Mount Sturgeon and Mount Abrupt.

He is proud that Dunkeld and nearby Penshurst were the only two Western District towns to increase their population in a demographic survey by Bernard Salt that highlighted the wasting of the west. Salt described Dunkeld as feeling 'the Royal Mail effect'.

Myers has been a subject of great media interest for many years and is not known for welcoming it, regularly keeping prospective

Allan Myers has imaginatively transformed the Royal Mail Hotel, now a modern facility for the district

profilers at bay. I approached him for interview prudently, and his secretary responded by asking if I could ring back ten days later at an appointed time. On cue, I was put through to a slightly irritated Myers, who asked plaintively, 'How long will this take?'

I assured him that I already knew enough about his public life to keep me going, but in this case I wanted to ask him about his memories of his Western District upbringing. An hour later, I put the phone down.

He was engaged, at ease with the world of his youth, and he revelled in telling his story. 'My family had been in Dunkeld since 1839,' he told me. His ancestors, James Griffith and Jane Brisbourne, had come up from Van Diemen's Land, where they were both convicts. 'When they had done their time, they came across to the Port Phillip settlement, changed their name by deed poll, adopted an Irish persona, concealing their Scots and Welsh origins, and settled in Dunkeld.'

For young Allan, Dunkeld was a welcoming place. 'I knew everyone and everyone knew me. I felt I could go to anyone's back door – probably walk in without knocking in most cases. Both my grandfathers were alive, and I remember them well. My love of the place is partly family.'

When he first went to school, his career received a boost from an unexpected source. 'I went to the Dunkeld State School, No. 183. We were very proud of its low or early number. I began in 1953. On that day, 64 children started school. We were accommodated in the Methodist Sunday school hall, because there was no room at the school. Ursula Griffin was the teacher. She had taught at Alexandra House in Hamilton but had married a farmer at Dunkeld.'

Wisely, Mrs Griffin decided that a class of 64 children was too big. There was a wide range of abilities; some of the students were 'hopeless', Myers said, and they stayed in the hall, but sixteen of them, including him, were put up to the next class.

His memories of the childhood that followed are mostly idyllic. 'My friends were the kids at the Dunkeld school. I had a wonderful life, running wild. There were plenty of rabbits, so from fairly early on, one made money by rabbiting. It was a town of working people. The railway line provided employment for a lot of people, the sawmill, the Country Roads Board, the local shire. There were plenty of shops.'

But the big negative was sectarianism. 'It was a terrible thing,' he said. 'As a Catholic, you were despised. It was awful. We were treated with condescension and disdain by many people who are still around. The likes of Stewart McArthur – he's a friend now, but he's definitely bigoted against Catholics. I always introduce him as a lapsed Catholic to ruffle him up a bit. I say, "I don't know a single McArthur who was not a Catholic. You are a Highlander. Your people were true to the faith. When did you turn?" He is always disconcerted, but he likes it in a way. The truth of the matter is that he was brought up to look down on Catholics.'

Myers suspected that the main drivers of bigotry were the Methodists and Presbyterians in Hamilton. He felt the effects as a high-school student at Monivae, the Catholic school in that town.

'They campaigned against Monivae boys being able to travel on the school bus from Dunkeld to Hamilton. It was a great worry for my parents, because one didn't know from one week to another that an edict wouldn't go out that non-State-school children were not allowed to travel on the school bus.'

Fortunately, the bus driver was a man called Terry Finnegan whose brother was a priest and sisters were nuns. Myers said, 'It would have been hard to give Terry instructions not to allow a Catholic boy or girl on the school bus. It is extraordinary when you think of it.'

Myers was at pains to disabuse me of the notion that the Catholic church in Dunkeld was predominantly an Irish institution. 'It's just not true to say the Scottish settlers were all Presbyterian – they clearly were not. The Presbyterians were mainly lowlanders, pseudo-Scotsmen, but the Highlanders who did their work for the squatters as indentured labourers were Catholic. The Catholic church in Dunkeld is a thoroughly Scots establishment. It was established by McArthurs, McIntyres, Lewises, McDonalds – all Scots from the Highlands who were cleared, emigrated and became indentured workers for the squatters.

'My great-great-grandmother was a Walker, a Highland Scot. They had come as labourers for the Chirnsides – signed up for three years, and then came to Dunkeld in 1840. My father can remember her as an old woman, and she still had a very distinct Scots accent, so they were Catholics of a very different timbre.'

When Myers was young, the area around Dunkeld was undergoing a significant shift of power, which would ultimately undermine the Protestant ascendancy reinforced by the squatters' presence. 'The squattocracy that surrounded the town were in retreat because the soldier-settlement scheme was in operation. Part of Woodhouse was taken, part of Blackwood. All of Mount Sturgeon was taken from the Armytage family trustees.'

It was just as well, because Dunkeld had just experienced a massive setback. The town had been burnt out in the 1944 bushfires, and many people couldn't bring themselves to stay after that. 'A lot of people who were burnt out did not bother to rebuild,' he said. 'They just left. If it were not for soldier settlement, it may not have survived.'

Myers recalled a speech by a local woman, Billie Young, to mark her 100th birthday. 'She said it was the soldier settlement scheme that saved the town and changed the character of the place. There were more people, more kids at the school, but they were also different people, a new class of people. Instead of working for the government or on properties owned by the squatters, these were people making their own lives on their own properties. Soldier settlement around Dunkeld was quite commercially successful – the places were of sufficient size, and the wool boom helped a great deal.'

These days, Allan Myers QC is sometimes described as Australia's richest lawyer, a phrase he loathes. He is certainly very wealthy, but he earned his real fortune outside the courtroom in middle age. After graduating from the University of Melbourne and Oxford, he became a commercial lawyer and barrister. Initially, he built a big practice in tax advocacy, mainly acting for Melbourne's Jewish community. He gained a reputation as a steel-trap mind for hire, and his clients soon included the rich and famous, including Gina Rinehart, Kerry Stokes, Lloyd Williams, John Elliott and Alan Bond.

Of all these luminaries, it was Bond who gave Myers lasting notoriety, if not his wealth. The legal fraternity adores good gossip, and its version of the story is that Myers, like Kerry Packer, had an unexpectedly profitable encounter with Bond.

The story offers a neat explanation of his wealth, but Myers dismisses it as apocryphal. 'There is not a skerrick of truth in that Bond story,' he says. 'I went to Poland before I met Alan Bond. It's beyond me why it's repeated. I acted for Alan Bond. He had some breweries. I bought some shares with my friend John Higgins in breweries in Poland. They are the facts. There is no connection, except that I am the same person involved in both stories. And why would Bond give me the shares? If he had, the liquidator would have had them long ago.'

Business Review Weekly supports his version. In 2016, it recorded that Myers and Higgins had bought the brewery just after the collapse of communism, paying a reported $US4.8 million ($AU6.4 million). Since then, beer consumption has risen sharply, and the Grupa Zywiec business is now listed on the Warsaw Stock Exchange with a market capitalisation of about $1.5 billion. Myers and Higgins still own stakes in the company valued at about $200 million each.

When I asked Myers for his own description of how he created his wealth, he replied, 'I worked hard as a barrister and invested some of the money I have earned successfully.' The Polish brewery was his best single investment, he said, but not the largest. 'I bought 25,000 acres in the Dunkeld area – you don't get that for nothing – and the amount of money I have spent around Dunkeld is very large indeed.'

I asked whether his land purchases around Dunkeld had benefited the old families, mentioning the case of Jim and Susie Clarke at Devon Park, who had sold him 1700 acres of land some years before, when they needed money to restructure.

Myers said, 'I don't know. I do know Jim was resentful of me. Terribly. Whether he had any good to say of me before that, I don't know, but he certainly had nothing good to say of me after that. I don't know. I suspect Jim wanted me to give him the money and not take the land. I don't know.'

Relations had improved since Jim Clarke's death. 'Susie of recent times has become a friend. She comes to things at our house in Dunkeld and sees my wife a bit, and our friends go out and visit Devon Park. It certainly didn't happen when Jim was alive.'

I asked whether he thought wealth earned off farm had been crucial to the Western District – for example, when money was brought in by wives from city-based families.

Myers thought about it and said, 'I don't think that's entirely true.

When Blackwood was for sale, I went out to have a look at it. Eda Ritchie was keen for me to buy it. I spoke to her son, and he told me – and I have no reason to doubt it – that the income from Blackwood from the 1890s to the 1950s was, year in year out, £200,000 a year. Now, that is an enormous income when ordinary people were earning between five and ten pounds a week.'

He mused about whether something like that could happen again. 'It's a bit hard seeing it, but it may do. Productivity still has to be increased. We have stopped investing in improving agriculture in Australia. We have rested on our laurels, and there isn't the scientific improvement in agricultural techniques that was the case for so long.'

But he still thought it possible to make a good income from land in Western Victoria. For example, he estimated that in 2013, when we discussed the question, if his company had been running the land more intensively, their 25,000 acres would have been producing 100,000 lambs and making $10 million a year.

He went back to my earlier proposition that pastoral wealth had often been created elsewhere. 'It is partly true,' he said, 'because people who have a lot of money like to live in nice places, and Western Victoria is a lovely place and is always going to attract a lot of people with a lot of money.'

Myers himself fits that description. He chooses to spend the working week in Melbourne because his legal practice, business and board commitments demand it, but he is very much a son of the Western District. 'When I went to Oxford,' he told me, 'I took one book to establish my cultural and intellectual credentials, and that was Margaret Kiddle's *Men of Yesterday*. It was about my part of the world, and was a beautifully written and truly scholarly work.'

What was it, I mused, that created such a fierce longing for the Western District in both of us?

'Because it is such beautiful country,' Myers said emphatically. 'Dunkeld is at the foot of the Grampians, the plains are not flat, the flora and fauna is rich, the rainfall is reliable, the seasons are variable, the coast is nearby. It's a very beautiful place. I've always revelled in the natural beauty, the natural attributes of the Western District. I have travelled down the rivers, the Wannon and the Glenelg, from the source to the sea. I've walked over most of the Grampians a number of times, and I've climbed Mount Sturgeon many times.'

Knowing he had recently purchased paintings by Eugene von Guérard, I asked what had attracted him to the works.

He explained that his wife Maria owned more than ten, and they both loved von Guérard's paintings. 'He was the greatest romantic painter of Australia in the nineteenth century – a tremendous technique and wonderful powers of composition. He depicted the Western District as he saw it.'

When I remarked that some people weren't taken by his paintings, Myers laughed. 'Then they don't have much appreciation of nineteenth-century painting. No one can criticise him on any ground. He had technique – one of the great Romantic painters north or south of the equator, and we are so fortunate that he recorded so much of Australia.'

He added that many Germans had contributed to civil society in Victoria, including von Guérard and the botanist Ferdinand von Mueller. 'It should be a reminder – although we have a British constitution, the really important founders of our society were from other places, including Germany.'

I asked about Susie Clarke's remark that it was striking how little parts of the Western District had changed since von Guérard produced his paintings.

'I don't think that is right,' Myers replied. 'A lot of the land has been cleared and developed. The trees that are there are in straight lines, in plantations. One of the pictures in the exhibition was of the view from Mount Rouse back across to the Grampians, viewed from between Penshurst and Dunkeld. It was full of swamps and blackwoods. It looks quite different country now.'

I asked him about a remark he had made suggesting that he could have been happy elsewhere.

'I suppose that is true,' he said, 'but I have chosen not to. My actions belie my words. Anyone who says he is doing something other than what he wants to do is probably not telling the truth.'

When I asked what inspired his philanthropic activities, he replied, 'My father taught me to have a very deep commitment to advancing the needs of the community, and I want to see a better and stronger society. That's why I do what I can. I am by instinct a builder and like to add to the strength of institutions, which are really the skeleton on which society is built. This means a commitment of people who have education and money. I see it as a duty. I guess I would be a liar if I said it wasn't a good feeling doing good things, and to a limited extent I don't mind the recognition.'

On the other hand, recognition could be a two-edged sword, he said. 'A lot of people can be pretty envious. So it's wise to keep a pretty low profile, although it's good to get some recognition so that it may encourage others.'

Myers knows the risks of being viewed as a patron. In this context, he tells me the story of Dunkeld's putative sports stadium. Myers offered to donate $3 million to build a stadium for the town, matched on a dollar-for-dollar basis by the federal government, but his offer has so far been rejected, because Myers made it a condition of the gift that alcohol not be served or sold on the premises. The locals uncharitably maintain that Myers is protecting his own liquor outlet at the Royal Mail, but he is adamant that his aim is simply to encourage young players to participate in sport without subjecting them to an alcohol-fuelled environment.

Reflecting on his work around Dunkeld, he told me, 'Whether

or not people are appreciative depends I suppose on whether or not they share my view of the world. Some people in life don't want to change. They prefer to be miserable and blame someone else for their failures.'

I asked if he thought the squattocracy was dead, and he replied, 'It's dead as the squattocracy, I think, because they don't have the social pre-eminence that wealth gave them, nor the political influence, but the connection between those families is still quite strong. A dinner party in the Dunkeld district is likely to consist of people with large parcels of land whose families have been there for a long time. But the attitude towards land is changing, and this is affecting the whole society.'

He speculated that we might be moving toward a situation where land is simply valued according to the profit that can be made from it, not as a sign of social position.

Myers didn't waste much sympathy on the old squatting families who were selling large parcels of land, often under pressure.

He said, 'They should have been selling that land fifty years ago or at least a generation ago, and they would have received relatively much more for the land. The big houses are a nuisance to most people,' he added.

Myers saw the future of the Western District as being finely balanced. 'Fewer and fewer people want to live in the country,' he said, 'and the force of gravity of Melbourne is enormous. It sucks everything into it. If you are 150 kilometres out of Melbourne, then you have got difficulties. Most of the shires in the Western District have suffered declines of population of between 10 and 15 per cent in the last 20 years.'

He saw a future for the region in tourism and education. Agriculture would become more efficient and productive, but probably wouldn't make more money or provide a great deal of employment. He believes any enterprise will succeed, unless it is ill chosen, provided that the proprietor puts in enough capital and gets enough attention.

Myers and his contemporaries are part of the new Western District, just as important as the mightiest of the nineteen-century squatters such as Niel Black or George Russell. I do get a sense, though, that more time will be needed for their contribution to be fully acknowledged and understood. Out on the plains, you earn respect by doing hard things well, but in the end reputation comes from how long you last.

33

Melbourne Land Boomers and the New Order

Melbourne has an enduring connection with the Western District, where urban magnates can enjoy the romance of owning rural land while keeping a home base in the city. Their reasons for acquiring country are many and varied. Some have bought in response to tectonic shifts in world affairs, such as the rise of new markets in Asia and the Middle East; others have sought an outlet for windfall profits. On the other side, landed magnates have used the stock market to reinvest profits from rural booms; for example, Western District landowners were among the first investors in line when BHP was founded in the late 1880s.

The Melbourne-financed Mann family began what has become a dynasty spanning four generations and four properties when they bought Brie Brie at Glenthompson in 1936. Speaking to Richard Allen, Ted Mann said his parents had taken a big risk: they bought during the Depression, and the property was rabbit-infested. The whole family had to be very careful with money into the early 1950s. Eventually, however, Brie Brie became the basis for a significant family enterprise embracing the nearby property at Larra and extensive interests in Camperdown dairying.

The influx of wealth from the city gathered momentum after the Second World War, when blueblood John Baillieu purchased Yarram

Park and a vast slab of farmland west of Melbourne, which is now being transformed into a commuter suburb. After the stockmarket crash of 1987, stockbroker John McIntosh annexed Terinallum. In 2006, former VFL footballer Stewart Gull implanted his boots on Banongill after selling part of his retirement home business for $23 million. The shifting sands of station ownership now form a complex web, which has widened to include the Murdoch matriarchs around Hamilton, US superannuation funds, Chinese corporations and Qatar sheiks.

Rupert Murdoch's involvement in the industry reached its peak in the 1970s, when he strode the Riverina as master of the famed F.S. Falkiner and Son mosaic of wool-growing estates. The personalities taking up vacated squatting empires also have included the odd carpetbagger – Alan Bond and Rene Rivkin both felt the momentary urge to put their hands on woolly backs at Wormbete and Purrumbete, for example.

Many of the new investors have one thing in common: they are all absentee landlords. In 1989, when CRA executive Mark Rayner began searching for a Western District property, one of his preconditions was that the place had to be large enough to support a full-time manager. He also wanted a property with views and preferably a comfortable house and garden. In 1992, he found all these qualities in Mokanger, a 2850-acre property on the Wannon River. For the Rayners, Mokanger became a family retreat, but they kept their house in East Melbourne.

The Western District is a manager's domain. Australia-wide, actual farmer numbers have been declining by two per cent a year. It is a seismic shift that changes everything. The old saying used to be that the owner's boots were the best fertiliser. But today, with management graphs recording today's cash flow data and instant communication through teleconferencing, the emphasis is on accountability and productivity.

I decided to visit some of the famous properties where very long-term squatting families have sold out to new investors bringing money from outside the industry.

Echoes of the past swirl irresistibly around Skipton's famed Carranballac, which was owned by members of the Chirnside family for 150 years. I have passed by the gatehouse at the Glenelg Highway entrance, imagining the paradise beyond, and here I am now, on a sultry January day in 2017, finally trekking the interminable driveway that leads to the homestead, beginning under sugar gums that close above the red gravel drive like the roof of a gothic cathedral.

The current owner of Carranballac is Melbourne investor Ian McNaughton, who divides his time between the property and a South Yarra schloss. I walk through a maze of charming breezeway verandas into a house of renovated timelessness, where I eventually find the lady of the house, Brighton-born Libby McNaughton, in the homestead kitchen. Libby, an effervescent force of positivity, has been in residence for 30 years, a mere blink in these parts, and is resolutely non-proprietorial. 'It's not our history' she says. 'It goes without saying, we are custodians. We owe it to the family before to maintain it'.

The McNaughtons harbour no desire to rid the imprint of time on Carranballac. Its working bluestone woolshed, stables and stalwart homestead are reminders of how life was lived on the plains. At the same time, the property is a live demonstration of the connection between Melbourne wealth and Western District heritage.

The McNaughtons' ownership of the landmark property has been unremarkable, as Libby's husband Ian would prefer. His business is private, his life the same. He was not at Carranballac the day I called. Ian and his younger brother Pip bought Carranballac as a partnership

A later Chirnside generation (and not the sellers of Caranballac),
émigrés to the coast Judy and 'Wumpty' Chirnside
in their Geelong flower shop

in 1986 from Robert and Judy Chirnside. Judy was a Western District personality of stunning beauty. Libby recalls the sweet scent of her perfume as she tripped up the stairs during fun-filled visits to her former home.

At the time of their purchase, however, Carranballac was declining. There had been a dip in the Chirnsides' fortunes, and the couple had also been affected by their middle son's suicide. A decade earlier, the property had been offered for sale only to be spectacularly withdrawn on auction day, when news came that a wealthy aunt had died in England and left a bequest that would ease the financial burden on Carranballac. It wasn't the first or last time that a Western District property had been saved by a random inheritance or desperately needed dowry.

Ian McNaughton, 75, like Libby, was Brighton born. After Melbourne Grammar, he and his brother plunged enthusiastically into Melbourne's land boom in the east around Eltham and Dandenong, where their entrepreneurial father had with commendable foresight

Libby McNaughton with Peter Learmonth at Carranballac

bought farming land. With Melbourne's suburbs spreading towards the Dandenongs, the McNaughtons prospered. Then, in the late 1980s, as the stock market crashed, they were able to spread their wings into rural investment, developing industrial and housing land on the Bellarine Peninsula and increasingly popular surfing spot Bells Beach near Anglesea. In reality, McNaughton has owned Western District property for 50 years, holding a property at Camperdown since 1967, but today he is settled into city life.

Libby is philosophical about the duality and goes with the flow, enjoying life at her home in South Yarra and her committee role at the Alexandra Club, a women's club in Collins Street with strong roots as a Western District outpost. The social cachet of owning broad acres has waned, she says. 'People who still live in the district are fascinated that Ian and I live here. They identify us as owners of Carranballac. Thirty years ago, people driving past our gate would

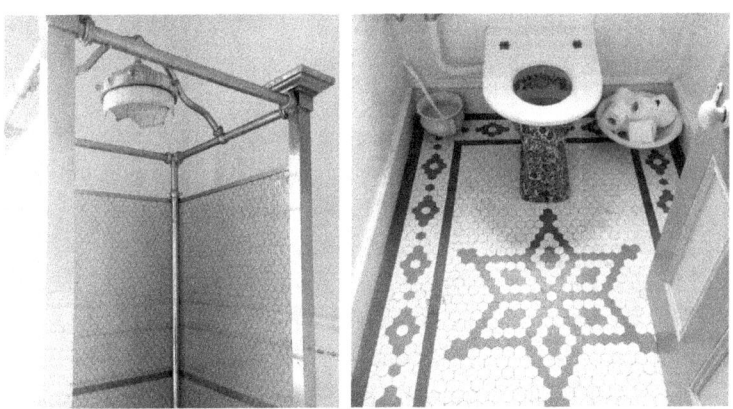

The hall at Carranballac, and the bathroom fittings

have thought "those awful Melbourne people", but I think we have proved to them that we love the place.'

Carranballac's homestead and stables overlook a bountiful stretch of Mount Emu Creek, a sizeable lake that can accommodate a motorboat, held up by an imposing 25-foot cement weir. Libby explained how permission for the weir was granted. 'Gordon Chirnside built the weir in 1918 with the highly innovative aim of hydro-electricity power generation. To get the permit to build the weir in the first place, Gordon told the powers that be, "I will bring power to Skipton." He didn't but the whole property was electrified, including a dozen cottages, the shearing shed, main house – the first in the district to have electric light.'

Carranballac, a jewel in the Chirnside empire, at times in the nineteenth century extended to 250,000 acres. It is now just 2500 acres. It was established when brothers Thomas and Andrew Chirnside rode over the Skipton plains just three years after Major Mitchell had crossed there. Enlivened by the ubiquitous kangaroo grass, basalt soil and fresh water in Mount Emu Creek, they claimed up to 70,000 acres as their own in 1839. Andrew later fell in love with Mary, his brother's betrothed, whom he was supposedly chaperoning on the long voyage from Scotland, and with his cuckolded sibling's permission, the couple had nine children. Today Simon Chirnside is the last to churn the soil of the fertile prairie.

'Something went wrong in these families, in their development,' Libby remarks. 'When you have children, you have a responsibility to train them to carry on. You must make sure the next generation keep it, and for some reason the Western District families didn't.'

Libby explains that in the McNaughton succession plans, there is a hiatus but no plans to sell. 'We have a 41-year-old daughter, Lynda, and Pip has a son, Lachie. Both love Carranballac, but neither would live here. But properties around here are changing hands so rapidly and in different ways. Apart from the US superannuation funds and foreign investors, some are going to relatives of the family or sons-in-law. A decision will have to be made, because Ian and I are at an age and stage where he has more interests in Melbourne and I have a wonderful life there.'

Born of the city, Libby has adapted to country living, a trait her father would never have suspected. 'Dad adored Ian,' he says, 'but when he asked for my hand in marriage, Dad said, "Well, young man, I don't know how you are going to keep my little social butterfly down on the farm." He lived to see me as a farmer's wife embrace a rural community with all it offers. But our lives have altered. Ian likes to be here when the work is on, shearing, weaning cattle, and bushfire season. It means we are here quite a bit at different times of the year. Ian was always sorry he didn't buy more. When land came up on our boundaries, Ian had just invested in something in Melbourne or Dandenong and wasn't able to expand.'

Expansion is something that Gordon Dickinson, the owner of Nareen, understands instinctively through years as a city banker, after spending his youth as a country boy. He has made seven land purchases adjoining Nareen since 1996, including Brian Learmonth's 6000-acre Baramar in 2000 and ten years later 2500 acres for winter grazing in four lots north of Robe. His carrying capacity of 25,000 ewes and 3000 cows has made him a player among the Western District's elite.

Dickinson bought Nareen after highly secretive dealings with Malcolm Fraser. He later joked that he had spent an extra $1 million 'because it was Malcolm's place'. For all its political currency, though, the picture-perfect woodland property north of Coleraine has contributed nothing to Dickinson's wider public profile, which I suspect is exactly how he likes it.

A Melbourne Scotch College old boy, Dickinson dropped out of university law school after seven weeks and headed bush to jackaroo, then in 1977 began a course in agriculture and farm management at Marcus Oldham College near Geelong. Dickinson's instincts were rural but after a few years on his father's property south of Nareen at Koonongwootong he was wrestling with his economic future and doubting the financial rewards of farming when a job offer fortuitously came from Ord Minnett, a private wealth manager in a sector that was about to take off.

Colleagues say Dickinson was immediately at home in a foreign world. His career advancement came in a series of superior job offers and culminated with him spending almost a decade as Executive Chairman of UBS in Sydney, a Swiss global financial services group. Here he used his analytical skills as a long-term planner and cool-headed decision-maker, all the time building a personal bank, including a $25 million 'golden handshake', which he would use to launch into the rural sector.

In 1996, around the time when Nareen came onto his radar, he had an opportunity to buy an apartment in the Circular Quay residential building known colloquially as the 'Toaster' for about the same amount of money, $5 million. This time, the hard-nosed banker allowed his heart into the equation.

Dickinson at 60 chairs three companies from his Melbourne base and spends more than half his time at Nareen, where staff report the boss is a hands-on operator. He does this within the comfort zone of knowing what he is doing. When in doubt, he can ask his grazier partners while wandering the Barwon Heads links with a golf stick in hand and a little white ball as the enemy.

A rutted bitumen lane leads to the Barwon Heads Golf Club, three storeys of angles, windows and Scottish defiance rearing above an exposed bluff and the boisterous Southern Ocean. The course was deliberately built along the same lines as those on the east coast of Scotland. The spirit of the grasslands ends here, at this home of the plainsman's sporting soul. Some wit dubbed it the Western District's gift to civilization.

Warned not to wear jeans, I have made it into the cloistered club as the guest of an adopted son of the west, David Robertson, whose father was pioneer surgeon Guy Robertson of Mount Gambier.

We're talking in the clubhouse over the soup of the day, a self-serve pea and ham. David knew Gordon Dickinson from their time together at Scotch College, and he is a director of Dickinson's Nareen Station Pty Ltd. A technically skilled grazier, David also farms Austral Park, a stretch of classic Coleraine red-gum country his father Guy bought when he retired.

For David Robertson, farming is strictly business. 'I inherited 1700 acres with a small debt and have built that to 5000 acres, also with a small debt,' he tells me. He was part of the generation that went to agricultural college in the late 1970s and began to apply business principles to farming.

Today, he says, good farmers and stockowners analyse everything, and it pays off. For instance, they monitor the condition of their stock closely. They won't bother sending a thin ewe to market when a fat one the same age can command a much better price. They're far more aware of death rates, particularly at lambing time, and they've lifted their lambing rates by 20 or 30 per cent by improving the health of the ewes. There has also been a move from lambing in autumn to late winter and spring, because conception rates are much better at the end of summer.

Farming these days isn't a matter of guesswork. 'There is a lot of scientific evidence used, ' David says. 'We do a lot of soil testing, put out a lot of fertilizer – potassium, sulphur and cobalt.' Much more attention is paid to soil acidity, and there is more use of lime to neutralise acid soils. There is also more emphasis on grazing techniques to make pastures last longer, as it's wasteful and expensive to be constantly re-sowing.

'And there are specialists to help you,' David adds. This has obviously been a major change. 'The veterinarians have diversified and moved into farm advice. Where they were purely pregnancy testing or pulling calves, now they are into management, or trying to eliminate drench resistance.' Today's vets can advise on finances and stocking rates, and farmers can also call on the expertise of agricultural scientists who have joined the commercial world after being laid off from government programs.

David says the younger generation of farmers have moved into the use of machinery. 'Diesel is in their blood,' he remarks. One reason for this is the change in the type of sheep they breed. 'They have moved from Merino sheep to crossbreds, and they aren't 50-kilo sheep, which you could handle yourself. They are 100- or 120-kilo sheep, and you can't handle them. So now they need machines.'

In Hamilton alone, he says, there are three outlets selling machines that grab and hold the sheep, but it's hard to handle them even then. At shearing time, the sheep are too heavy for the shearers to drag out, and there's talk about employing specific sheep catchers, one for each two shearers.

David is a strong believer in the future of raising sheep. 'There are not many sheep in the world,' he says, 'and no country can do it like us. People eat sheep meat all over the world. I am a firm believer in the sheep industry.'

He is also a supporter of the Western District's cropping potential. 'Raised beds have changed the landscape,' he says. 'Anywhere south of the Glenelg Highway is now suitable for cropping.' Farmers there get far higher yields than their counterparts in the Mallee or the Wimmera.

David travels around the district, sometimes speaking to groups of farmers. The conversations invariably follow the same pattern, he tells me. He begins by asking, 'What are you here for?' The farmers will always say that they're there for the lifestyle.

'OK, so what is a good lifestyle?'

'Oh, go on holidays, buy a good car, join Barwon Heads Golf Club.'

'How do you do that?'

'Make money.'

'And how do you do that?' At this point, David takes over. 'By running the business at its potential, not at its maximum. You have to find a niche in there. It's no good putting out tonnes and tonnes of fertilizer if you're not going to utilise the feed, or hundreds of cattle if there's no feed.'

The new generation, he says, can see the benefits of the lifestyle, and they can achieve it with new technology and expertise. 'Let's use it,' he says. 'The old families never used it. They never sucked the information out of the research arms, and so they are finished.' He is aware that this has produced a certain Western District malaise.

'There is guilt in selling old family land,' he says. 'I have seen it where I live.'

He has cleverly refurbished a derelict cottage a couple of streets down the bitumen lane from the golf club. He paid $1 million for it as an unliveable pile without views and restricted by heritage orders. The cost then was an indication of real-estate prices in fashionable Barwon Heads. He recently rejected a $3.5 million offer for what is now a spacious, high-ceilinged house with living spaces for three generations of Robertsons.

David has also set out to overcome the succession dilemma. Rather than dividing the farm at Austral Park between his two sons, he has included them in the farm's expansion. The property has remained an economic entity owned by the family, and their combined strength has made it possible to buy more land. By growing together, they've avoided the old practice of dividing properties down the middle, which weakened sibling relationships and led so many families to sell up and emigrate to the coast.

In January 2017, Tim Hutton sold Cheviot Hills in the dramatic rock-strewn country beneath Mount Rouse, just outside Penshurst. The property had been in his family for 164 years.

When I spoke to Tim, his three children – all in their thirties and working in London, Sydney and Melbourne – had just spent their last weekend at home.

'They were gutted,' Tim says. 'But I knew I had to sell, otherwise it would have killed me.'

I ask him what he means.

'It's very dangerous terrain,' he tells me. 'It's really horse country, but we get around on four-wheel motorbikes.' There are serious health and safety issues with the bikes. 'You have to wear helmets and safety gear, and it's easy to hit something and break a wrist or arm.'

The land has heart-breaking stony ridges littered with sharp volcanic rocks that even horses baulk at. But, in Tim's words, it also has 'beautiful flats – wall-to-wall clover, green all summer and autumn, growing in the lava flow'.

The path to the Huttons' ownership of Cheviot Hills is as diverse as the terrain. A Hutton ancestor docked in Tasmania in 1824, and the first Hutton arrived in these parts before Penshurst was founded. The property itself was part of the Mount Rouse Aboriginal Protectorate in the early 1840s, but was then hived off and offered for lease. The Huttons took up 8100 acres there in 1852, after some of the earlier lessees left to join the Victorian gold rush.

Now named Cheviot Hills, the property reached 15,000 acres at one point, but subdivision has since reduced it to less than 5000 acres. Around the time of the Second World War, Tim's father sold some

Cheviot Hills, the Hutton family home for 150 years, now owned by British billionaire Sir Michael Hintze

of the extra land he had acquired to shield the property from the attention of the government purchasing commissioners, who were identifying properties of more than 5000 acres to be subdivided for soldier settlement.

The size of the property was a problem, though. It was too much for one man to work, but Tim was in a bind. 'I couldn't afford a manager,' he says. 'He would need $80,000 – the same as I draw a year.'

The new owner, Sir Michael Hintze, a billionaire London-based hedge fund operator, paid $10 million for the property and had already employed a Penshurst couple to manage it.

'They have big plans.' Tim says. 'Maybe they will build roads through the place, but it's a different and difficult place. You can't flog it. I had stocking strategies that depended on when it rained. You had to have strict pasture management and careful budgeting. They will find out.'

Tim and his wife Jen have bought another property, Nigretta, which is a much softer management option. Nigretta has a gentle frontage to the Wannon River and a romantic two-storey timber house built in 1929 to a Canadian-influenced design. The homestead is currently half renovated, but there is plenty of room for improvement.

Tim is happy to stay in harness, but fears for the future of the Western District. 'It will become a land of managers,' he says. 'It's all corporate, and they are ruthless. Money, money, money. They will sink money into a property at the beginning and then flog the guts out of it. And the managers, it is a nine-to-five job for them. They don't care.'

He can see the industry moving towards roving work parties of ten men operating ten properties in turn. They will do up the shearers' quarters and move on, then a different group might turn up to do the lambing, dip and mark the sheep, shear and so on.

'The wealth has been stripped out of the land and the families,' Tim says. Tony Gurry, a long-time Hamilton accountant, once told Tim that when he started working in the 1960s, 'the wealth in the Western District was just staggering. And it's all gone. Now the corporations are coming in because the families can't afford the big properties on a return of two per cent.'

Then there's the succession problem. Even when younger family members are willing to take on a property, Tim says, 'The next generation can't buy the rest of the family out.'

And yet for Tim the prospects are hardly bleak. He has sold in a rising market. He now has a new property, a happy bank manager and an exciting project to restore a famously different house. And he has avoided migrating to Barwon Heads, unlike many of his friends. Beachside retirement holds no attraction for Tim Hutton. 'I couldn't imagine anything worse,' he says.

In a different twist to the coastal saga, some émigrés have bought hobby farms on the Bellarine Peninsula, a decompression chamber where they can adjust to life without the worries that attend the ownership of big properties. I have a poignant memory of visiting Russell Chirnside on his farmlet near Barwon Heads. A gentle man well into his eighties, Russell had everything in place on his small acreage – fences, gates, yards, all in miniature, including a corrugated-iron woolshed that would fit inside one pen of the sprawling bluestone landmark at his old home.

I left him to drive along the Geelong–Barwon Heads commuter strip, on a road lined with realtors' billboards extolling the raptures of 'country life' in the region's 'village estates', with their hundreds of houses pinned together, a vision of shimmering colourbond roofs that offer none of the pledged rustic charm. Country life is not to be found on the ersatz border of Barwon Heads. It is two hours drive west, in a foreign place where most of the original inhabitants have fled and man and nature still combat each other – a place where nothing is certain.

34

Generational Shift

> *Of all my peers, Digby Crozier and his wife Jill are the only ones who built their own place.*
>
> Malcolm Fraser

There are men of the Western District who lived in it, and the country got inside them. They had no anxiety about belonging as first settlers. They were men with a farmer's eye, like Niel Black and George Russell, the legendary Scots of the 1850s, and more moderns than it is manners to mention. The Western District made them, and they made the Western District.

But what of the men who were not born of the Western District yet emerged seamlessly to embrace its ruling-class attitudes and fashioned politics to fit their adopted heritage? Malcolm Fraser was one of these, Digby Crozier another. Their stories illustrate the rules that governed the plains. It is arguable that both had their lives laid out for them by the unwritten instructions of a social elite. There is no literature to tell us what they thought of that none-too-subtle pressure, but when I asked Digby Crozier, he ventured a beguiling, 'There could be some of that.'

Malcolm and Digby had much in common. They were both from political families and born on the cusp of the 1930s, and they lived on properties 26 kilometres apart, Fraser on the red-gum country near Coleraine, Crozier north of Casterton towards Edenhope, on less kind land. They also chose different paths, though both in the traditionalist ethic of the Menzies Liberal Party; and eventually they both abandoned their rural holdings towards the end of their lives. Fraser was three years younger than Crozier. They attended different private schools – Melbourne Grammar for Fraser, Geelong Grammar for Crozier – and then Fraser went to Oxford while Crozier chose Cambridge. They also came home to the land with different priorities. Malcolm allegedly rode roughshod over the jackaroos on Nareen, but Digby rolled up his sleeves and began clearing the yakka bush and ferns on his farm at Kalabity, a block of determinedly thin soil that had already broken some smallholders' hearts.

These stark differences marked the friendship – and they were friends, although Digby has described Fraser as 'a hard man to know'. Malcolm strode into the political fray 20 years before Crozier came down from his D2 Caterpillar bulldozer and secured Liberal endorsement for the Victorian upper house seat of Western Province. At various stages in the 1970s and 1980s, both were ministers in their various governments. Malcolm's term as prime minister ended as Crozier took the Victorian lower house seat of Portland. He held the seat from 1985 to 1988 before handing over to future premier Denis Napthine, a man whose background was determinedly different. Napthine was one of ten children of a Catholic farming family at Winchelsea; he graduated in veterinary science after being told by an imperious vet that his schoolboy dream 'would be very hard for a country boy like you'.

The seismic political shifts that have gone on in the Western District – from Crozier to Napthine in Portland, and from Fraser to David Hawker and then Dan Tehan in Wannon – were emblematic of the erosion of confidence undermining the Western District's famed bravado. When the evacuation began, Fraser and Crozier were not immune. Malcolm was the first to go, selling Nareen in 1996 and retiring to the Mornington Peninsula, while Digby sold his 6400-acre property in 2007 and found some solace with the lost white tribe at Ocean Grove on the Bellarine Peninsula.

Both men sold for financial and family reasons. Malcolm said farming was a young man's game, and his children weren't interested, but it was a business outside grazing that had brought him undone. Fraser had become a Lloyd's of London 'name' with the aim of earning off-farm income, but was liable for a portion of any underwriting losses. He ended in a series of loss-making syndicates, which eventually cost him Nareen. After Malcolm and Tamie joined the emigrants, a reluctant Digby followed, recognising the exigencies of succession. One of his sons, John, wanted to venture away from sheep farming, and his two daughters, Georgie and Annabel, were due their share.

'We were told there wasn't a satisfactory plan to look after our four children, so we grabbed the nettle,' Digby said. His son Will, 49, was happily running the farm with his father, but when the hard line to sell was drawn, he was sadly compliant. 'I couldn't buy my sisters out at half the price,' he told me. 'I said to Dad, "It has to be sold up." It means a lot to sell. It is hard to divorce business from emotion. In our case, we made a sound, very smart business decision for our family. But it was bloody hard and took its toll on everyone.' Will has since become a farm consultant to Chinese investors.

It was a huge effort to leave the farm after so many years, Will said. 'We had two months to get out and 20,000 sheep to sell. All very confronting logistically. For my father it was hard. He loved the place – he and my mother Jill had developed and cleared the land and built a beautiful homestead sited on 15 acres of water that dad had dammed. This put an extra layer of emotion on the sale. It's heart-wrenching to tear away a piece of your soul,' he added.

Fraser died in 2015 and Digby's wife Jill a year later. When I spoke to Digby, who turned 90 in May 2017, he was visiting a gym three times a week. Tamie Fraser, a close friend of Jill's, continues to live on the Mornington Peninsula. Tamie and Jill were Western District matriarchs, students of its mores, playing pivotal roles in their husband's political careers, stalwart rocks both on and off the farm.

Digby's daughters were the most affected by the sale, their passion for the land heightened as the day of leaving came closer. 'They were hit hardest,' Will said. 'They would come home and have a Sunday barbecue roast down by the Glenelg River and it would be exquisite. They would invite all their friends to the perfect setting. I still don't think they have got over losing it.'

Reflecting on his father among the émigrés on the coast, Will offered an interesting insight. 'There is a sadness amongst the Western District people on the Peninsula. It's God's catching pen.' On the other hand, he said, the Western District people down there do look after each other. 'They play bridge and golf together, and probably see more of each other than they did when they were farming.'

I asked him, 'Are they the lost white tribe?'

Will replied, 'Yes, that's exactly what they are. But often after selling the farm they have a nice house down there, smelling the ozone. I think a lot of them don't miss the actual farm.'

When I mentioned the title of this book to Digby Crozier, a great big laugh came down the line. 'Having joined the tribe,' he said, 'I must say I am glad to be at arm's length at Ocean Grove and away from Barwon Heads.' It was said without malice.

Will told me of one of the great ironies of his own family's Western District experience. He was certain that the well-run family farm was at the apex of commercial agriculture. He backed it up with research conducted while running the ruler over a number of properties, potential purchases for Chinese investors. He told me that the private accounting records proved beyond doubt that the soundest operations were family-owned and operated.

Will's analysis of farm records was helped along when the Croziers were invited to join Mutual Trust, which the *Sydney Morning Herald* has described as 'an integrated financial services adviser to the well-heeled'. The trust was established in 1951 by the Baillieus, with the aim of lifting the commercial performance of their own farms by benchmarking them against other places.

At that time, David Goodfellow was chief executive of Mutual Trust. He had 28 farms worth $480 million on his books, and he told me the job involved 'getting me on farms every week, learning what makes farms tick. Because I was doing the figures, we had some really powerful benchmarking going on. We could quickly work out who was going well and who wasn't, where the high levels of profits were coming from and how to exploit that and how to avoid the pitfalls.'

When I spoke to David Goodfellow, he'd recently become the boss of Rifa. A few months earlier, when he came aboard, the company had bought Blackwood, and he was investigating other Western District properties that would lend themselves to integrated management. Blackwood is one of those properties. Hearing Goodfellow talk, it was clear that one of his prime considerations was how properties could work together. 'Now we can buy any property we like,' he said, 'because it fits with Blackwood. We could buy a place suitable for breeding and fatten at Blackwood or vice versa.'

Goodfellow's research into the commercial property market in the Western District supported Will Crozier's conclusions about the superiority of family-operated farms, adding to the irony of the great farming exodus.

Goodfellow had a finely tuned appreciation of what Western District properties would suit his Chinese investors. 'The big trophy places', he said, 'lend themselves to Melbourne lawyers or people with a lot of money who can afford to appreciate the great houses and lifestyle benefits.' But, he added, the people making money out of agriculture in the Western District 'are not those sitting in the bluestone mansions or castles. It's the guys who have put together big acres of genuine producing country, places that do a bit of everything.'

He told me that this was where the family farms came in. 'That is the challenge for corporates in the Western District wanting to buy land. You are really up against the successful family farmers, and it can get pretty expensive. Corporates will never run a farm as well as a good, organised family. Corporates can't get near them because of the massive overheads, the compliance and regulatory costs of managing other people's money and those sorts of expenses that families don't have.'

I wondered how this would sit with the farmers who had sold out. Maybe it would just confirm what they already knew.

Goodfellow saw the meat trade, especially, as having infinite potention. He told me, 'The Chinese have a fascination for the safety of our food. While we may complain of red tape, we have some of the best-quality food in the world, so they have an interest in getting our meat back there. Already frozen meat is going back into China, and now fresh meat is heading that way too. The abattoirs licensed to export fresh meat will double in the next couple of years.'

With all this growth in fresh meat exports to Asia and premium prices paid by their consumers, Goodfellow and Will Crozier were both facing problems finding good properties. It was especially difficult to source the bigger acreages that suited their business plan. 'Land prices are very resilient,' Goodfellow told me. 'Good land just doesn't come up very often.'

He said that many of the Western District that had recently sold were those bought 20 years ago from the dynastic families. 'When you look at the big historic places that have sold, they are properties that have been bought within the last generation. Banongill, Terinallum, Bundooran and Mt Fyans all fit that bill, and all have had the benefit of new cashed-up owners. They have each had a personal touch put on them by the owners of the modern era, and each one has been different.'

He ran through what had happened in the last two decades on each of these iconic properties. 'Terinallum has seen its infrastructure, its housing and guest accommodation significantly upgraded. It is just a beautiful place to take people to enjoy the Western District countryside. At Mt Fyans, the Earl of Stradbroke – an eccentric but true-blue English aristocrat with 15 children from two wives but no one to inherit the property – realised his ambition to grow by buying six or seven surrounding soldier-settler places to build up to 14,600 acres. Banongill also acquired more land, but spent a considerable amount of money clearing the land of stones and putting drainage through paddocks that were previously badly drained.' Both Banongill and Bundooran were also re-fenced and money was spent on pastures.

These properties were attractive to corporate investors, he said. 'Mt Fyans definitely was, and we tried hard to buy Bundooran, because it was so close to Blackwood and we would have run those two properties in conjunction with each other. The problem for us is the economic land size is always over 4000 acres, and normally in the Western District a place that size has a bluestone mansion on it.'

He said corporates could handle one of those overcapitalised properties, but then they need a bunch of undercapitalised ones to balance it. 'We had genuine interest in Bundooran because it doesn't have a big lavish homestead on it – it has a beautiful but sensible home, but not a ridiculous house like Minjah or Terinallum. Those properties lend themselves to someone who has substantial financial means and is happy to spend money on themselves.'

Goodfellow and his team are more pragmatic. 'We are looking at properties that have put all their money into capital infrastructure rather than flash homesteads or just pure beauty, which can become a noose around your neck. We are in it for the money.'

Epilogue

Place speaks to me more than the dogmas of any religion, and it speaks of very fundamental things: time, death, what we have in common with the animals, what things are like when we stop to look.

Charles Tomlinson

The Western District's white tribe has incurred many losses as a result of leaving the land that defined them. It's a permanent loss for the people, a more arguable defeat for the landscape. It's a loss spread through family dynasties and ineffable stories of personal grief.

In leaving, the pastoralists have forfeited their own history, their connection with place and much of the meaning in their lives, their morning, noon and night emptied by the evaporation of familiarity and the fundamentals.

The English poet Charles Tomlinson speaks to the heart of this transformative dispersion, but I often wonder if the Western District needs to be reminded of his notion of stopping to look. People in the district don't talk of forsaken family land or the hazy doubt about what replaces it. If the subject is raised, they become self-righteous. I suspect that the men feel it most, in leaving they are turning their backs on their whole working lives. Their wives sweep new brooms, practising golf and bridge. The chatter blows by on the wind.

There, along the shoreline of Western Victoria, enclaves of émigrés occupy large coastal retreats as their children disappear into the commerce of the cities. The loss of meaning is sweetened by cash emoluments from the sale of their properties. They gather at soirées or funerals, emboldened and distinguished by pedigree, often seeming slightly shocked by the change.

While there is no divine right to land or guarantee of perpetuity, it's difficult to explain why these descendants of the district's pastoral elite had a seemingly unshakeable grasp and then simply released their grip, leaving us with the mystery of their going. Their private grieving opened a wound, and those that were left scrambled to survive. As Jane Calvert from Hopkins Hill told me, 'There is something that has gone.'

The reason for this book is to find that 'something' and so preserve the dignity of the place. It's not to denigrate or disentangle lives, but to remember and cherish the sanctity of uniqueness, to discover what lies behind Charles Tomlinson's words, developing an awareness of the past and a connection to the basic but important things they have left.

Nature writers insist that to have some idea of our own identity, we must have a deep and abiding sense of place. In their thinking, there are two worlds, both in this one. There is the everyday world of commerce and conflict, and the real world, which begins with land and sky and the mystery embodied in the place where we live.

And who better to talk of the land and sky, of light fingers breaking cloud after rain, trees dancing in the wind, temperatures soaring on the skin, than the farming people who lived and breathed it? I have been with graziers who knew every blade of grass on their 4000 acres. Their eyes were filled with the picture in front of them and memories of things that had happened in that gully or beyond that rise. They felt no need to translate it for public consumption, for this was the place where they lived.

Or the place they no longer live. One former farmer told me that what he missed most was not the obvious things like the smell of welcome rain or the magpies' song at first light, but the imaginary life he led. 'I liked nothing more than the moments of silence and aloneness on your own place,' he said. 'In that time I had an imaginary life where I remembered my dad, my brothers who have gone, and

Epilogue

Port Fairy on the Moyne, now home for many
Western Districts émigrés

what they did at a certain time. It transported me to a more generous, warmer place of animals we bred, dogs, seasons, the future. It's gone now, drowned out by the town around me.'

Of course, there were other factors disrupting his life and that of the people around him – the marginalisation of the wool industry, increasing international competition in commodity markets, the great uncertainty of cropping in high rainfall areas, climate change affecting the balance between the north and south of the district, degradation of pastures through lack of farm investment. These are all real obstacles, but the squattocracy, instead of grasping a world that has turned, have interpreted it as a cruel realignment in an unjust age that has no need of them.

The Frasers, Streets, Fairbairns and the rest who upheld the standard are no longer there to protect them or hold sway in the Liberal Party. In business, BHP, the NAB, the Collins House companies, the Australian Wool Council and the VRC, once part of the Western District's DNA, look further afield for investment and inspiration. Only the Melbourne Club, that grim monolith at the 'Paris end' of the city, reaches out to the sons of its Western District forebears.

Certainly the remaining squatters' postcodes would still feature heavily on the share registers of blue-chip companies, but the flow of off-farm wealth from Australia's cities into the Western District has largely become a luxury of the past. Workaday farmers now have to survive by using improved techniques, developing systems to ensure cost/price sensitivity and constantly renewing their intimacy with the land that nourishes them.

The Western District is traditionally silent about its core and remiss about its myths. In the brutal years since its belle époque, goodwill has been dispersed. Cynicism is a pitiless killer of fond memory. Yet most of those born there instinctively refer to the Western District as home. It's the place of their desires, a part of their soul. There is an eloquence in their silence. It's not always easy to come clean about failure.

The Western District is experiencing convulsive change. Ownership is often international, and the mindset could not be more different from that of the families who made it their home for 150 years. Chinese corporations are establishing cattle enterprises to deliver 'safe beef' to high-end shoppers in Shanghai, while American super funds buy trophy places with plans as fluid as the markets. The district is infiltrated by managers, consultants, spreadsheets and new faces.

Meanwhile, the pastoral families that remain are learning to admire the loveliness of the region again and respect its ability to heal any feelings of social isolation that lingered from the past. They live on a prairie of great scope and breathtaking beauty, nurtured by nature with a bit of help from humans.

Landowners today can no longer retreat from nature. Stockmen and greenies are closer than they think, the earth the common denominator. Conservation efforts are everywhere: from single farmers to organised Landcare groups experimenting with kangaroo grass or tearing out capeweed. There's mutual support to prevent ecological destruction and erosion, while dryland salinity has all but been defeated.

At Dunkeld, Allan Myers has fenced long sections of Wannon River frontage and set aside 3000 acres for conservation. His Dunkeld Pastoral Company has a breeding program for local endangered species and two full-time workers engaged in preservation, plus a conservation director for its Australian properties.

John Fenton at Lanark near Branxholme has revitalised 2000 bleak and windswept acres. Sixty years after inheriting the land, he has some 100,000 trees, areas permanently retired from grazing – including wildlife corridors, wetlands and native grassland – with other sections partially grazed or cropped, leaving the less environmentally sensitive areas for continuous high production.

The Reids at Waratah have five waterbird sanctuaries in fenced, dual-purpose dams. On his property, David Robertson plants a hundred trees for every one that falls, while on the Wando estate, Harry Youngman produces 7000 tonnes of compost every year to enrich his paddocks. None of them do this because of sentiment; they do it because it works.

Tim Winton has said, 'Land is my family.' Speaking of a different place, Stephen Henschke says that in his vineyard, Hill of Grace, he can recall 'the spirits of the generations that have come before me'. The same mystique of generational ownership echoes around the vales of those magical places still retained in the Western District.

But you don't hear a murmur of it.

It's time we did.

Time can erode but it mustn't destroy.

Emblematic of the district's decline:
the former Coleraine drapery

Acknowledgements

David Armstrong and Allan Myers are both subjects and of enormous influence on this book. David inducted his school mate, a wide-eyed eight-year-old into the magical mystery that is the Western District in 1953 and Allan allowed with unyielding support, sixty-four years later, an attempt to explain that astonishment.

David and Allan's Western District genetics reach back 170 years of familial connection and are at the core of this story of overwhelming adoration and then bewilderment at a Vanished Land if that is what an exodus and sacrifice of pastoral identity can be called.

I am indebted to them both and to those who granted interviews and who continued to graciously help me uncover the truths of life on the volcanic plains, for me a lost land. I do know of its ability to bounce around the economic parameters of success and failure and it just might be entering that upswing today. I trust it's in good hands.

Peter Learmonth, a Lion of the Western District, was central to the discussion that sowed the seeds for this book and instrumental in locating many of its voices as he grew into a great friend on those lonely roads he drives with such knowing and sympathy.

My thanks also to Chas Armytage, Peter Allen, Norman Anderson, Chris Lucock, Andrew Clark, Richard and Jane Jamieson, Bim and Anna Affleck, Keith Urquhart, John Goold, John and Jenny Gubbins, David and Kaye Blackburn, Clive and Kate McEachern, David and Pauline Barry, Stewart McArthur, Tim and Jen Hutton, David Robertson, Brian Wood, Bill Woods, Peter Groves, Wumpty and Judy Chirnside, David and Penny Hawker, Bruce Allen, Russell Chirnside, Richard and Julie Mann, Hugh Beggs, Jim Hay, Stirling Draffen, Campbell McKellar, Colin McKenna, Tyrrell Evans, Ken

Satchell, James Kimpton, Peter Yule, Marston Nicholas, Hugh McLachlan, Wally Merriman, Andrew Reid, Rev David Schulz, Bruce Whitson, Paula Learmonth, Jane Zachariah, and in the spirit of the AFLW and in no particular order Chris Alexander, Eda Ritchie, Susie Clarke, Catherine Winter-Cooke, Fleur Mein, Trisha McKenzie, Helen Watson, Georgina Weir, Libby McNaughton, Mary Schlight and Joy Potter.

Finally it came down to a question of pre-natal protocol and procedure. Somebody had to do it. I was lucky to find Jenny Lee, an editor of vast experience. Jenny gave me the necessary practice of solidity and strategy, as did my partner Sarah Hyde who as a proud South Australian has more areas to champion like the Fleurieu or the Barossa than a place she has visited twice. Her forbearance was as remarkable as I hope you, my readers are.

Additional reading

A Fortunate Life, A.B. Facey, Penguin.

A Single Tree, compiled by Don Watson, Penguin-Hamish Hamilton.

Australia's Second Chance, George Megalogenis, Penguin-Hamish Hamilton.

Australia, A Biography of a Nation, Phillip Knightley, Vintage.

Australia, A Cultural History, John Rickard, Longman.

The Bush, Travels in the Heart of Australia, Don Watson. Penguin-Hamish Hamilton.

The Water Dreamers, The Remarkable History of Our Dry Continent, Michael Cathcart, Text Publishing.

Breaking the Sheep's Back, Charles Massy, UQP.

From Forest, Swamp and Stones, A History of the Shire of Minhamite, P.L. Yule, Warrnambool Institute Press.

Girt, The Unauthorised History of Australia, David Hunt, Black Inc.

Men of Yesterday, A Social History of the Western District of Victoria, 1834–1890, Margaret Kiddle, Melbourne University Press.

My Blood's Country, A Journey Through the Landscape that Inspired Judith Wright's Poetry, Fiona Capp, Allen and Unwin.

Narrapumelap and The Lions of Wickliffe, Allan Willingham, author.

Phillipsland: Country Hitherto Designated Port Phillip, John Dunmore Lang, Thomas Constable, Edinburgh.

Kidman, The Forgotten King, Jill Bowen, Fourth Estate.

Habitats, Grasslands, Julia Waterlow, Wayland.

The Fatal Shore, Robert Hughes, Colins Harvill.

The Big Picture, Bernard Salt, Hardie Grant Books.

The Squatters, Geoffrey Dutton, Viking O'Neil.

The Plains, Gerald Murnane, Text Classics.

Great Properties of Country Victoria, The Western District's Golden Age. Richard Allen and Kimbal Baker, The Miegunyah Press.

Heads You Win, A History of the Barwon Heads Golf Club, Weston Bate, Barwon Heads Gold Club.

History of Lake Bolac 1841–1966. Lake Bolac and District Historical Society.

Scotland's Empire, The Origins of the Global Diaspora, T.M. Devine, Penguin.

The Shepherd's Life, A Tale of the Lake District, James Rebanks, Allen Lane.

Skye, Derek Cooper, RKP.

The House That Wool Built, Nine Valentine. Book Committee Queen's and Ballarat Grammar Schools.

Thicker Than Water, History, Secrets and Guilt: A Memoir, Cal Flynn, William Collins.

Vanished Kingdoms, The Rise and Fall of States and Nations, Norman Davies, Viking.

Wanganella, and the Merino Aristocrats, Timothy Lee, Hardie Grant Books.

Wimmera, The Work of Philip Hunter, Ashley Crawford, Thames and Hudson.

Index

A

Abbott, Tony 174, 220, 246–248
Affleck, 'Bim' 142, 195
Affleck family 16, 54
Alfred D'Orsay Tennyson Dickens Library 66
Allen, Bruce 22
Allen, Jim 128–130
Allen, Peter 128
Apsley 245
Ararat 30
Ardno 168, 171
Armstrong, David 5–14, 227, 244
Armstrong, Ian 51
Armstrong, Pauline 15
Armytage, Chas 189, 219–223
Armytage family 67
Asimus, David 100, 101, 117, 118
Austin, Thomas 18
Austin, Tom 52
Austral Park 285

B

Baillieu, Antony 33, 78
Baillieu family 59, 78, 80, 293
Baillieu, John 33, 274
Ballarat 29, 38, 42, 51, 55, 57, 60, 67, 106, 113, 222, 246

Balmoral 70, 81, 204, 220
Banongill 124–126, 275, 295, 296
Barber, John 134
Barr Smith family 219
Barry, David 88, 237
Barton 123
Barunah Plains 134, 135
Barwon Heads 14, 60, 253, 257, 282, 285, 288, 289, 293
Barwon Park 18
Batesford 25
Baulch, David 222, 249, 250
Baulch, Geoff 242
Beggs, Hugh 82, 100, 109, 110–119, 128, 190
Beggs, Richard 113
Bellarine Peninsula 18, 35, 107, 177, 278, 289, 291
Bentley (cars) 197, 201
Biddicombe, John 134
Birregurra 18, 19, 20
Blackburn, David and Kaye 106
Black, Niel 22, 42, 178, 273, 290
Blackwood 61, 75, 109, 116, 120, 121, 122, 123, 126, 216, 266, 269, 294, 296
Blainey, Geoffrey 84, 87, 88, 89
Bolac Plains 88, 143, 238

Bond, Alan 267, 275
Boonerah 141, 142, 224–229
Boortkoi 29, 37, 38, 210
Branxholme 178, 213, 301
Brie Brie 215, 274
Brinkworth, Tom 123
Bromell, Hugh 107, 177
Bromell, John 'Jack' 172, 174, 175
Bundooran 295, 296
Burrumbeet 139, 180

C

Calvert, Jane 298
Calvert, Keith and Flo 157
Calvert, Rod 52
Camelot 5
Camperdown 19, 21, 41, 50, 147, 179–185, 207, 211, 227, 274, 278
Caramut 30, 81, 142, 195, 215
Carngham 38
Carranballac 103, 170, 276–280
Cassab, Judy 165
Casterton 29, 71, 81, 105, 290
Cavendish 197
Chatsworth 28, 38, 43, 82, 109, 126
Chatwin, Bruce 25
Cheviot Hills 286
Chirnside family 16, 33, 216, 219, 266, 276, 280
Chirnside, Gordon 280
Chirnside, Robert and Judy 277
Chirnside, Russell 103, 162, 289
Chirnside, 'Wumpty' 277

Clark, Andrew 97
Clark, Daryl 35
Clarke family 16, 61, 191, 193
Clarke, Jim and Susie 268
Clarke, Susie 190–195
Clarke, Trevor 19, 57, 186–191
Clarke, W.J.T. 'Big' 186
Clark, Geoff 94, 95
Colac 87, 182, 227
Coleraine 26, 71, 105, 177, 281, 283, 290
Collinsville 70, 145, 225
Condah 92, 131, 177
Coolana 37, 250, 253
Corangamite electorate 22, 63, 207
Cotter, Peter 35
Croft, Graeme 31
Crozier, Digby 290, 293
Crozier, Will 295
Cumming family 209, 216
Cumming, Roger 34
Currie, John 32

D

Daimler (cars) 61, 62, 115
Darlington 33, 34, 170, 209
Davidson and Henderson, architects 32
Dawson, James 41
Dawson, Meredith 53
Delaney family 33
Dennys Lascelles 36, 166, 207

Index

Devon Park 61, 75, 150, 186–196, 268
Dickinson, Gordon 281, 282, 283
Draffen, Stirling 255, 257–261
Dunkeld 73, 75, 76, 120, 180, 186, 189, 190, 219, 222, 262–272, 301

E

Edenhope 243, 290
Eilyer 106
Elephant Bridge 33–35
Elliott, John 36, 267
Ennerdale 135, 142, 237
Ercildoune 139
Evans, Tyrrell 67, 121, 172–178

F

Fairbairn family 125
Fairbairn, James 33
Fenton, John 301
Flannery, Tim 84
Framlingham 41, 96
Fraser, Malcolm 109–113, 221, 243–246, 263, 281, 290–292, 292, 299
Fraser, Tamie 109, 110, 244, 292

G

Gammage, Bill 84, 85, 87, 88, 89, 90, 95
Gardiner, Andy 176
Geelong 17, 25, 29, 32, 75, 81, 134, 168, 187, 207, 211, 217, 260, 277, 282

Geelong Grammar 67, 104, 109, 121, 147, 199, 217, 222, 227, 291
Gibbs, David 61, 62
Gibbs, Fleur 61
Gilbertson family 31
Glenfine 31
Glenormiston 22
Glenthompson 30, 82, 274
Golf Hill 133, 134
Golsworthy, Eric 33
Goodfellow, David 294–296
Grampians 73, 75, 77, 88, 204, 236, 237, 262, 263, 269, 270
Grasmere 172
Great Ocean Road 18, 22
Gubbins, Arthur 37
Gubbins, Jenny and John 252
Gubbins, Simon 251, 252
Gull, Stewart 125, 275
Gunditjmara 77, 92
Gunn, Noel 67
Gunn, Sir William 99, 117
Gurry, Tony 67

H

Hamilton 1–2, 12, 13, 23, 29, 36, 44, 45, 46, 48, 50, 51, 60, 61, 64–71, 82, 91, 92, 93, 107, 109, 117, 120, 131, 135, 167, 169, 170, 172–177, 183, 194, 197, 198, 201, 213, 217, 222, 244, 251, 253, 265, 266, 275, 284, 288
Hamilton College 2, 12, 46, 48, 69, 70, 174, 198, 217

Handbury, Geoff 69, 70, 174
Hawke, Bob 112, 244
Hawker, David 174, 243, 245, 245–248, 291
Hawkesdale 30, 81, 242
Hay, Jim 43, 59, 135
Henty, Edward 97
Hexham Park 5, 8, 9, 36, 51, 225
Heywood 18, 91, 92
Hintze, Sir Michael 287
Hood family 176
Hood, Robert 258
Hopkins Hill 125, 298
Horsham 17, 71
Hurrey, Mick 176
Hutton, Tim 286, 288

I

Illira 172, 173, 175, 177
Injemira 172, 256

J

Jaensch, Gary 79, 80
Jamieson, Mr 35
Jamieson, Richard 143
Jamieson, Rosie 35
Jellalabad 34

K

Kalabity 291
Kaladro 123
Kelly family 176
Kenna, Ted, VC 29

Kennett, Jeff 185
Kerin, John 101, 118
Kimpton, James 53
Kinonvie 67
Koolamurt 25
Koonongwootong 282

L

Laidlaw, Hal 48, 78
Laidlaw, Ralph 250
Lake Bolac 19, 30, 106, 107, 208, 222, 238, 240
Lake Condah 92
Lake Keilambete 22, 148
Lake, Marilyn 77
Lanark 301
Langi Willi 62, 63
Lang, John Dunmore 86, 87
Lang, P.H. 32
Learmonth, Peter 25, 26, 67, 103, 120, 130, 147, 166, 168, 189, 250, 278, 281
Le Louvre 55, 56
Lewis family 266
Lismore 30, 32
Lovett family 91
Lucock, Chris 142

M

Mackinnon, Claire (nee Adams) 153, 159–165
Mackinnon family 16, 49, 63, 161, 162, 233, 234
Mackinnon, L.K.S. 233

Index

Mackinnon, Scobie 153, 159–165, 234
Maclennan, Dr John 234
Manifold, Andrew 250
Manifold family 16, 37, 43, 176, 193, 208, 209, 261
Manifold, John 147
Manifold, Sir Chester 179–182, 184
Mann family 176, 274
Mann, Richard 213–216
Mann, Ted 274
Marriner, David 183
Marshall, Alan 148
Matterdale 235, 236
McArthur family 107, 266
McArthur, Stewart 50, 207
McConachie, Jim 67
McCullough, David 38
McDonald family 266
McEachern, Clive 167–172
McEachern, Kate 166
McEachern, Ralph 131, 166
McEwen, 'Black Jack' 99
McGavin, Tim 124
McIntosh, John 275
McIntyre family 266
McKellar, Kim 106
McKenna, Colin 255–256
McKenzie, Patricia 62
McLachlan, Gillon 19
McLachlan, Hugh 103
McLeod, Rev. Neil 45, 46

McNaughton, Ian 276, 277
McNaughton, Libby 276, 278
Medlin, Leigh 135
Megalogenis, George 84, 85
Meningoort 50, 210, 212
Menuhin, Hephzibah 153–159, 162, 163, 168
Merrang 257
Minjah 54, 195, 296
Moffatt family 16, 38
Moffatt, John 43
Mokanger 275
Monivae School 69, 70, 265
Moodie, Bill 175
Mooramong 49, 63, 153, 154, 159–165, 233
Mortlake 6, 13, 14, 15, 21, 30, 33, 35, 36, 81, 94, 104, 105, 128, 141, 170, 176, 189, 209, 224, 226, 250, 260
Mount Abrupt 73
Mount Duneed 75
Mount Elephant 27, 32, 33, 41, 139
Mount Hesse 135
Mount Rouse 75, 270, 286
Mount Shadwell 36
Mount Sturgeon 73, 74, 176, 220, 221, 263, 266, 270
Mount William 75, 219
Moyne River 24
Moyston 123
Mt Fyans 295, 296
Murdoch family 68
Murdoch, Rupert 68, 174, 275

Murnane, Gerald 149
Murndal 62
Murray, Reg 'Bomber' 92
Murroa 251, 252, 254
Myers, Allan 70, 220, 262, 263, 264, 267, 301

N

Napthine, Denis 291
Nareeb Nareeb 109, 110, 113, 114, 115, 116, 119, 125, 128
Nareen 110, 112, 113, 244, 281, 282, 283, 291, 292
Naringal 31
Nicholas, Lindsay 153, 166
Nicholas, Marston 156–158
Nigretta 287, 288
Noorat 34, 148, 149

O

Oldham, Marcus 187

P

Paterson, Rowly 69
Plimer, Ian 246, 247
Port Fairy 14, 23, 24, 60, 68, 113, 121, 177, 217, 253
Portland 17, 26, 40, 86, 97, 120, 178, 247, 291
Port Phillip 3, 40, 41, 86, 264
'Princeland' 97
Proudfoot, Helen 37
Purrumbete 43, 147, 183, 275
Puyuun, Wombeetch 41

R

Rayner, Mark 275
Rebanks, James 230, 231, 235, 242
Reid, Andrew 198–204
Reid, Charles 197, 204
Reid, Don 201
Reid, Elizabeth 199, 201
Rippon 67
The Rises 70, 231
Ritchie, Eda 60, 61, 109, 111, 121, 122, 124, 219, 269
Ritchie family 16, 61, 75, 120, 123, 193, 216
Ritchie, James 41, 120
Ritchie, Jason and Kate 120, 122
Ritchie, Robin 121
Rivkin, Rene 183, 275
Robertson, David 283, 285, 301
Rockgrove 35
Rolls-Royce (cars) 48, 49, 65, 68, 78, 160, 161, 163
Rowe, Bill 31
Rowe family 16, 31
Royal Mail Hotel 263, 264
Russell family 38
Russell, Geordie 134, 136
Russell, George 42, 133, 137, 171, 273, 290
Russell, Philip 134

S

Salt Creek 237
Satchell, Ken 131

Schlight, Mary 181, 182, 183, 185
Schulz, David 46
Shelford 18
Shipley 53
Skipton 19, 29, 30, 32, 81, 82, 89, 103, 112, 124, 153, 159, 163, 164, 276, 280
Smythesdale 30
South Boorook 128, 129, 130, 131, 135
St Andrews Presbyterian Church 44, 46
Stephens, Jack 260
Strathdownie 123, 168, 171
Streatham 19, 31, 35, 82, 208
Streeton, Arthur 74, 75, 151, 236

T

Talindert 183, 183–185
Tattyoon 30
Tehan, Dan 113, 263, 291
Terang 22, 81, 227
Terinallum 153–158, 163–168, 170, 275, 295, 296
Timboon 22
Titanga 32
Toolang 61, 62
Toomey, Reg 67
Toora 48, 49, 78
Tower Hill 23

U

Urquhart, Keith 141, 224
Urquhart, Nick and Helen 224

V

von Guérard, Eugene 85, 151, 194, 196, 270

W

Wachmeister, Carl Gustav 33
Walling, Edna 31
Wando 71, 301
Wando Vale 71
Wannon electorate 113, 150, 174, 221, 243–245, 263, 270, 275, 288, 291, 301
Waratah 197–206, 301
Warrnambool 14, 18, 22–24, 51, 53, 67, 68, 71, 94–96, 172, 244–247
Warrnambool Racing Club 53, 249
Watson, Don 84, 85, 150, 151
Watson, Helen 171
Weatherly, Lionel 139
Weatherlys 176
Weir, Georgina 55, 57–59, 190, 192
Werribee 40
Wettenhall, Gib 75
Whitson, Robert 5, 7, 105
Wightman, Lillian 55–57
Willaura 70, 78–80, 82
Wills, Alastair 31
Wilson, Jean 235
Wimmera 138, 237, 243, 284
Winchelsea 18, 291
Wingiel 135, 168, 169, 171
Winter Cooke family 62, 67, 107
Wirrincourt 70

Wood, Bill 102
Woodhouse 78, 215, 266
Woolongoon 139, 227
Woolsthorpe 255
Woorndoo 237, 242
Wormbete 275
Wright, Tony 18, 92

Y

Yarram Park 59, 78–80, 274
Youngman, Harry 301

Wakefield Press is an independent publishing and
distribution company based in Adelaide, South Australia.
We love good stories and publish beautiful books.
To see our full range of books, please visit our website at
www.wakefieldpress.com.au
where all titles are available for purchase.

Find us!

Twitter: www.twitter.com/wakefieldpress
Facebook: www.facebook.com/wakefield.press
Instagram: instagram.com/wakefieldpress

www.ingramcontent.com/pod-product-compliance
Lightning Source LLC
Chambersburg PA
CBHW061427300426
44114CB00014B/1580